Wordsworth in Time

Wordsworth in Time

WORDSWORTH
IN TIME

❃ ❃

John Beer

FABER AND FABER

London & Boston

First published in 1979
by Faber and Faber Limited
3 Queen Square London WC1
Printed in Great Britain by
The Bowering Press Ltd
Plymouth and London
All rights reserved

© John Beer, 1979

British Library Cataloguing in Publication Data

Beer, John Bernard
    Wordsworth in time.
    1. Wordsworth, William—Criticism and interpretation
    I. Title
    821'.7   PR5888

    ISBN 0–571–09621–2

Me this unchartered freedom tires;
I feel the weight of chance-desires:
My hopes no more must change their name,
I long for a repose that ever is the same.

Wordsworth, *Ode to Duty*

It was only later that one discovered his power of choice—he was like a mind racing between separate madnesses. . . .

Norman Mailer, *An American Dream*

. . . I understood how we lived a contradiction. . . . For an instant out of time, the two worlds existed side by side. The one I inhabited by nature: the world of miracle drew me strongly. To give up the burning bush, the water from the rock, the spittle on the eyes was to give up a portion of myself, a dark and inward and fruitful portion. . . .

William Golding, *Free Fall*

Contents

Preface and Acknowledgements

The idea that it is wrong to treat Wordsworth as anything but a simple poet dies hard, particularly in England. There may be a concealed tribute here to the persuasiveness of the *Lyrical Ballads* preface as a statement about the need for poets to communicate with their fellow men—a plea which has by no means lost its point.

In recent years, nevertheless, a number of fine thematic studies, including those by Geoffrey Hartman, David Ferry, David Perkins, Colin Clarke, Christopher Salvesen, Geoffrey Durrant and Donald Wesling have, by dwelling on particular elements in his work, made it difficult to ignore its complexities or to resist the sense of his intellectual power. If uncertainty remains, in fact, it is more likely to be due to the very diversity of the themes that have been educed—the apocalyptic element in his writing, his preoccupation with death, the fascination of memory. It is not easy to find a central strand: his thinking is not found to fall readily into a particular tradition; he does not even seem to have been fond of reading works of philosophy. The reader is left asking how such a writer came to write so perceptively on topics (the mind's relationship to nature, knowledge of one's own mind and so on) which are normally regarded as the province of professional philosophers.

Inasmuch as the present book is a contribution to that discussion, it springs from a longstanding conviction that the high quality of Wordsworth's thought and writing—particularly between 1797 and 1805—owes much to his friendship and frequent conversations with Coleridge. The idea is not in itself new, of course. Melvin Rader's searching examination of Wordsworth's ideas (first published in 1931 and re-published as *Wordsworth: a Philosophical Approach* (Oxford 1967)) includes the thesis that Wordsworth learned of contemporary movements in philosophy largely through what Coleridge was able to tell him of them. But I believe the debt to have been less straightforward or obvious than is usually assumed—that before he went to

Preface and Acknowledgements

Germany Coleridge was already developing a body of thought about the relationship between the human mind and nature which, though related to what was going on abroad, contained original elements of its own, and which, though vulnerable in certain respects, was also brilliantly suggestive, helping Wordsworth to focus his mind in a new way on nature and the workings of his own mind. Certain elements in Wordsworth's achievement are on this argument associated with what Thomas McFarland has termed the 'Wordsworth-Coleridge Symbiosis'—to be seen on my terms as embodying the impact of some unusual and provocative ideas upon a mind which was powerful but also, left to itself, rather static. My reconstruction of Coleridge's developing ideas has been set out in a number of articles and books, most notably in the recent *Coleridge's Poetic Intelligence*, and is summarized here. (In view of some continuing reverberations from Norman Fruman's discussion of Coleridge's plagiarisms, I should refer the reader to my review of his book in *Review of English Studies* (1973, XXIV, 346–53) and to Thomas McFarland's 'Coleridge's Plagiarisms Once More' (*Yale Review*, Winter 1974, 252–84). The question needs further extended discussion but it is not, in my view, directly relevant to Coleridge's early thinking, which showed considerable originality.) It is no part of my purpose to argue for Coleridge's superiority, however. I see his role rather as resembling that of Shakespeare's Cleopatra—exerting an influence under which other things—including Wordsworth's genius—'become themselves'. Despite the attention given to Coleridge in the early chapters, the hero of this book is intended to be Wordsworth.

It should also be stressed that the thesis here does not offer to sum up his achievement. The question of human relationships, for instance, another central concern of his, has beeen reserved for a separate study entitled *Wordsworth and the Human Heart*, to be published at about the same time as this one. The mutual effects of the relationship upon their respective attitudes to previous literature and to language generally also calls for consideration, which I hope to give it later. To work with Wordsworth for long is to become steadily more aware of his many-sidedness—a point aptly made by Herbert Lindenberger when he remarked that his book on *The Prelude* might well have been called 'Thirteen Ways of looking at *The Prelude*'. It is a presupposition of my approach that Wordsworth's poetry grows in stature—and consistency—as one looks at it in different lights.

11

Preface and Acknowledgements

Some of my thinking on this subject was stimulated some years ago by Eugene Stelzig, who came to me in Cambridge to discuss his project of writing on Wordsworth and time when he was first thinking about it. Since then he has carried out his own work and published it under the title *All Shades of Consciousness* (The Hague, 1975); the study will be found to complement the present one by setting Wordsworth's ideas further into the context of previous and contemporary theories. I should mention with gratitude also Richard Wordsworth and participants in successive sessions of the annual Wordsworth Summer Conference, where some of the ideas in the book were given a first run; I have also gained much from conversations with Hugh Sykes Davies, Thomas McFarland, Bryce Gallie, John Woolford and a number of students, including one who came up after a lecture one morning and talked for a few minutes about Wordsworth's fears of madness.

It is a pleasure to acknowledge the help of the Librarians and staff of the Cambridge University Library, the Bodleian and the British Library and of the libraries of Peterhouse and St John's College, Cambridge. I am grateful to the Trustees of the Dove Cottage Library for their kindness in allowing me to use their collection, to the curators for their kindness and help and to Mr Jonathan Wordsworth who, as chairman of the Trust, gave me permission to quote one or two readings from the original manuscripts. He also facilitated my work by making available certain of his materials ahead of publication. I owe much to Mrs Olive Page and Mrs Hazel Dunn for their patience and accuracy in typing the various manuscripts involved, and to Miss J. L. Fellows for compiling the index. My greatest debt is, as always, to my wife.

A Note on Texts and Editions

During the past few years the scholarly materials for the study of Wordsworth have been improved by some splendid new works, including the Owen/Smyser edition of the prose, the re-editing of the Letters, M. L. Reed's *Chronology* and Mary Moorman's biography. The volumes of the Cornell Wordsworth, which have at the time of writing just begun to appear, are doing a similar service for the poetry.

After some thought, I have decided wherever possible to quote the earliest complete text of particular poems and passages. Although this sometimes means missing a later improvement or addition, such losses are, I believe, counterbalanced by the advantages of seeing Wordsworth's text nearest to the original process of composition. In particular, the early versions often bring out the original *movement* of a poem: later revisions are sometimes purchased at the expense of a dulling of that movement.

In quoting from *The Prelude*, similarly, I have quoted from the letters and MSS in which passages first appeared where possible,* and then from the text of 1805, making reference to the 1850 version only where it is a source of further illumination.

In quoting from Dorothy Wordsworth's *Journals* I have followed recent practice in using Mary Moorman's slightly better text for the passages covered by her Oxford Paperbacks edition and de Selincourt's for the remainder.

* For the reader's convenience, references are given to the main line-numbering of the 1799 *Prelude*, as in the Cornell Wordsworth edition.

A Dialect of Disturbance

Wordsworth's words always *mean* the whole of their
possible Meaning
Coleridge, 1803[1]

'Shall I ever have a name?' The question, half eager, half despairing,
is tucked away in one of Wordsworth's early notebooks;[2] and it
echoes in the mind. Its eighteenth-century sense is quite clear: shall
I ever achieve an eminence which will secure wide respect, and so
justify my existence? But even by Wordsworth's time the desire for
a name in that sense is also beginning to acquire more desperate
overtones. Shall I ever have a name rather than a label? Will it ever
be possible for someone hearing of me to think not merely of
the pictured face or the reported behaviour, but of the self which
I myself know but cannot normally express? For that matter,
can I acquire an identity which will be recognizable even to
myself?

The eighteenth century was not, of course, the first period during
which problems of self-identification were felt: human beings had
been aware of them since the Renaissance, as they began to sense
that important areas of their own inner nature did not correspond
to the rationally arranged, quantitatively measured universe which
was being organized around them. Hamlet was a representative
figure as well as a prophetic one. Just before the rise of Romanticism,
however, the problem tended to polarize itself for some into a
straightforward alternative between sanity and madness. So long as
a man chose 'sanity', society offered him various ways of life, any
one of which, once embraced, would endow him with a 'character'.
The rare individual who could not accept any of these modes, on
the other hand, found it difficult to avoid some form of mental
alienation. The eighteenth-century urge to retirement then turned
into a more headlong retreat, spurred on by the need to avoid the
collision with contemporary society and its established demands

that might leave one placed in the last and damning category of madness.

At the end of the century, however, materials for exploring problems of self-identification more confidently, and even creatively, began to be devised. Instead of retiring to seclusion or submitting to the cell of madness, an intelligent artist who wished to escape the limitations of the contemporary intellectual structure might embark on the enterprise of projecting for himself an imaginative universe, its structure more intimately related to that of his own human nature, which he could enter not, like his predecessors, as a world of fantasy, but as a genuine complement to the accepted universe of space and time around him.

What such an artist was seeking was not, in one sense, excessive. He was simply looking for the kind of structural security that Milton had still been able to enjoy in creating *Paradise Lost*. Yet the problems which greeted Blake, chief pioneer in this enterprise, when he tried to create a contemporary equivalent for Milton's poem, vividly illustrate the difficulties involved. Allegory gives place to symbolism; a universe that could in Milton be represented by a diagram becomes one that must be recreated by the reader moment by moment in the act of reading. Despite the apparent confidence with which Blake presents his visionary universe, it is not a model that can be appropriated; it acts rather as a challenge to the reader to exercise his own mind and imagination at full stretch. Communication in the more ordinary sense of the word is often, as a result, in jeopardy.

Wordsworth's strategy in dealing with the same situation was more ingenious: it involved a genuine approach to the world of his contemporaries which yet masked a preoccupation with the role of human consciousness itself. His art has a complicated existence, therefore. A typical poem of his will be carefully structured and presented in the familiar eighteenth-century world of time and space; it will have a straightforward moral point, to link it with the moral universe of the common reader: yet there will often be, in addition, an unexplained residue. It may be simply the distinctive usage of a single word, or it may be the existence of some apparently unguarded absurdity; whatever its nature, it leaves the sensitive reader with an uneasy sense that the poem contains either some element of failure or some further point which he has not quite grasped.

The extreme form of this phenomenon is found in Wordsworth's treatment of the world of nature. He carries forward and develops the eighteenth-century predilection for the picturesque, presenting us with a steadily observed view of particular landscapes, such as those of the Lake District. Yet these landscapes are rarely as concretely and immediately presented as in, say, Dorothy Wordsworth's *Journals*: We become aware that in spite of familiar names and identifiable vistas this universe is one which is being recreated and reorganized in Wordsworth's own mind—that the features of it which recur are in some sense selected features, constituting a universe which exists not simply as a landscape in time and space but as a psychoscape, reflecting some area of his own nature. Behind the exoteric world of nature which can teach us some straightforward moral lessons about our human status there looms a universe hardly less visionary than Blake's, yet more carefully guarded since presented with the commonsense aspect always uppermost.

Although the critical problems involved in dealing with Wordsworth seem less complicated than those involved in dealing with Blake, then, since Wordsworth can be approached as a public poet, recognizing the normal conventions of communication, further investigation shivers the illusion. We come to discover him as one of the most carefully masked of poets, his 'public' face, though certainly adapted to the conventions, indicating only one side of his personality. In *The Prelude* he recalls how on his lonely walks he would take a dog with him, to bark if someone approached, since he was afraid that anyone hearing the loud noise of his composition would spread a report that he was mad.[3] The critic must ask himself whether there is not sometimes a bark of the diversionary dog in the poems as well, drawing away attention from more disturbing undertones.

This is only one of the critical problems that beckon the modern reader. A more immediate one is related to traditional 'Wordsworthianism'. In the nineteenth century there was a strong predisposition to take the Wordsworth of old age at his face value. Despite his isolation he had shown a sharp sense of the coming age and its needs when he propounded his great twin values of duty and affection: for many disillusioned Victorians these concepts provided an acceptable foundation on which to rebuild a shattered philosophy.

Some twentieth-century readers, on the other hand, see this same Wordsworth as a propagator of dangerous attitudes. In the context of two world wars and a discredited imperialism, duty and affection sound too much like the veiling hypocrisies by which an establishment may seek to perpetuate itself at the expense of general human sacrifice. Such readers, looking for the moments when his statements ring true for themselves, look to the passages of drama, energetic expression and human realism.

They also tend to agree about the shape of Wordsworth's career, maintaining that it came to an early climax with 'The Ruined Cottage', the poem felt to be most directly shaped by a harmonized working of all the poet's powers. After this achievement directness of utterance is to be traced more fitfully, though a critic as sensitive as Leavis can discern it in poetry written much later—in some of the Duddon sonnets, for example. When it appears it is characterized partly by a sense of *ease*—not in the simple eighteenth-century sense (though Pope's use of the term would not be irrelevant) but in a more subtle one, suggesting a considerable pressure of intelligence transmuted into a style responsive to subtle shifts of contour in the subject and changes of focus in the poet's mind.

But this is not the note which one associates with the great body of Wordsworth's work, nor is it characteristic of any of the great Romantic writers of his generation. In Blake and Coleridge, also, one can trace initial progress to a climax in which expressive powers are seen at their most fully integrated (as in Coleridge's major poems, or Blake's *Songs of Experience*) followed by a later period of less direct communication. The reason may lie with the particular circumstances of the time. These poets, the first to be touched by the French Revolution, were simultaneously stimulated and oppressed. The intellectual ferment moved them to positive utterances, the natural thrust of excited feelings, while the problems and failures inherent in the effects of the revolution called on them to suffer more than they could act. It is impossible to acquire an extensive response to these writers, therefore, unless one is prepared to see the very terms of their art as a kind of matrix, where a struggle for unity of interpretation is taking place.

The language which they evolve is in each case coloured by the complexity of the situation. For the first time, no 'agreed style' is available to the poet: if he is to be as sincere as the events demand he will inevitably need different forms. Wordsworth's poetry is the writing of a man who has at least cracked the existing moulds. He does not pursue a more radical change; he is by no means willing to entrust himself, like Blake, to the bounding line of expressive form.

His desire to remain true to the *whole* of his experience sets him rather in the world of paradox, needing both a moving expression, adequate to his feelings, and a firm structure to maintain the assurance he admires in his predecessors.

Although neither the Victorian adulation of Wordsworth nor the more astringent reappraisals of recent years can show us the full extent of this paradoxical world, however, they indicate its extremes dramatically. To read Wordsworth's more admiring nineteenth-century critics with full sympathy requires the almost impossible effort of imagination which would restore us to a world where the voice of the 'official' Wordsworth was hardly distinguishable from the purified voice of God required by the age; while the best 'modernist' criticism, even if it fails to offer a way in to the poetry at large, jolts us into awareness of his extraordinary expressive power.

Wordsworth has been seen in other lights as well—particularly by men whose primary concerns were not literary. A. N. Whitehead saw him as a major figure in the movement to bridge what seemed to him the most important gap in Western thinking—the split between scientific thinking and religious intuition. For him, Wordsworth's great contribution was that of a man who opposed to the scientific study of change a sense of the concreteness of things—who was 'haunted by the great permanences of nature'. As such he was a major prophet of Whitehead's God, defined as the 'principle of concretion'. Whitehead analyses his position finely:

> Now it is emphatically not the case that Wordsworth hands over inorganic matter to the mercy of science, and concentrates on the faith that in the living organism there is some element that science cannot analyse. Of course he recognizes, what no one doubts, that in some sense living things are different from lifeless things. But that is not his main point. It is the brooding presence of the hills which haunts him. His theme is nature *in solido*, that is to say, he dwells on that mysterious presence of surrounding things, which imposes itself on any separate element that we set up as an individual for its own sake. He always grasps the whole of nature as involved in the tonality of the particular instance.[4]

This analysis catches the main features of the drive to objectivity in Wordsworth's writing. But the word 'haunted'—used in two separate places—points to an area that is left unexplained. And there is a similar lack in Whitehead's more general analysis of Wordsworth's attitude.

> Wordsworth was passionately absorbed in nature. It has been said of Spinoza, that he was drunk with God. It is equally true that Wordsworth was drunk with nature. But he was a thoughtful, well-read man, with philosophical interests, and sane even to the point of prosiness. In addition, he was a genius.[5]

This again leaves unexamined the question whether Wordsworth's 'sanity to the point of prosiness' was simply a result of thoughtfulness and wide reading—whether, perhaps, a covert fear of insanity was not also involved.

Nor is it every thinker who has been so straightforwardly impressed by the prosaic quality of Wordsworth. Another audience has responded to the mystical element in his work, as exemplified in the *Immortality Ode*. Although there are few passages which touch the opening of that poem for direct rendering of imaginative power, moreover, a visionary presence may be sensed throughout his work. Havelock Ellis went so far as to make a statement which may surprise modern readers: writing in 1897 of mescal he said,

> . . . a large part of its charm lies in the halo of beauty which it casts around the simplest and commonest things . . . If it should ever chance that the consumption of mescal becomes a habit, the favorite poet of the mescal drinker will certainly be Wordsworth. Not only the general attitude of Wordsworth, but many of his most memorable poems and phrases can not—one is almost tempted to say—be appreciated in their full significance by one who has never been under the influence of mescal.[6]

Although there is an element of exaggeration somewhere here (after all, Wordsworth himself did not take mescal), Havelock Ellis's report is evidently true for at least one man who was normally inclined to concentrate on the processes of rationalism. And it suggests something which one need not be a mescal-taker to suspect—that there was in Wordsworth a strong streak of visionary power which was not simply a gift of early childhood but continued to haunt him in various ways throughout life, half-emerging as an elusive presence in the later poetry, even if it rarely achieved direct and immediately recognizable expression. If this is so, it suggests again that the type of distinction which one is tempted to make between his poetry and that of more committed visionary poets, such as Blake, needs to be modified. If there was a region of the human personality which both Blake and Wordsworth knew well, the real difference between them may lie rather in their respective attitudes to their own visionary experiences.

It follows that the critical problems involved in dealing with Wordsworth may in one respect be more difficult than those involved in dealing with Blake. Once he has committed himself to a sympathetic reading of Blake, the main question which faces a critic is to decide how far he is willing to follow him into his private and imaginative universe. He must make his own answer to the question whether Blake's failures of communication represent a factor in his verse which is fundamentally disabling or whether success in communication is simply an irrelevant criterion.

In the case of Wordsworth the problem is more complicated, since —at least at one level—communication is always made. But if what is directly communicated also turns out to mask a more oblique utterance, the critic will be faced by a more difficult choice: he must either ignore the indirect utterance entirely, arguing its irrelevance to the direct verbal and syntactical presentation on the page, or commit himself to an attempted evaluation of hints, yearnings and hauntings which are only half present in the text. And this does seem to be the case with Wordsworth: the surface diction follows one pattern, yet one's imagination is sometimes engaged also by an undertone, or even a contrary projection, which seems to be expressing a different one.

This undertone (it might be misleading to call it a voice, since it does not always find verbal articulation) is the utterance of a man who has known some of the same visionary experiences as Blake, yet has withdrawn from them—not without an occasional spasm of fear. The critic is perfectly entitled to reject the undertone in favour of the immediately presented verbal structure, but the consequences of such a dismissal must also be recognized. To accept that dismissal is also to accept the principle which underlies it—that the language of poetry is a single, graspable medium which is brought into focus at the point where the mind of the educated audience succeeds in deriving from it a common meaning.

For many of those who do accept this assumption, Wordsworth's poetry dies as their eye lights on it. Locked into the rather drab typography provided by many publishers, it assumes to their eyes the format of one of the less inspiring sections of the Old Testament. Reading it becomes an act of moral discipline rather than an absorption of engaged intelligence. They are likely to find themselves returning the book to the shelf, reflecting in self-defence that a man who could entitle a section of his work 'Poems on the Naming of Places' must always have had strong reserves of dreariness fairly near the surface.

Yet it is not uncommon to discover that even when Wordsworth has been dismissed he continues, against expectation, to hold one's attention. It is not easy finally to have done with him. The reader may even feel disturbed by the sense of a power which is still at work on him and for which he is at a loss to account. To explore the sources of that power, moreover, involves an unusual critical enterprise, for which established criteria are only partially useful. Wordsworth's diction exists neither as a vehicle for spontaneous ejaculations of feeling nor as a medium for the construction of carefully moulded artifacts, but as a larger theatre, in which these and other impulses play together, looking for resolution. We cannot, in fact, form theories about Wordsworth's diction without forming theories about his personality. If there are dislocations in the diction, they correspond to dislocations there as well.

It is not difficult to suggest causes for that dislocation. The loss of both parents, one when he was seven, the other at thirteen, may well have been decisive in interrupting the natural development of his subliminal self, that physical element in the personality which anchors a human being to the earth and links him to human society. What is certain is that in childhood certain inward forces in him were unusually strong and vivid. They could visit him with a sense of splendour so compelling as to transform his vision of the universe until everything around him shone with its own inward light; they could also grip him with intense fear. Or the splendour and the fear might intertwine:

> Many times while going to school have I grasped at a wall or tree to recall myself from this abyss of idealism to the reality. At that time I was afraid of such processes.[7]

By the time that he was a young man this force was much less active; the more specifically chemical senses seem also to have played a minimal part in his experience. Southey went so far as to say that Wordsworth had no sense of smell, backing the assertion by his account of an experience at Racedown:

> Once, and once only in his life, the dormant power awakened; it was by a bed of stocks in full bloom, at a house which he inhabited in Dorsetshire, some five and twenty years ago; and he says it was like a vision of Paradise to him; but it lasted only a few minutes, and the faculty has continued torpid from that time.[8x]*

One suspects that the key-word is really 'torpid' and that Wordsworth's lack was not of a sense of smell as such (to which he alludes from time to time in his poetry) but the experience of being possessed by a scent in much the same way that he had been possessed by vision in his childhood—that here, as elsewhere, the subliminal forces in his personality were not lost, but dislocated. Instead of moving in harmony with his rational self, reinforcing, encouraging, even covering deficiencies where necessary, they now existed as a separate and sometimes divergent force. Wordsworth was later to say, speaking of the gap between the present and the remembered past,

> ... sometimes, when I think of it, I seem
> Two consciousnesses, conscious of myself
> And of some other Being.

1805 ii 31–3

It may be argued that the activity of memory mattered precisely because it allowed such consciousnesses to exist side by side.

At the same time he seems frequently to have been fascinated by a 'double vision' in his dealings with nature. The same landscape which could seem starkly objective in one mood could in another link itself directly with the observer, impressing him with a sense of connecting passion.

The phenomenon could sometimes be nightmarish. It could express itself in an experience like that of dealing with a person who presents all the outword signs of normality and reasonableness yet who also impresses one with an elusive air of menace. Near the beginning of his pamphlet on the Convention of Cintra, Wordsworth writes that the event was

* The suffix 'x' to a note indicator signifies that the note contains further information, as opposed to simple references and cross-references.

by none received as an open and measurable affliction: it had indeed features bold and intelligible to every one; but there was an under-expression which was strange, dark, and mysterious—and, accordingly as different notions prevailed, or the object was looked at in different points of view, we were astonished like men who are overwhelmed without forewarning—fearful like men who feel themselves to be helpless, and indignant and angry like men who are betrayed.

PrW I 224

The coinage 'under-expression' in this passage is matched by similar formations, ('under-agents', 'under-consciousness', 'under-powers') in *The Prelude*, where the double consciousness is thought of in more benevolent terms.[9x]

As we consider the implications of this play of powers in Wordsworth, the contrast with Blake asserts itself again. Faced with a similar split between the activity of his rational, measuring consciousness and the subliminal forces of expressive vision, Blake felt more threatened by the former. He identified it as Urizen and forswore allegiance as far as possible in favour of a wooing of the subliminal by cultivation of energy in all its forms. Wordsworth, on the other hand, who was as frightened and fascinated by the irrational forces in himself as Blake was by Urizen, clung to the palpable. Though not so extreme a devotee of solid forms as Johnson, who kicked the stone to refute Berkeley and insisted on measuring the ruins which he travelled miles to see, Wordsworth had something of the same obsessional concern with the actualities of things in themselves, freed from any colouring supplied by the observing eye.

The underlying state of tension between a conscious self which was always threatening to fix the universe into a single and final mathematical order and a subliminal self which would feel extinguished by such absolute constraint was often shunted on to a tension between the evidence of eye and ear—particularly when Wordsworth was looking at a landscape. While his eye was organizing a scene into an ordered whole and mentally resolving it into unity, his ear would pick up those elements in the scene which did not fit that unity—the mocking noise of echoes, for example, or the sombre hollow sound of roaring torrents. From time to time, also, he could express this duality of response either in terms of a conflict between his dominant senses as he contemplated a scene which was presently and quantitatively extended in space before him, or, more often, as a harmony between them, the apparently discordant elements being somehow incorporated into a further pattern. But the tension, or the harmony, between organizing and subliminal consciousnesses could be more naturally observed when he was contemplating a landscape or a situation *in time*. To equate the world of the eye with the conscious and that of the ear with the subliminal offers a field for artistic activity, but necessarily a limited and precarious one; the relationship between a present scene and a scene remembered, on the other hand, invokes the subliminal powers directly, through the operation of memory. If one returns to a scene of passionate engagement many years later and discovers that the identical passion, forgotten in between, leaps nonchalantly back into existence as if no barrier of time existed, one finds oneself in the presence of a human phenomenon to which the laws of space and time are strangely irrelevant. For this reason the processes of memory were talismanic for Wordsworth: when enjoying them directly and when contemplating them through some further operation of recall he could hold the two worlds of his consciousness more readily in balance.

At the same time, it is doubtful whether the subliminal powers of his consciousness would have been allowed so large a role in his poetry had it not been for his friendship with Coleridge. In face of his own tendency to put the more passionate elements of his childhood experiences behind him and assume the mantle of sobriety and maturity expected by his contemporaries, Coleridge's delicate psychological probings held out the possibility of an alternative universe, in which his instinctive life might be seen as possessing an importance and validity of its own. While Wordsworth's own inclination was always towards direct harmonization and concretion of his experience into large and detailed poetic patterns, Coleridge's speculations were a subversive presence, capable of infiltrating the defences of Wordsworth's character and rousing his instinctive energies to play a more active part in the creative process.

Although Coleridge shared Wordsworth's puritanism, his fear of the power of the subliminal was marked by fascination at some of its potentialities. This offered Wordsworth ways of approaching his own experience. As a result, the periods of intimacy (or recent intimacy) with Coleridge were always periods of maximum subliminal disturbance in his own work. When alone and self-sufficient he could move towards the elaboration of that philosophy of duty and affection which so impressed his immediate successors; but when drawn into Coleridge's orbit the tides of his imaginative powers began to move, producing poems which would fascinate (and puzzle) a later generation more than the monuments of his straightforward 'natural piety'.

One way of exploring such poems is to see in Wordsworth a major instance of 'dissociated sensibility'. If so, however, the dissociation in question is something more than the split between expression of thought and of emotion which Eliot sketched in his famous discussion,[10] since this suggests a dissociation between forms of experience which are in some sense of the same order. If it is ultimately possible to 'feel one's thought as immediately as the odour of a rose', the two experiences are thereby placed in the same synaesthetic spectrum. But the dislocation in the work of poets such as Wordsworth lay at a deeper level: it involved an awareness that the different *kinds* of activity involved, say, in thinking at full stretch and in reviving past memories through sensuous experience could never be fully reconciled. We can still share Eliot's enthusiasm for the type of poetry which restores wholeness—to make thought passionate and passion definite—but we go astray if we do not also recognize that for certain human beings in certain situations the two elements must be mutually exclusive.

Without embarking on a full-dress discussion, we may simply remark that so long as the development of Western civilization continues to be based on further mastery of the resources of nature by techniques of measurement and quantification, the human consciousness must inevitably continue to be trained to separate those of its functions which are suited to that activity from those which are more instinctive. And while that training continues to be powerfully reinforced and rewarded by society at large, the achievement of the metaphysical poets in recognizing and giving eloquent expression to the resulting state of mind is as unlikely to be followed by a convincing reunification of the poetic psyche as it was in its own time.

Wordsworth commands attention by his recognition of this dilemma. He only rarely achieves the sort of poetry which succeeds in reconciling the rational and the subliminal, though, like the best of the metaphysicals, he was a man in whom the rational urge to apprehend, measure and control the universe, and the subliminal drive to enter into immediate union with it, were equally strong. At its best, the subliminal might transfigure the rational; more often he found its operation an irritation, a disturbance—even a pressure threatening insanity.[11] This too is faithfully reflected in his poetry.

At its most extreme the phenomenon results in a curious effect, hard to match elsewhere in literature. Possible parallel examples might be *Wuthering Heights*, where the commonsense narrative of Nelly Dean bears in and in on an emotion which common sense cannot comprehend—and which is thus released vicariously if at all; or Yeats's *Last Poems*, where the pressure of faced reality eventually releases the trip-catch of the reader's imagination, to illuminate the stark scene with a splendour not to be accounted for by the immediate effect of the words themselves.

In Wordsworth, similarly, the most patient evocation of a landscape of objective reality can sometimes transform itself (behind the poet's back, as it were) into a psychoscape of his own imagination. The clinging to the palpable is both a refuge from the power of the mysterious and unknown and an affirmation of paradox, the paradox of Jacob's stone : 'This is none other but the house of God, and this is the gate of heaven'. What is primarily presented is the blank rock-face, but we cannot stare at it for ever without knowing that it is open to the sound of hidden torrents, or that, at the touch of sunlight, it is thrown into a more bearable relief.

The critic who wishes to approach Wordsworth sympathetically must therefore be prepared for an unusual exercise of his powers. The very exercise of consciousness by which he bends to analysis automatically excludes and damps the subliminal forces in his own psyche; and when the subliminal is as withdrawn as this, he may be tempted to deny its effects altogether. If he nevertheless believes in the importance of Wordsworth's absconded imagination and wishes to pursue it, however, one very simple and straightforward mode of approach may be proposed. It is that he should look first not for the homogeneity of Wordsworth's diction but for the disturbances in it— the moments, for example, where he uses an unexpected word, or even a normal one with some unexpected heightening of effect. The more puzzling the usage, the more likely it is that the key will be found in some subterranean working of Wordsworth's imagination (inviting, in turn, reappraisal of some of his more commonplace expressions).

A Dialect of Disturbance

The critic who has already satisfied himself concerning those passages in Wordsworth which express the voice of true feeling and has proceeded into this more wary passage, will look at such points for indications that their commonplace setting holds in check some other excitement or concern. He may also find himself drawn to a further proposition—that when Wordsworth is being most evidently absurd, this is the time for greatest vigilance. If one has once come to see Wordsworth's poetry as a context of cross-currents and contrary impulses, it becomes logical to assume that even the absurdities of so self-conscious and self-critical a man may be pointing to the subsistence of some central preoccupation, powerful enough to make him overlook, or even disregard, his audience's more obvious and comfortable response.

Most of all, of course, such a critic will be attracted to those areas of disturbance in Wordsworth which reflect some disjunction in the time-process, for there, we have suggested, contemplation of the two processes of his consciousness is facilitated, enabling him to be more faithful to both. In this case, however, the passages in question will be found to correspond with some of his most memorable and accepted achievements, the stature of which is merely enhanced the more the characters imposed by his later poetic stance are seen to be inter-penetrated by the moving lineaments of revived emotion.

Cycles and Occasions

The phenomenon which revealed itself as a dislocation of sensibility in a few individuals at the end of the eighteenth century was to gain in consequence during the next hundred years. By the time that T. S. Eliot wrote his essay on the metaphysical poets, indeed, it can be seen as having extended itself to the whole culture within which he is writing:

> Our civilization comprehends great variety and complexity, and this variety and complexity, playing upon a refined sensibility, must produce various and complex results. The poet must become more and more comprehensive, more allusive, more indirect, in order to force, to dislocate if necessary, language into his meaning.[1]

Taking it for granted that Western civilization has lost its sense of unity, Eliot is prescribing for the poet a posture of heroic isolation, from which he must reach out to impose a pattern upon experience, using in the process certain resources peculiar to language. Wordsworth, writing at a much earlier stage, was in a different situation. In his time the main pressures upon the poet were still towards conformity: disturbances and dislocations insinuated themselves into his consciousness by stealth, finding expression through language as best they could—often by passive acknowledgment and absorption rather than through any new and active initiative.

This was particularly so with the poet's attitude to the universe in which he found himself. Eighteenth-century thinking was dominated by the sense that time was essentially a quantitative mode, to be dealt with in a similar manner to space. It could primarily be visualized as a steadily self-extending line—capable of being plotted, if necessary, on a chart.

There were always, of course, those who recognized that in the human consciousness time behaved in quite other ways, so that remembered experiences, for example, could rise into it without sense of differing distance. It was around this recognition, after all, that

Sterne had constructed the action of *Tristram Shandy*. In the eighteenth century, however, Newton's prestige made this conception almost necessarily comic or whimsical.

Later, the curious behaviour of time in the human consciousness would be attended to with increasing seriousness.[2x] At its extreme, it was to evoke the epic treatment accorded to it by Proust; but it would also come to be recognized on a smaller scale by novelists as justifying new experiments with the treatment of serial time. A succinct and racy version of that recognition is to be found, for example, in Golding's *Free Fall*, where an early rumination by the hero gives open voice to the novelist's purpose and forthcoming strategy.

> For time is not to be laid out endlessly like a row of bricks. That straight line from the first hiccup to the last gasp is a dead thing. Time is two modes. The one is an effortless perception native to us as water to the mackerel. The other is a memory, a sense of shuffle fold and coil, of that day nearer than that because more important, of that event mirroring this, or those three set apart, exceptional and out of the straight line altogether.[3]

Such recognitions are naturally most vivid in personal experience. In the case of corporate memory the compelling clarity of revived sense-experience is inevitably lost, to be replaced, if at all, by the dramatic power of recorded historical episodes and the myths which have evolved or been created around them.

In his book *The Sense of an Ending*, Frank Kermode has helped to formulate the more general issues involved by reinvoking two Greek words for time, *chronos* and *kairos*.[4] *Chronos* may be used simply for the passing time of scientific quantification and of common speech; *kairos*, by comparison, makes room for the conception that certain times are more significant than others. The latter word had already become fashionable in recent theology, in fact, largely through the influence of Paul Tillich, who used it to express his concept of 'crisis'; others had employed it to denote the sense of a 'due season', or 'the fullness of time'. The foundation in biblical Greek for such detailed ascriptions has been shown to be doubtful, to say the least, but as Professor Kermode points out, it remains significant that several distinguished theologians should have found the need for them in the development of their own thinking about time.[5x]

When, under his tutelage, the basic distinction is carried over into the realm of fiction, it acquires an even greater usefulness. For the chief value of 'kairos', whether interpreted as 'time of crisis', 'time of opportunity' or 'significant season', is that it renders possible a certain kind of discourse without prematurely defining its limits. The critic is thus enabled to talk about certain treatments of time in fiction as more significant than others, without being forced to settle too quickly on the *kind* of significance involved. The moment of judgment, the moment of decision, the sudden illumination, the sudden despair, the Apocalypse itself—all are examples of *kairos*, united by the fact that in some sense they stand apart from the time-process in which they participate.

It is possible to make a further and slightly different discrimination, however, by resorting to the more limited use made of *kairos* in earlier iconography. Panofsky has pointed out that our familiar figure of Father Time, with his scythe and hourglass, results (by way of a resemblance of names between scythe-bearing Kronos, the Greek god corresponding to Saturn, and Chronos, the Greek word for time) from a Renaissance conflation of simple personified Time with the frightening figure of Saturn. In classical art, he points out, the case had been otherwise. There

> Time was depicted only as either fleeting Opportunity ('Kairos') or creative Eternity ('Aion').[6]

These two great figures, which Panofsky ascribes to the classical world, indicate an attitude to Time in which the quantitative perception of Chronos (and consequent melancholia at the inevitability of impermanence) plays a strictly subordinate part. 'Kairos' (or Opportunity) is normally represented as a young man with wings at shoulders and heels, and scales—originally balanced on the edge of a shaving-knife, and later on one or two wheels; he has a forelock which can be seized. 'Aion' has two forms: connected with Mithra, he may appear as a grim winged figure with lion's head and lion's claws, tightly enveloped by a huge snake and carrying a key in either hand; alternatively, however, he appears as the Orphic divinity commonly known as Phanes, a beautiful winged youth, surrounded by a zodiac, equipped with various attributes of cosmic power, and (likewise) encircled by the coils of a snake.[7]

In this older context, it will be observed, the concept of Kairos was more closely defined than in its modern reappearances. Primarily it depicted time as offering repeated opportunities—which in turn called for an agile readiness that could turn them to account. The Orphic Aion, similarly, offered a view of eternity as an ever-resurgent youthfulness, a sense which had later come to be sapped, as eternity was increasingly identified with an unending sequence of time, stretching limitlessly into the future.

While these earlier conceptions of Time could hardly now be revived in their original form, they are at another level virtually indestructible, inasmuch as they correspond to permanent tendencies of the human mind. For while, to the contemplative eye, time may stretch out as an endless line, the human being, once involved in its processes, sees himself in different relationships with it, corresponding to needs and attitudes of his own. He can intervene actively to seize an offered opportunity, presenting a positive front to Time; or he may, in more passive states, acknowledge the existence of other forces under the influence of which his own sense of passing time is temporarily annulled. In both cases the bleak contemplation of time as process is superseded. The one state might be said to realize itself in the sense of *Occasion* (*occasio* being the Latin equivalent for the Greek *kairos*), the other in an influx of *visionary* power : the one commemorates moments when a human being feels himself to be actively and totally fitted to the world about him, the other those when he or she is so possessed by inward imagination as to feel no transience in the passing of time. Wordsworth's account of himself skating as a boy with his companions,

> When we had given our bodies to the wind,
> And all the shadowy banks, on either side,
> Came sweeping through the darkness, spinning still
> The rapid line of motion . . .

1805 i 479–82

offers an early example of Occasion perfected; the same boy, at those times when, as he later put it,

> I was . . . unable to think of external things as having external existence, and I communed with all that I saw as something not apart from, but inherent in, my own immaterial nature . . .[8]

was experiencing Vision in an extreme form. Sometimes both states might be experienced in succession, as when he would leave the main pack of skaters to go off on his own and, in quietness and isolation, feel an influx of revelation from the natural scene beyond, or when in alternate bouts of ambling and galloping on horseback he would successively experience a passive sense of the breathing life of nature or an active sense of identification with its positive powers:

> Even in this joyous time I sometimes felt
> Your presence, when, with slacken'd step, we breathed
> Along the sides of the steep hills, or when,
> Lightened by gleams of moonlight from the sea,
> We beat with thundering hoofs the level sand.

1799 ii 135–9

The sense of nature's breathing tenderness, felt during a temporary respite from galloping energy, looks forward to other such moments in *The Prelude*. The sublimity of the moonlight gleams on the sea, on the other hand, glimpsed in utmost excitement, indicates a less common Wordsworthian Occasion: that of feeling himself both elevated in spirits and polarized with his fellows, so that his being, while vividly felt, is neither asserted above nor submerged below theirs. It was a feeling akin to that which he was also to feel during the early days of the Revolution, a sense of men living in individual self-fulfilment yet all touched by the gleam of a common emotion. In such states, the human being was rescued from the oppressions of that more familiar Time, the figure of Chronos who stepped with measured pace, carrying his hourglass and scythe.

Eighteenth-century poets such as Pope or Cowper had given little attention to such alternatives. If they spoke of Time it was without sense of crisis or, indeed, of undue oppression, since its dominance was accounted inevitable. If there is a metaphor in the work of these poets which looks beyond Newtonian models, it is the ancient Heracleitan image of time as a stream:

> Oh! while along the stream of Time thy name
> Expanded flies, and gathers all its fame,
> Say, shall my little bark attendant sail,
> Pursue the triumph, and partake the gale?

writes Pope in the *Essay on Man*; Cowper declares, more straightforwardly,

> The lapse of time and rivers is the same

—and pursues the comparison through a twelve-line poem.[9] In the most famous formulation of all (Isaac Watts's), 'Time, like an ever-rolling stream, / Bears all its sons away'.

To see time as a river rather than as an extended line is to take some account, at least, of its mysterious nature. The controlling form of the image, nevertheless, is a spatial one and in general eighteenth-century views of civilization were conceived predominantly in such terms.[10x] When a poet considered possible changes in his civilization, similarly, he was liable to think of a series of new, spatial *constructions*. Dryden (as Walter Jackson Bate has pointed out) saw the civilization of the age before him in the form of a temple, which his own age was striving to rival.

> Our Builders were, with want of Genius, curst;
> The Second Temple was not like the First.[11x]

Even in contemplating the French Revolution some minds would still favour this imagery. One writer was to comment: 'From the ruins of tyranny and the rubbish of popery a beautiful and finely framed edifice would in time have been constructed.'[12]

For many, however, the American and French Revolutions were more challenging, marking a period of decisive change in the very pattern by which historical events were to be viewed. They found it necessary to shift their emphasis on civilization as a spatial organization, within which familiar forms decayed and needed to be renewed, and to focus upon it as a temporal process, in which entirely new kinds of event could happen, creating discontinuities and fresh departures. The most immediate participants in these events, of course, found the needs of the moment too pressing to admit of long theoretical consideration. Faced with the need to find forms and institutions for the new civilization, their first instinct was to look back to the civilizations they most admired and build upon the patterns which they found offered there.

On the simplest of such interpretations, the French were called upon to produce a new version of the Roman republic. Madame Roland and others, brought up on writers such as Livy and Plutarch, had seen parallels to be imitated.[13] Others, however (including Marat, who had travelled in England and been convinced against his will) argued that the conditions of life in a modern commercially developed state made it impossible to look for renewal of the Roman system, based as it had been on sobrieties and austerities.[14x] Although many speeches during and after the Revolution carried references to the Roman past, therefore, some of the most thoughtful *philosophes* had already turned their attention elsewhere. The evolution of the

American constitution, in particular, had made it possible to think about such matters in radically new ways. Insofar as the revolutionaries now looked to the classical past, in other words, they were no longer seeing it as an unimpeachable ideal, to be imitated as extensively as possible, but rather as a repository of basic forms, from which the patterns for particular new developments might be selected. And beneath this change of emphasis there can be discerned a fundamental change in the view of time itself.

To appreciate its nature we need to turn back to the conception of time as a continuously self-extending line, and to recall that that line had sometimes been conceived not as straight but as moving naturally in a circling process. Once again, this view did not originate in the eighteenth century or even in the Renaissance. So long as men had noticed cosmic recurrence, whether in the seasons of the year or in the circlings of the heavens, it had been natural for the time-process itself to be viewed in a similar manner. The Stoics had used the concept: Aristotle had been attracted to it, partly by his fondness for the image of the sphere and partly by its susceptibility to numerical organization.[15x] Christian thought, on the other hand, had looked on it with less favour, since it seemed to question the supremacy of divine providence. While it might be used for large typological patterns, such as the rounding fulfilment of creation in the final moment of apocalypse, or the initiation of the New Dispensation when the sin that began with the Tree in Eden was vanquished on the Tree of Calvary, most Christian thinkers followed St Augustine[16x] in avoiding further or more general use of the idea. The one indulged exception in mediaeval times was the Wheel of Fortune, a piece of intellectual licence which enabled the wanton changes and chances of mortal existence to be viewed as the result of unexpected and unpredictable circlings.

When the cyclical mode did find a place in Renaissance Christian thought, it was as part of a defence against the fashionable notion that all was in decay. Jean Bodin wrote much on the power of cycles, both astronomic and chronological, as playing a part in the Divine providence.[17] He was ready to ridicule those who could see no possibility of new growth, but his main concern was with the maintenance of stability and with combating those who believed that the state of nature was necessarily in decline. George Hakewill, similarly, a seventeenth-century clergyman who thought in cyclical terms and collected many instances of modern superiority over the ancients, did so in aid of his censure of 'the common errour touching natures perpetual and universal decay.'[18x]

With the establishment of the Copernican view of the universe, on the other hand, and with the discoveries of Newton, the sense of circling process took on a new access of strength, for these enforced with telling power the sense of a universe inhabited by bodies in continual circulation. It may even be that the new philosophy modified the idea of revolution in the political sphere. When one reads of revolutions in the mediaeval world one often senses in the background the image of the wheel of fortune, which, in a simple movement of itself, can precipitate a man or a kingdom from the position formerly held. In the seventeenth century, by contrast, the term is most used to describe two particular events: the restitution of the monarchy in 1660 and the expulsion of the Stuart monarchy in favour of William and Mary in 1688.[19] If not totally conservative in tone, it carries a strong suggestion that the state has found a way of rejecting a false order and aligning itself with a truer one. The change is, in other words, from the image of a dominating wheel which may by its revolution precipitate an event, to that of events seen as actually participating in a revolving order.

There were many permutations of these varying patterns, as Frank Manuel has noted.[20] With the rise in France of movements associated with the Revolution, on the other hand (as he also points out) a further factor intervened—a leaning towards patterns which could take up the cyclic concept, with its conservative implications, and combine it with progressivism. Baron Turgot, in one of his addresses at the Sorbonne, had spoken 'on the Historical Progress of the Human Mind'; the idea was developed by Condorcet in his *Outlines of an Historical View of the Progress of the Human Mind* (1795). While accepting that many things in nature were in the grip of cycling repetition, he argued that scientific progress, at least, was non-reversible:

The phenomena of nature, subject to constant laws, are enclosed in a circle of revolutions that are always the same. Everything is reborn, everything perishes, and through successive generations in which vegetation and animal life reproduce themselves, time merely restores at each instant the image it has caused to disappear.

The succession of men, however, presents a changing spectacle
from century to century. Reason, the passions, liberty, produce
new events without end . . .[21]

This twofold assertion can be seen to have been developed in
France by the revolutionaries also and so to transform the very
idea of 'revolution' once again. For although at first sight, as we
have seen, that word carried the implicit assumption of a wheeling
process in action, the idea of the change involved had varied from
one century to another. The most recent form, based on the Newtonian model, might suggest that all so-called revolutions in human
affairs would be seen on a larger view simply as dreary repetitions,
forced back into the same patterns by larger laws. Insistence on the
progress of the human mind, by contrast, made it possible to initiate
a sense of revolution which combined recognition of inevitable
circlings in the universe with that of possible new events in the
spirit of man. On this assumption, human civilization in time was
not a repetitive circling but a spiralling process, cognizant of echoes
from the past but thrusting forward into organizations which were
unprecedented. A generation later, the idea that the circling process of human affairs was being penetrated and transformed by
significant changes in the human spirit would have entered firmly
into English poetry, as in Shelley's

> The world's great age begins anew,
>   The golden years return,
> The earth doth like a snake renew
>   Her winter weeds outworn:
> Heaven smiles, and faiths and empires gleam,
> Like wrecks of a dissolving dream.[22]

Keats, similarly, would couple his insistence that those who listened
intently could hear in his age 'the hum of mighty workings' with
the assertion that 'Great spirits now on earth are sojourning'—and
name as his first example

> He of the cloud, the cataract, the lake,
>   Who on Helvellyn's summit, wide awake,
> Catches his freshness from Archangel's wing . . .[23]

By 1816, then, Wordsworth could emerge as a prime example of a
new spirit among the 'mighty workings'. But how far would the

young Wordsworth consciously have entertained such a view of his own destiny?

It is not altogether easy to gauge the exact extent of his knowledge or reflections on the subject at the time. The idea of time's cycles had sometimes been expressed in English poetry, as for example by Samuel Daniel;[24] the wheel of fortune had appeared in Chaucer and Shakespeare.[25] *Tristram Shandy*, with its wanton dislocations of time, was, by his own testimony, one of the few works of modern literature that Wordsworth had recently read in 1791.[26] But any detailed knowledge of the more sophisticated attitudes that were emerging in France would in all likelihood have been derived from conversations with educated men whom he met in France and books which were circulating there. Given his general involvement with the revolutionary movement, on the other hand, there is good reason to believe that he would have been drawn to ideas which were so closely bound up with current events.

The sense of time as a series of wheelings was certainly likely to have impressed itself upon an observer brought up in the eighteenth-century English tradition, moreover, dominated as it was by Newtonian physics and all that it indicated of planetary wheelings and ineluctable law. Wordsworth had completed his education in the university where Newton's laws were first propounded, and where they still dominated intellectual life. Newton's statue stood in the chapel of Trinity College, not far from his own college room;[27] his discoveries were expounded by men who continued to see them as reflecting the work of a benevolent creator. In such minds, however, the natural and moral universes interlocked without deeply challenging one another: if they came together it was simply to reinforce the authority of over-riding Law.

Wordsworth had not been altogether at home in such a dispensation. For one thing, the predominance of mathematics and science had not proved beneficial to poetry: Thomas Gray, despite his stature, could hardly be thought of as a second Milton. Yet the university offered an enlightened and benevolent setting for a cultivated young man, with opportunities for combining study of classics and mathematics with a more dilettante interest in the arts and in the political and religious issues of the day:

> Friendships, acquaintances, were welcome all;
> We saunter'd, play'd, we rioted, we talk'd

Unprofitable talk at morning hours,
Drifted about along the streets and walks,
Read lazily in lazy books, went forth
To gallop through the country in blind zeal
Of senseless horsemanship, or on the breast
Of Cam sail'd boisterously; and let the stars
Come out, perhaps without one quiet thought.

1805 iii 250–8

While Wordsworth's self-portrait shows himself taking up the pre-ferred modes of his society there was, nevertheless, something un-satisfied under the surface—hinted at in the last line of that passage and best indicated perhaps as a sense of possibilities which had opened out during his last years at school and not yet found fulfil-ment. His enjoyment of poetry during the period had included a passion for some poems which a more developed taste told him to be inferior; yet he could not escape the sense that the feelings aroused had had an authenticity which survived his adverse critical judge-ments. Similar feelings were experienced in Cambridge only when he wandered out alone to the Backs at night.[28] Even his contemporaries, nevertheless, noticed that on certain topics he might stray beyond the easy elegance of normal conversations. One of them wrote,

> I remember his speaking very highly in praise of the beauties of the North; with a warmth indeed which, at that time, appeared to me hardly short of enthusiasm. He mentioned too . . . that he had received the whole of his education in the very bosom of the Lakes, at a small seminary, which has produced of late years in our University several names which have done it very considerable credit.[29]

Despite his occasional misgivings, Wordsworth at Cambridge was, by his own account, slipping comfortably enough into the stream of time. The learned professions offered pleasant prospects to a young man of ability: the way lay open for him to embark upon a useful career. And so, indeed, it might have proved, had he not chosen dur-ing the long vacation of 1790 to visit France with his friend, Robert Jones. There is little indication that he had intended this to be more than an undergraduate walking-tour in search of the picturesque: the two men, making their way swiftly to the Alps, stumbled across the effects of the Revolution, as it were, by chance. Landing in

Calais on Federation Day, however, and finding the place *en fête*, he was deeply impressed. As he would later recall:

> A homeless sound of joy was in the sky:
> From hour to hour the antiquated Earth
> Beat like the heart of Man: songs, garlands, mirth,
> Banners, and happy faces, far and nigh . . .[30]

Or again,

> Far other show
> My youth here witnessed, in a prouder time;
> The senselessness of joy was then sublime![31]

Two words here invite attention by their dislocation of normal usage: 'homeless' and 'senselessness'. They speak to an awareness that the release of joy knows no dimensions of time and space, no organization by the organs of sense. It is a moment of *aion*. Yet Wordsworth is also giving the words an overlay of warning, the effect of a subsequent recognition that human beings need to be linked to a home, that 'senselessness' (the word also used by him in describing the excitement of galloping on horseback) is not a good state in which to live permanently.

That is a later reflection. At the time, the signs that they were not just witnessing an important event but living in a period of *kairos*, the occasion of something altogether new in human history, were hard to evade. The very imagery in his most famous description is of a renovating moment in time:

> Bliss was it in that dawn to be alive,
> But to be young was very Heaven; O times,
> In which the meagre, stale, forbidding ways
> Of custom, law, and statute took at once
> The attraction of a Country in Romance . . .
>
> 1805 x 692–6

The sense of a new season in the affairs of men was reinforced, he says elsewhere, by the natural republicanism that he had experienced in the society of the Lakes, where men took for granted a natural equality with one another. The new order in France, linking itself to what he had known there, appeared therefore like a natural fulfilment. In his manuscript Letter to the Bishop of Llandaff, drafted in 1793, he could still argue for the course of defending a hard-won liberty by violence as a 'stern necessity', part of a 'convulsion from which is to spring a fairer order of things'.[32]

However precarious the joy was to prove in retrospect, then, it was at the time overpowering. Wordsworth catches the double sense finely in three lines of *The Prelude*:

> . . . 'twas a time when Europe was rejoiced,
> France standing on the top of golden hours,
> And human nature seeming born again.

> 1805 vi 352-4

The suggestions of *aion* in the image of the mountain-top, the word 'golden' and the temporary assurance of rebirth are undermined only by the suggestion that the 'top' might be that not of a mountain but of a wheel, the hours not the dancing graces of classical mythology but the inevitable circlings and reversals of time.

This vulnerability applied to the cyclical ideal generally. In less propitious circumstances a disillusioned mind would easily revert to its older mode of perception. If the hoped-for progress in human affairs turned out not to be taking place, if old evils seemed simply to be consolidating themselves more firmly, the cyclical pattern of history would be seen once again not as a progressive spiral, gradually circling upwards, but as a series of rounds incessantly repeating themselves, from which human beings struggled to break out only at the expense of finding themselves more firmly bound. In Wordsworth's case, the sense of inexorability induced by such a reversal was likely to be subtly reinforced by his contact in France with intellectuals whose acceptance of Newton's laws was accompanied not by the belief in Divine benevolence expressed by Newton and most of his English followers, but by atheism.

Certainly the Terror, when it came, affected his sensibility powerfully. Living in Paris at the time and lying awake in fear one night, his imagination conjured up strange images and 'dim admonishments':

> 'The horse is taught his manage, and the wind
> Of heaven wheels round and treads in his own steps,
> Year follows year, the tide returns again,
> Day follows day, all things have second birth;
> The earthquake is not satisfied at once.'

> 1805 x 70-4

The force of the circling imagery (horses in a ring, the heavens wheeling round inexorably, the years recurring, the tides returning, the earthquake repeating itself) was all the more powerful, it seems, in the shadow of its more happy earlier associations of spiral and progress, here transformed into nightmare wheeling and enclosure.

The implied image of a wheel turning faster and faster and rolling inexorably into vortex then re-emerges (though transposed into a minor key) when Wordsworth finds a likeness for the revolutionaries and their rapacious carnage ('Head after head, and never heads enough / For those who bade them fall') in the behaviour of children:

> . . . they found their joy,
> They made it, ever thirsty as a Child,
> If light desires of innocent little Ones
> May with such heinous appetites be match'd,
> Having a toy, a wind-mill, though the air
> Do of itself blow fresh, and makes the vane
> Spin in his eyesight, he is not content,
> But with the play-thing at arm's length he sets
> His front against the blast, and runs amain,
> To make it whirl the faster.
>
> 1805 x 336–45

This sense that the nightmarish, vortical conclusion to what had begun in such hope was endemic in human nature, resulting from a tendency to press experience to extremes which could be traced even in small children, was crucial to Wordsworth's development. The contrast between established *chronos* and revolutionary *kairos* had presented itself with apparent decisiveness in the course of human history, only to be thwarted in its optimistic implications. The image of an aged Father Time being replaced by a new and vital young spirit had failed. Wordsworth would never again identify the looked-for *kairos* with an opportunity in the political sphere; and at this time he found himself embarked upon a more sombre course of thinking. The harsher face of nature, rearing itself tyrannically in the Terror, was showing him in a more fearful form the kind of phenomenon which had led his hero John Milton to write, 'New *Presbyter* is but old *Priest* writ large.'[33] And when he saw his own country taking up arms against the troubled infant republic

the cynical circle seemed complete, turning him away from the
beckonings of optimism into a sense of wilderness wanderings. The
effect, as described in *The Prelude*, was a kind of negative revolution—and of revolution concealed in an older mode at that:

> Not in my single self alone I found,
> But in the minds of all ingenious Youth,
> Change and subversion from this hour. No shock
> Given to my moral nature had I known
> Down to that very moment; neither lapse
> Nor turn of sentiment that might be nam'd
> A revolution, save at this one time,
> All else was progress on the self-same path
> On which with a diversity of pace
> I had been travelling; this a stride at once
> Into another region

> 1805 x 231–41

He also recalls his divided feelings:

> A conflict of sensations without name,
> Of which he only who may love the sight
> Of a Village Steeple as I do can judge
> When in the Congregation, bending all
> To their great Father, prayers were offer'd up,
> Or praises for our Country's Victories,
> And 'mid the simple worshippers, perchance,
> I only, like an uninvited Guest
> Whom no one owned sate silent, shall I add,
> Fed on the day of vengeance yet to come?

> 1805 x 265–74

During the summer which witnessed this blow both to his own
sense of loyalty and to his hopes of marriage in the near future (since
he could no longer visit Annette Vallon, whose child he had fathered
during an earlier stay in France)[34] Wordsworth had undertaken one
of the most momentous expeditions of his life, his journey across
Salisbury Plain. Having stayed on the Isle of Wight

in view of the fleet which was then preparing for sea off Ports-
mouth at the commencement of the war, I left the place with
melancholy forebodings. The American war was still fresh in

memory. The struggle which was beginning, and which many thought would be brought to a speedy close by the irresistible arms of Great Britain being added to those of the Allies, I was assured in my own mind would be of long continuance, and productive of distress and misery beyond all possible calculation. This conviction was pressed upon me by having been a witness, during a long residence in revolutionary France, of the spirit which prevailed in that country.[35]

Any physical comfort in the journey ended abruptly, moreover, when the carriage in which he and his companion were travelling broke down and he was forced to carry on alone. The Plain, with its prehistoric remains and general starkness, was a fitting background to the thoughts which were dogging him:

> The moments and traces of antiquity, scattered in abundance over that region, led me unavoidably to compare what we know or guess of those remote times with certain aspects of modern society, and with calamities, principally those consequent upon war, to which, more than other classes of men, the poor are subject.

He was prompted to plan, against the same scene, a poetic narrative about destitute travellers.

The resulting poem, which began as 'A Night on Salisbury Plain', was not finally published until 1842, when it bore the title 'Guilt and Sorrow'.[36x] Throughout the various revisions one main theme survives, overriding the particular sequence of events: it is an awesome sense of human beings trapped in a sequence of events from which they are powerless to escape. In the first version that sense is voiced directly, through a question:

> Must Law with iron scourge
> Still torture crimes that grew a monstrous band
> Formed by his care and still his victims urge
> With voice that breathes despair to death's tremendous verge?[37]

That version concludes by forthrightly urging the 'Heroes of Truth' to

> pursue your toils till not a trace
> Be left on earth of Superstition's reign,
> Save that eternal pile which frowns on Sarum's plain.[38]

He could not remain totally bound by his own dreary vision, however, even on the plain itself. As he passed across it and saw its ominous prehistoric circles, with their grim suggestions of human sacrifice, he was also visited by a quite different vision of the Druids as natural harmonizers, interpreting the movements of the heavens with the aid of the great circles they constructed:

> . . . when 'twas my chance
> To have before me on the downy Plain
> Lines, circles, mounts, a mystery of shapes
> Such as in many quarters yet survive,
> With intricate profusion figuring o'er
> The untill'd ground, the work, as some divine,
> Of infant science, imitative forms
> By which the Druids covertly express'd
> Their knowledge of the heavens, and imaged forth
> The constellations, I was gently charm'd,
> Albeit with an antiquarian's dream,
> I saw the bearded Teachers, with white wands
> Uplifted, pointing to the starry sky
> Alternately, and Plain below, while breath
> Of music seem'd to guide them, and the Waste
> Was chear'd with stillness and a pleasant sound.
>
> 1805 xii 338–53

This was no more than a visionary moment, perhaps, to be treated from that limited perspective; but it was valuable as a release from the depression that was dogging him. Nor did the expedition end on Salisbury Plain—though the sequel is usually discussed separately. Wordsworth continued over the Severn and up the Wye to see Jones, his former companion in France, who was now a clergyman at Plas-yn-Llan. This latter part of the journey was marked by encounters with at least two memorable figures: the little girl who was to become the heroine of 'We are Seven', and the 'rover' who gave Wordsworth the idea for *Peter Bell*.[39] The indications are that Wordsworth was thinking about the mysteries of human nature, particularly as they revealed themselves in a little girl who could not fully realise the concept of mortality and a grown man who was unresponsive to the beauties of nature.

The exact nature of these encounters can only be inferred from the poems that were afterwards created about them; the most significant event of all, however, the first visit to Tintern, was to be described more directly, when Wordsworth later tried to recall

> what I was when first
> I came among these hills; when like a roe
> I bounded o'er the mountains, by the sides
> Of the deep rivers, and the lonely streams,
> Wherever nature led: more like a man
> Flying from something that he dreads than one
> Who sought the thing he loved.
>
> PW II 261

This passage, and the well-known one that follows are, once set in the original context of events, surprising. Everything else that we know about this expedition suggests sober meditation of a rather pessimistic kind; these lines are fraught with wildness. The sounding cataract 'haunted' him; the great forms of mountain and gloomy wood were 'an appetite, a feeling and a love . . .'

Yet the two versions of himself are not irreconcilable. Wordsworth, at this particular juncture, emerges as a complicated figure, his moments of depression as he surveyed the cyclical workings of human history set off by tensely passionate responses to particular experiences in nature.

There was to be one occasion, moreover, when the passions moved yet more strongly, inspiring a belief, momentarily at least, that the ideal he thought he had glimpsed in France might still be about to reveal itself in human history. In the following year, walking by the Leven estuary on a day of unusual splendour, he watched a company of travellers wading across the estuary at low tide. The first of the band, instead of throwing out a conventional greeting, cried, 'Robespierre is dead!' It was a little time before Wordsworth could grasp the full significance of the news, but when he did his dream of the French Revolution sprang back into sudden life. All might yet be fulfilled, the aspirations of the revolutionaries might after all be realized. He passed into a rhapsodic mood as he walked along by the river bank and allowed himself to dream of a new Golden Age. And as he looked back on this event, in *The Prelude*, it seemed strangely fitting that it should have happened in the very place where he had previously felt his own identity most strongly—

... that very Shore which I had skimm'd
In former times, when, spurring from the Vale
Of Nightshade, and St Mary's mouldering Fane,
And the Stone Abbot, after circuit made
In wantonness of heart, a joyous Crew
Of School-boys, hastening to their distant home,
Along the margin of the moonlight Sea,
We beat with thundering hoofs the level Sand.

1805 x 559–66

The taking over of the last line, intact, from his earlier description of a rapturous boyhood excursion indicates the kind of significance that Wordsworth attached to this revival of former hopes. Once again, he had the sense of perhaps assisting at a great occasion in history, a re-establishment of correspondence between human society and the inner aspirations of man.

Great was my glee of spirit, great my joy
In vengeance, and eternal justice, thus
Made manifest. 'Come now ye golden times,'
Said I, forth-breathing on those open Sands
A Hymn of triumph, 'as the morning comes
Out of the bosom of the night, come Ye:
Thus far our trust is verified; behold!
They who with clumsy desperation brought
Rivers of Blood, and preached that nothing else
Could cleanse the Augean Stable, by the might
Of their own helper have been swept away;
Their madness is declared and visible,
Elsewhere will safety now be sought, and Earth
March firmly towards righteousness and peace.'

1805 x 539–52

Despite the force of his rhetoric, the presence of individual words such as 'glee' and 'vengeance' once again infuses an admonitory note at the beginning—a suggestion that his emotions, though genuine, had been immature and faulty, insufficiently rooted in experience and understanding of human nature. The glory in nature which had encouraged them, equally, was only one of her manifestations, to be set alongside many other moods.

Viewed from a distance of years, therefore, the incident could be

47

viewed as a moment of unusual rapture, cheering to look back on with an indulgent eye but also, essentially, a divergence from his main path of development, which had continued with the search at Racedown for a more solid basis to his human philosophy. He describes in successive later versions of *The Prelude* how he concluded his period of scientific analysis by abandoning all moral questions and resolving to turn 'towards mathematics, and their clear / And solid evidence'

> . . . and there sought
> Work for the reasoning faculty enthroned
> Where the disturbances of space and time—
> Whether in matter's various properties
> Inherent, or from human will and power
> Derived—find no admission.
>
> 1850 xi 328–33

With this resolve he reached one of the extremes in his development, a posture in which, indeed, he might well have been lost as a poet. So compelling was it in its own terms that he could move out of it only by a large change of concern, one which would enlarge his whole view of things by enabling him to shift his attention from political possibilities to observation of nature coupled with personal introspection and to explore the possibility that, when looked at in certain ways, the structure of nature could be seen to be fitted to that of the human mind in ways hardly dreamt of in eighteenth-century philosophy.

His later accounts would suggest that he was directed into this path, once again, by rediscovering aspects of himself that were not easily contained within the sharp boundaries imposed by his own analysing reason. In particular it was Dorothy who at this time

> Maintain'd for me a saving intercourse
> With my true self; for, though impair'd and changed
> Much, as it seem'd, I was no further changed
> Than as a clouded, not a waning moon . . .[40x]

Her own openness of heart, which kept in being his feeling for humanity, ensured a future course, not through the oppositions of rationalism (which might have resulted in further sterilities of the sardonic) but through the polarized forces of his own feelings.

These forces were still organizing themselves around the eighteenth-century modes of sublimity and pathos. By now, however, they had begun to crystallize into more particular forms. Sublimity had localized itself more firmly in the semi-mystical and passionate experiences which he had begun to encounter at the end of his school-days and which had continued to haunt him occasionally in Cambridge: his private sense of initiation into a world dominated by passions (terror, love, beauty) which were also revealed in nature herself could be peculiarly satisfying:

> I had a world about me; 'twas my own,
> I made it; for it only liv'd to me,
> And to the God who look'd into my mind.
> Such sympathies would sometimes shew themselves
> By outward gestures and by visible looks.
> Some call'd it madness: such, indeed, it was,
> If child-like fruitfulness in passing joy,
> If steady moods of thoughtfulness, matur'd
> To inspiration, sort with such a name;
> If prophecy be madness . . .

1805 iii 142–51

The emotions which are remembered with so much assurance in 1805 had been approached with less confidence at the time, however. In other obsessions of passionate sense, Wordsworth could then feel that he might truly be coming close to madness:

> I crossed the dreary moor
> In the clear moonlight: when I reached the hut
> I entered in, but all was still and dark,
> Only within the ruin I beheld
> At a small distance, on the dusky ground
> A broken pane which glittered in the moon
> And seemed akin to life. There is a mood
> A settled temper of the heart, when grief,
> Become an instinct, fastening on all things
> That promise food, doth like a sucking babe
> Create it where it is not. From this time
> That speck of glass was dearer to my soul
> Than was the moon in heaven.

PW I 314

Hauntings such as this, some exciting him with a sense of revealed knowledge, others appalling by an effect of irrational yet irresistible attraction, were climactic among attachments to the natural world which seized him from time to time. He needed to come to terms with them, but could for the time being do no more than give them expression.

In this respect, the parallel with Blake is again suggestive. There is evidence that from his youth onwards Blake had been pondering issues similar to those which had come to oppress Wordsworth, including the sense of an implacable Necessity at work in human affairs. The results appear most extensively in a series of drawings which he made in his Notebook and which were eventually drawn upon for the briefer series of engravings entitled 'The Gates of Paradise'. These include, for example, a design with the inscription (from Donne) addressed to Destiny

> Whose changeless brow
> Ne'er smiles nor frowns.[41]

In 'There is No Natural Religion', on the other hand, Blake not only posed the dark implications of contemporary natural philosophy but set against them the achievement of the poet or prophet:

> If it were not for the Poetic or Prophetic character the Philosophic & Experimental would soon be at the ratio of all things, & stand still, unable to do other than repeat the same dull round over again.
>
> BW 97

For Blake the contrast was primarily that between the static, 'vegetative' element in human consciousness and the different state created in the exercise of energy. To the 'Corporeal Vegetative Eye', Time and Space are fixed (the Sunflower is 'weary of time').[42] Once the human being rises up in energy, on the other hand, the dull round of time is transcended. 'Between two moments bliss is ripe,' cries Blake's Oothoon, spirit of free desire; his 'devil' of Energy proclaims confidently that 'Eternity is in love with the productions of time.'[43] It is the same with the act of poetic creation in *Milton*:

> Every time less than a pulsation of the artery
> Is equal in its period & value to Six Thousand Years,
> For in this Period the Poet's Work is Done . . .
>
> BW 516 (28: 61–29: 1)

Blake, more than anyone else of his period, understood the ways in which time could be transcended by active energy. Yet he was always conscious how alien to the dominant intellectual modes that notion was, how liable to be encroached upon by more conventional views:

> The Greeks represent Chronos or Time as a very Aged Man; this is Fable, but the Real Vision of Time is in Eternal Youth. I have, however, somewhat accomodated my Figure of Time to the common opinion, as I myself am also infected with it & my Visions also infected, & I see Time Aged, alas, too much so.
>
> BW 614

Wordsworth, who as a child had suffered experiences of vision so powerful that the orderings of the external world dropped away, making it necessary for him to clutch at a gate or post to reassure himself of the material existence of things, but who had also suffered a sharp decline in that power, was more oppressed by the precariousness of any such deliverance from time, more heavily aware of the encroachments made upon experiences of vision by his own maturing consciousness. For him they remained no more than a possible key—even if they enabled him still to set up, in however shadowy a form, a dialectic between *kairos* and *aion*. In his first poetic productions he had been able to celebrate an occasion (the exercise of sensibility against a fitting landscape) in 'An Evening Walk' and then, in 'Descriptive Sketches', to express aionic hauntings of the sublime. These were rudimentary forms, however; before he could progress as a poet he needed to develop them beyond thir contemporary acceptation—both to discover modes by which, despite the oppressions of his darker awarenesses, single occasions could be rendered into universality, and to develop a 'Poetic or Prophetic character' through which normal commonplace existence, instead of simply repeating 'the same dull round over again' would be seen to be in a state of perpetual renovation.

Blake, before him, had offered a brisk way forward. In *The Gates of Paradise* his images of despair were followed by a crucial plate bearing the inscription, 'Fear & Hope are—Vision' and another expressing the subsequent sense of liberation: 'The Traveller hasteth in the Evening'.[44] Wordsworth, by contrast, moving through similar territory and also drawn to the relationship between fear, hope and vision, was to find in it matter to brood upon for a lifetime. The journey of this mental traveller could not be undertaken in haste— nor, indeed, could he find a true way forward until he fell into the company of Coleridge.

Springs

When Coleridge died, Wordsworth said, among other things, that he
was 'the most *wonderful* man that he had ever known—'[1] He was
not a man to use words extravagantly, particularly in his later years,
and the adjective was evidently chosen with care. It pointed to something he felt as essential in his friend—an enthusiasm, an intelligence delighted in its own exercise, a sense of informing imagination.

Descriptions of the relationship often suggest little more than a
loose association between two men with similar interests, Coleridge
throwing out various ideas and images, some of which Wordsworth
was able to take up and use for his own purposes, Wordsworth, in
return, impressing Coleridge with his own feeling for nature. Some
direct debts undoubtedly exist; one can trace a line from Coleridge's
description of the view of the Bristol Channel—

> It seem'd like Omnipresence! God, methought,
> Had built him there a Temple: the whole World
> Seem'd *imag'd* in its vast circumference . . .

to Wordsworth's

> sense sublime
> Of something far more deeply interfused,
> Whose dwelling is the light of setting suns,
> And the round ocean and the living air,
> And the blue sky, and in the mind of man . . .[2]

or from Coleridge's use of conversational language in poetry ('Well,
they are gone, and here must I remain,/This lime-tree bower my
prison!') to Wordsworth's ('Once again I see / These hedge-rows,
hardly hedge-rows, little lines / Of sportive wood run wild . . .').[3]
Yet even in these cases one is immediately forced to notice both the
greater scope and range of Wordsworth's pantheistic landscape (indicating a further refinement of the idea) and the existence of a
conversational tradition, particularly in Cowper, on which they could

both draw. Although each is sometimes attracted into the other's most characteristic diction, moreover, the results, on Coleridge's side at least, are not impressive—his contribution to 'The Three Graves' does not represent his best writing. The movement between the two minds is better when more subtle, as when one poet is drawing from some idea of the other's while pursuing a preoccupation of his own. One need only mention how Coleridge uses a story similar to that of Oswald from *The Borderers* in his own 'Ancient Mariner', and how Wordsworth then counters other features of Coleridge's poem by writing *Peter Bell*, to suggest the scope of the mutual interaction at its best.

When it comes to interaction at the level of ideas, critics have found themselves in more difficult territory. They have usually been content to suggest that Coleridge acted as an intermediary for philosophical theories which Wordsworth would not have known from his own reading, introducing him to the systems of Hartley, Berkeley and Spinoza—followed later, perhaps, by Kant and the Germans.[4]

So long as Coleridge's own intellectual progress is seen as a steady progress through the systems of these thinkers, such a theory suggests a plausible shape for larger and more general movements in Wordsworth's thought; it fails in important ways, however, to account for the precise detail of his poetry. And it is possible to see the development of Coleridge's mind during these years differently: not as a simple progress through rival systems but as embodying a dual process of its own, a series of engagements with the political, social and religious issues of his time being accompanied by the growth of a body of esoteric speculations, dating from the metaphysical enthusiasms of his schooldays and continuing, whenever circumstances were propitious, to engage his mind.

Here it is only possible to summarize these speculations, the evidences for which are set out at greater length elsewhere.[5] In brief outline, they are as follows. As a deeply imaginative adolescent, I have argued, Coleridge found himself attracted at an early stage by certain doctrines, such as those of Swedenborgianism, which held that in the universe there existed points of correspondence with the divine order through which the nature of the true God was revealed. He was also attracted by ideas such as those of Boehme and the Neoplatonists, which gave metaphysical status to the imagination and energy of human beings, arguing that they were matched by similar phenomena in the universe at large. In this way the common eighteenth-century picture of a universe distanced and ordered in terms of time and space could be complemented by a sense that under certain conditions human perception broke through that laid-out order to achieve an immediate and vivid experience of the reality at the heart of things. Coleridge's enthusiasm, on this account of the matter, was not simply motivated by a pleasure in exotic ideas for their own sake: he really believed that it might be possible to recover from such mystic and philosophical writers clues concerning the nature of the universe which would bear a relation to the more mysterious discoveries of contemporary science and perhaps resolve the dilemma created by the mechanistic theories of Newton and Locke.

The first of these ideas bore heavily on the Newtonian universe. It was that the *central* 'fact' of the universe lay not in the mathematical laws by which astronomers had learned to chart the movements of the planets but in the existence of vast centres of energy here and there, as in our sun. In a sense this too was a part of contemporary science, but Coleridge's particular contribution to the conception lay in his supposition (carried over from certain earlier writers) that the proper descriptive image for the sun was not that of a ball of fire, gradually burning itself out, but *a perpetual and self-renewing fountain*, attracting to itself the energies of the universe and then giving them back again, in much the same way that the heart persistently renewed the blood in the human body, and thus linking itself with all other living centres of energy.[6]

Our present concern, of course, is not with the truth or otherwise of the theory (which owed some of its contemporary plausibility—at least as a literal proposition—to the fact that the Laws of Thermodynamics had not as yet been propounded) but with the further reasons which would make it attractive to a thinker at the end of the eighteenth century in England.

At the surface level, where it was taken to indicate a fact about the sun in the physical universe, it was attractive as offering a possible point of major correspondence between the human being and his natural surroundings. But even if one rejected the actual physical correspondence, such a view might still be held to have general physical truth, to indicate wherein the true 'life of things' lay. The importance of such a concept at this remove would be to indicate that (independently of the behaviour of the actual physical sun) the central energies of the universe were those of life, not death. If they were viewed in the form of a ball of fire which was slowly burning itself out, then the universe at large became a vast machine, kept running by that furnace and destined to run down as the sun slowly cooled. If, on the other hand, they were in some sense vitally self-renewing, the universe need no longer be seen as a machine which would inevitably come to a stop. The cosmic despair which drove men to obsessive preoccupation with death might then be tempered by an awareness of life as always self-renewing—despite the deaths of particular individuals.

Traditionally men had avoided such despair by their belief in another order—separate from the one investigated by Newton— which imposed a moral law on mankind and promised them an immortality which would be accompanied by rewards and punishments commensurate with the standard of their earthly behaviour. Under this dispensation man found himself living simultaneously under two orders: the one, dominated by space and time and the processes of cause and effect within their dominion, helping to organize his sense-experience, the other abstract and ultimately transcendental, concerning itself with the nature and quality of his actions during his lifetime. Neither order, however, did full justice to the creative powers of human beings—or indeed to their capacities of communication. The advantage of the 'sun-fountain' theory was that it offered another dimension to life on earth here and now, suggesting the existence of links between all living things which need not be charted in terms of space and time. In the world of self-renewing energy, 'we are all one life'.[7x] One might even go further and propose that it offered a model for human nature, by which the light and energies of the sun could be related to the light of intellect and the energies of the heart, so that the truly alive human being would be thought of as he who best reconciled the two in his own body.

In its more general form this theory seems to have attracted Coleridge from his school-days; certainly by the time that he wrote his 'Greek Ode on Astronomy' at Cambridge he was picturing Newton not as the traditional figure of eighteenth-century iconography, with outstretched compasses,[8] but as a genius presiding over 'the spring/Ebullient with creative energy'[9]. The following year, at the height of his enthusiasm for Pantisocracy (his scheme to set up a small egalitarian community in America), he wrote 'My head, my heart, are all alive . . . the Head shall be the Mass—the Heart the fiery Spirit, that fills, informs and agitates the whole.'[10] It was probably in 1795, however, that he returned to this range of thinking and began to explore its psychological implications more closely.

The new idea to engage him was, in brief, that all men were born with a fund of magnetizing energy, associated with the heart, and that the process of human development involved a gradual organization and disposition of this energy. At the time of birth their magnetic field was, so to speak, 'open to infinity', so that they were still in direct communication with the infinite fountain in the universe which was God; but by the processes of adaptation to the world in which they found themselves they were increasingly oriented to the world of space and time, until virtually the whole of their human perception was governed by measurings and calculations in the world of sense. Nevertheless, this was always in some sense an artificial organization, superimposed upon their primitive spring of unorganized energy. The hypnotist who could, by his particular art, communicate with his patient's subconscious, causing him to do things which he had not himself willed and of which his normal consciousness knew nothing, was bypassing the superstructure to tap that underlying spring. And although this concept was for Coleridge intimately related to the concept of 'genius' (for genius, in the broader sense, could be identified with that hidden spring), the universality of hypnotic phenomena suggested that the man of genius was merely displaying in a more overt form a power which was present in all men and (though staled in most by custom) the key to their ultimate being.[11]

One important effect of this skein of reasoning, I have further argued, was that it opened the mind to awareness of a level of consciousness subsisting below that of normal rational activity, and acting, in certain important respects, in what might seem a qualitatively different mode. The workings of the unconscious, which were to be the subject of so much attention later, could thus be investigated in a rewarding manner—even if the point of view differed from that to be adopted by more analytically-minded investigators such as Freud.

So far I have been enumerating a sequence of speculations which I believe to have been operating in Coleridge's mind at this time; it is more difficult to convey the sense of a skein of interlocking correspondences, so that any of the series might interact with, and modify, any other—all being assumed to link at that unconscious level to which the hypnotist had limited access. Thus if the sun is linked to the image of a self-replenishing fountain, and the fountain to the physical fountain in the human heart (which also gains something of the splendour of the sun), all three are linked to, and modify, the idea that life itself provides a key to the phenomenon of genius, as well as to that of the creative process which operates in dreams (and, indeed, in all those acts of perception by which we see the world in unities, as opposed to particulars). The whole body of speculation, in turn, provides a scheme for the interpretation of the supernatural in human experience and the romantic in art.

Such a scheme might further help with the growing contemporary debate concerning science and religion. If it were valid, the apparent contradiction between the worlds of science and religion could be resolved by reinterpretation of the phenomenon involved. When men were in a state of waking consciousness, it could be argued, they were automatically 'magnetized' to the world of space and time; but in other states, as in nightmare, trance or hypnotism, their 'primary consciousness' would be brought into play, exposing them to greater life-forces at large in the universe and creating a sense of the numinous that existed in the same continuum as religious belief. Coleridge was evidently always in two minds about the matter. The 'religious' sense which was rescued by such a theory was not necessarily identifiable with Christianity, which from other points of view he valued and was anxious to preserve. Nor is it likely that his scientific friends would have accepted without scepticism his postulates about magnetism and solar energy, even in that speculative period. Yet it is a curiously haunting skein of ideas, even now, since it both provides an unusually imaginative framework within which to consider certain problems concerning the nature of consciousness which are important in their own right.

In Coleridge's day, finally, it possessed the further local advantage that it could provide the poet with a new account of sublimity and pathos. On this interpretation it was the activity of the primary consciousness which provided a man with his experiences of the sublime—so that fear, or nightmare, or other experiences which brought that consciousness into play, were also more likely to induce a sense of sublimity. When he returned from such an experience to the light of common day, moreover, he would see the world of space and time, the normal outer framework of his thinking, in a new light. The fact that in this world life feeds on life might then be seen as a fact of generous pathos, instead of imposing that sense of cruelly amoral mechanical process which might more logically engage the eye of rationalism. And the air which circulates around human beings could be seen as a phenomenon of the most elevated pathos— for this is one food of man which does not involve the consumption of other lives: it is the 'living air' which blows on all alike, and which, in the form of the breeze blowing against him, cherishes a man's awareness of himself as a separate identity, preserving him from nightmare extremes in which he feels himself either totally alienated from nature or merely an extension of its mindless rocks, stones and trees.

In presupposing that Coleridge's thinking developed in this way and that Wordsworth responded in this way or that, we are necessarily moving in a somewhat speculative area, since we are handling evidence which is indirect rather than direct. From our own knowledge of how dialogues proceed, similarly, we may suppose that Wordsworth was sometimes sceptical and questioning rather than straightforwardly receptive. Yet it is hard to account for the directions in which his poetry now moved unless one presupposes that some such dialogue was taking place. As was emphasized earlier, we are called upon to explain certain points of disturbance in his writing, the appearance there of themes which would not have been anticipated from his early work but which become more readily explicable in the context of exposure to ideas such as those just outlined. The full extent of them will become clear in subsequent chapters.

Such ideas could also be expected to have been attractive to Wordsworth in the years when he was recovering from his despondency. To a consciousness that had become obsessed by the awareness of mechanical and deathly processes in the universe they would be at once healing and vivifying, placing death in a context of life, rather than life in a context of death, and sustaining an awareness of the mercies of life in complement to that of the impersonal and antihuman forces of war and destruction. They might also enable him to come to terms with his own unusual experiences in nature. If his eye was magnetized to a piece of glass which he saw shining in a ruined building, for example,[12] this might be interpreted not as a sign of incipient madness but as a message from his primary consciousness that it had been neglected and was forcing some recognition of its importance and need for a secure point of focus. His experiences of direct communication with nature in boyhood and youth, equally, could be seen, not as aberrations from common sense, but as workings of the same consciousness, keeping alive an awareness of mysterious forces in the universe which were neglected by the majority of his fellows.

In the same way, the strange experiences of fear and trance which Wordsworth had been aware of throughout his childhood and youth, visiting him even on his journey across Salisbury Plain to Tintern, could now be persuasively accounted for. Viewed as movements in the primary consciousness, they could be regarded as corresponding to deeper forces in the universe at large. Coleridge's idea that the experience of fear could open the mind to important visionary experiences, culminating in motions of love, would be particularly suggestive in such a context, suggesting that Wordsworth's mood on his first visit to Tintern, 'more like a man/Flying from something that he dreads than one / Who sought the thing he loved', was in fact the most propitious for the revelation of beauty and harmony in nature that he had actually experienced in the Wye Valley on that occasion.

There is another, more subtle mode in which the Coleridgean ideas can be seen to have transformed conventional eighteenth-century imagery. As we have already seen, the most common way of viewing time then was through the image of a flowing river. Coleridge's favourite imagery of the spring, by transferring attention to another element in the paradigm, changed the points of emphasis. In those terms, the centre of the process was the perpetual self-renewal at the spring from which the river flowed, its steady flowing being a secondary and dependent process. Such a reflection could change one's mood even in contemplating an ordinary river, which was no longer to be seen primarily as a body of matter flowing to waste, but as part of a great self-renewing process in nature. It could also, in turn, change one's sense of the 'stream' of human consciousness, suggesting the constant intervention of acts of renewal within that consciousness through the creative powers of the human psyche. It also offered new ways of thinking about memory, and its ability to escape the 'stream' image altogether through its power of restoring instantly to the human consciousness moments revived from years before.

One final element in this line of thinking, related this time to the phenomena of organic life and growth, may be mentioned. Coleridge, throughout his life, interested himself in the differences between vegetable and animal life: vegetable life unfolding itself according to the inward idea contained in its seed, animal life characterized by a fund of energy which gave it freedom of movement in the world of sense. Whereas the vegetable unfolded itself directly in the course of time, the animal's growth was accompanied by instinctive movements of a free nature; these were then reflected in the more profoundly free activities of the human being. There were similarities as well as differences, however. In the vegetable, movements of energy, on the rare occasions when they became visible (as in the development of tendrils in the vine or the hop-bean), often took a spiralling form; in the animal, similarly, free movements of energy normally followed a circling or spiralling mode which could in turn be communally adapted to create patterns of movement—as in the play of flocks of birds, or the communal dance of flies.[13]

Certain aspects of this scheme will be seen to be unusually apposite to the patterns of obsessive thought traced in the previous chapter, since they actually take hold of the dominant imagery and transform it. The circling processes which had presented themselves to Wordsworth in nightmare form as he lay awake in his room in Paris might lose their imprisoning terror if he came to believe that a large upward-circling process was common to all life and growth. Once set against an alternative pattern of evolving spirals, those implacable revolvings might relax their insidious hold, and allow new hopes that the process which had failed in the French Revolution would yet, on a much larger time-scale, succeed, since the pattern of this slower growth would then appear to be ratified by the processes of nature herself.

If Coleridge's ideas worked in the way that I am suggesting (and it is not easy to account in other terms for the extraordinary efflorescence of mental activity which is evident in his own and Wordsworth's poetry of the time) it is important to see that Wordsworth's mind had already been partially prepared by certain of the more common ideas that had been circulating in Europe, particularly among the French *philosophes*.

In an important discussion,[14] H. W. Piper has described some of these ideas and their likely influence on Wordsworth and Coleridge. From his account we need only select two passages to illustrate the kind of thinking that was current. J.-B.-R. Robinet, in a book published in 1768, had written,

All matter is organic, living and animal. . . . In some aspects, the active power seems to reside in matter and to be an essential quality in it, though in other ways activity seems to be the substance, and matter only an instrument which this substance uses to deploy its energy. . . . The whole of nature thus offers to our contemplation two great objects, the progression of forces and the development of forms.[15]

Diderot had offered an even more striking account of the matter:

Each form has the happiness and the unhappiness which is proper to it. From the elephant to the flea, from the flea to the living, sensitive molecule there is not a point in all nature which does not suffer and rejoice.[16]

The ready availability of such statements encourages one to believe that during his residence in France Wordsworth had already been exposed to the concept of an 'active universe'. If so, it may be argued that in the company of Dorothy and Coleridge the whole idea was revived, to be at once deepened and broadened. From Dorothy, both as she now was and as she had been in childhood, he had learned the value of an active response to immediate situations in nature. Coleridge's theories, by suggesting that the sense of wonder evoked by certain of nature's activities was appropriate to the largest workings of the universe as well, directed his attention back to processes with which he had been familiar in childhood. To one brought up among the great forms and workings of a mountainous district, the transformation that takes place when forms that have remained bare throughout winter are suddenly changed to greenness and life, with trees budding at every point, was bound to be both striking and memorable. To one who was familiar with the great land-masses of such an area, equally, further possibilities of wonder inhered in the fact that even their winter bleakness was relieved by the omni-presence of water, presenting itself to eye and ear through strange processes of percolation, spring and torrent.

The immediate effect of Coleridge's theories, on this argument, was simply to focus Wordsworth's attention on familiar processes in a new way, enabling him to supersede the common eighteenth-century modes of perception which had come to dominate his mind. The man who wrote 'The Ruined Cottage' had still been describing nature through traditional modes of sensitive response to particular detail; by the time he wrote *Lyrical Ballads* he was concentrating on signs of vitalism in the scenes about him. A poem which began 'I heard a thousand blended notes' could now continue, by way of the asseveration,

> . . . 'tis my faith that every flower
> Enjoys the air it breathes . . .[17x]

to the suggestion (adopted explicitly in the teeth of a more sober judgement) that pleasure was an ineluctable feature of natural life:

> The birds around me hopp'd and play'd:
> Their thoughts I cannot measure,
> But the least motion which they made,
> It seem'd a thrill of pleasure.

There are scattered evidences throughout the year of the varying topics to which conversation on Coleridge's theories led. On the one hand there are touches of excitement, a sense of rediscovering truths that had somehow escaped the mass of mankind. These however give way to a sense of despondency at the unlikelihood of such beliefs making headway in modern civilization:

> If I these thoughts may not prevent,
> If such be of my creed the plan,
> Have I not reason to lament
> What man has made of man?

The temptation clearly was to see oneself as an 'Eye among the blind', the one sane person in a country where all are mad.[18] The figure of sardonic but sad isolation, of the one person who appreciates the beauty of a moonlit scene, for example, recurs in several poems by both men during this period.

More positively, the two poets turned to the problem of evil. If there were some such active force in nature, with which it was possible for human beings to align themselves beneficially, how did this relate to the facts of evil behaviour? Was there any sense, for example, in which straightforward and continued exposure to nature could be regarded as beneficial to them?

One striking treatment of the issues involved appears in the drafts for 'The Wanderings of Cain',[19] originally planned by the two poets as a collaborative poem. A guilt-ridden Cain is seen finding a natural correlative for his state of mind in sun-scorched deserts and wildernesses ('You might wander on and look round and round, and peep into the crevices of the rocks and discover nothing that acknowledged the influence of the seasons'), while for his innocent son Enos, the fertile 'moonlit wilderness' in which he is discovered picking fruits provides an equally appropriate setting. This project, intractable in itself, was followed by various explorations, on Coleridge's part, of the 'child of nature' theme. For him this phase of the dialogue came to a climax with the joint planning, around a scheme of guilt and supernatural vengeance, of 'The Rime of the Ancient Mariner'—a poem quickly taken over almost exclusively by his own imagination.[20]

Close study of the latter poem discloses the presence of some themes just touched upon. The Mariner is responsible for a deed that seems ordinary enough, yet which initiates him into a sense of guilt, exhibiting in the process a universe which is more mysterious than he had imagined. In that universe living organisms are bound together by unsuspected links; at its heart there is a central power which is a fountain of light and music. If the Mariner cannot understand what he has seen, he cannot forget it, either: he now moves through life with a consciousness radically different from those of the human beings about him.[21]

The motif of disturbed consciousness reappears throughout the original *Lyrical Ballads* volume. It is not the main unifying theme: that is to be sought rather in the sense of unity of life just mentioned, which, having been enunciated openly in 'The Ancient Mariner', reappears more obliquely in a series of characters who would hardly be noticed by the ordinary passer-by and who would appear in the fashionable poetry of the time only as figures of distanced pathos but who all, in varying ways, indicate the significance of the links of life that bind human beings together. Yet one can hardly understand certain features of Wordsworth's contributions unless we presuppose that unusual states of consciousness are also objects of his attention at this time.

Few hints as to the significance of this further interest appear in the surviving discussions of their collection by the poets themselves. There is, however, one statement which deserves to be looked at carefully. In the 1800 preface, Wordsworth says that it was a part of their aim to trace in situations of common life 'the primary laws of our nature', chiefly 'as regards the manner in which we associate ideas in a state of excitement'.[22] The implication would seem to be

that in such a state the forces of association by contiguity, as propounded by Hartley, cease to be dominant, giving way to other,
more profound activities related to the very ground of being. And it
is his interest in these various activities—often obsessional in
nature—we may argue, that causes Wordsworth, in the 1798 volume,
to bring on to his stage a series of figures who have something of
the same compulsive quality as Coleridge's Mariner—the difference
being that where the Mariner steps out to buttonhole a likely
listener Wordsworth's men and women tend to remain passive, either
telling their stories in even tones or revealing them only at the
behest of an importunate enquirer.

'The Female Vagrant' had in fact been written some years before,
as part of 'A Night on Salisbury Plain', so that it suggests something of what Wordsworth's views had been before he met Coleridge. Coleridge himself, walking through North Wales with Joseph
Hucks in 1794, had apparently discussed the effects of sublime
scenery on those who live in its neighbourhood and had concluded
that it was not automatically beneficial.[23] Wordsworth's poem deals
instead with a particular instance where a state of joy might be held
to have some connection with constant exposure to the sublime:

> Light was my sleep; my days in transport rolled
> With thoughtless joy I stretch'd along the shore
> My parent's nets, or watched when from the fold
> High o'er the cliffs I led my fleecy store
> A dizzy depth below ! his boat and twinkling oar.[24]

Her youthful happiness there is contrasted with her present state:
after many sufferings she has become a homeless beggar and lost her
happiness. Before meeting Coleridge, then, Wordsworth had already
suggested that the psychical security on which human happiness
partly depends might be fostered by an upbringing among sublime
scenes. In the 1798 collection, however, this hint is followed by
presentation of some stranger states of mind. In 'We are Seven', for
instance, the little girl encountered at Goodrich Castle becomes, by
her inability to admit that the number of her family is diminished
by the death of two of its members, a key representative of the
primary consciousness that knows nothing of death. The Mad
Mother and the Idiot Boy, similarly, appearing in successive poems,
form a natural pair, who display opposite extremes of disordered
consciousness. The one, who has been burning in mental agony after

being deserted by her lover, finds consolation only in the remaining link with her child, on which she builds all her hopes. The other, whose links with humankind have been kept alive through his mother's devotion, manifests a quiet joy in the cold beauties of nature (once again represented by moonlight and owl-cries) that he has not sufficient command of his wits to understand.

This aspect of the *Ballads* approaches its climax, in conventional terms, towards the end of the collection, with two figures who are presented against great perspectives of space. The Old Man Travelling, who moves so slowly and quietly that he seems to be a part of nature's stillness, turns out to be embarked upon an epic journey to see his son, dying in a faraway hospital; the Forsaken Indian Woman who has been left to die in the midst of great wastes of snow meets her fate by way of a meditation which moves in different directions, corresponding to what Wordsworth explicitly calls 'the flux and reflux' of her mind. In all these cases, the range of consciousness in the individuals concerned is shown to transcend the limits which a concern for their immediate situation and interests would impose. In the same way (to take a more complex instance) Simon Lee greets the narrator's kindly act in severing a tree-root for him, not with a word of thanks, but with a flood of tears.

One of the most interesting features of *Lyrical Ballads*, in terms of the dialogue here presupposed, is the presence of occasional passages in which a particular landscape is related directly to the state of mind of a character seen in the midst of it. This psychoscaping is more properly Coleridge's preserve, perhaps: in 'The Ancient Mariner' the strange oceanic scenes into which his characters are cast are constantly in interplay with the states of their minds; in 'The Foster-mother's Tale', similarly, it is the fitting fate of the child of nature that, having gone overseas, he soon afterwards,

> seized a boat,
> And all alone, set sail by silent moonlight
> Up a great river, great as any sea. . . .
>
> LB(1798) 57–8

Coleridge also includes some figures, such as the hermit in 'The Ancient Mariner' and the 'gentle maid' in 'The Nightingale' who find it natural to make their devotions in the open air.

In this collection Wordsworth's chief experiment in the mode is 'The Thorn', where, as we shall see later, he tries to imagine the

human being who might be drawn most naturally to such a manifestation of interpenetrating life and death as he observes in the aged
plant, bowed down by new and alien growths. Only occasionally
does he venture further towards the setting up of a subjective correlative by projecting his dominant state of mind into a natural
phenomenon, as in the 'Lines written near Richmond':

> Oh glide, fair stream! for ever so;
> Thy quiet soul on all bestowing,
> Till all our minds for ever flow,
> As thy deep waters now are flowing.
>
> Vain thought! yet be as now thou art,
> That in thy waters may be seen
> The image of a poet's heart,
> How bright, how solemn, how serene!

Here, however, all sense of disturbance is lost in a poem dominated
by eighteenth-century sensibility and reminiscences of Collins: and
one is not surprised to learn that the poem was written ten years
before.[25x] The significance of its appearance among these poems lies
rather in the fact that it should still, in 1798, be regarded as contributing importantly to the total work of the collection. It provides
a necessary note of still movement beneath agitation: a note which
will be picked up more strongly and centrally in the concluding
poem, 'Lines written above Tintern Abbey'.

It is to this poem, in fact, that we may look for the resolution of
many themes that have emerged in our discussion. It exhibits to the
full, for instance, the significant advance that has been made—at
least for the time being—from the intimations of dejection or madness that appeared during his previous phase. If his rhetoric is
being disturbed in this collection it is by a new factor: striking or
unfamiliar word-usages relate directly to a sense of active powers at
work in nature:

> Nor less I deem that there are powers,
> Which of themselves our minds *impress* . . .
>
> One *impulse* from a vernal wood
> May teach you more of man;

Of moral evil and of good,
Than all the sages can . . .

Our minds shall *drink* at every pore
The spirit of the season . . .[26]

The disturbance represented by my italicized words is a disturbance
caused by an intellectual excitement—rather as in 'Tintern Abbey'
itself he speaks of

> A presence that *disturbs* me with the joy
> Of elevated thoughts . . .

ll. 95–6

As we read the longer poem we discover further effects of that
excitement. Just as in 'To my Sister' he continues,

> And from the blessed power that rolls
>   About, below, above;
> We'll frame the measure of our souls,
>   They shall be tuned to love.

LB(1798)97

so in the longer poem, the whole structure of argument concerning
the relationship between response to beauty in nature and the
progress of the moral life is subtly strengthened by suggestions
(reflecting and extending Coleridge's speculations) that in going to
nature we are not simply acting self-indulgently but renewing ourselves in an actual—even physiological—sense, at one of the great
sources of life. Certain patterns of word-echoes mediate this sense
particularly: the word 'living' for instance. 'The living air' suggests
both a vibrancy of sense and an immediacy of contact, which is
supported by the phrase 'life and food' in the lines '. . . in this
moment there is life and food / For future years'. And these in
turn cast retrospective light on the earlier lines which describe

> that serene and blessed mood,
> In which the affections gently lead us on,
> Until, the breath of this corporeal frame,
> And even the motion of our human blood
> Almost suspended, we are laid asleep
> In body, and become a living soul. . .

ll. 42–7

68

Springs

The sense of an underflow to human consciousness which is receptive
to a similar underflow in the life of the universe is essential to any
final convincingness in these lines: it emerges into the full body of
the poem in Wordsworth's central attempt to evoke the mystical
experience. The presence that 'disturbs' him with 'the joy / Of elevated thoughts' is, we learn,

> a sense sublime
> Of something far more deeply interfused,
> Whose dwelling is the light of setting suns,
> And the round ocean, and the living air,
> And the blue sky, and in the mind of man,
> A motion and a spirit, that impels
> All thinking things, all objects of all thought,
> And rolls through all things.

ll. 96–103

Some features of this passage are new for Wordsworth—the images
which he selects for his illustration, for example, and the stress on
this 'motion' as *impelling* all thought as well as rolling through
all things.

It is in these lines, in fact, that the impress of Coleridge's mind
is most clearly discernible. The movement from 'setting suns' to 'the
round ocean' has something of Coleridge's conjuring imagination
about it: at the time of sunset the infinite light of the sun is more
nearly apprehended by human sight than in the full day; it is
natural to move from this tempered sense of infinite light and energy
to the dizzy actualization of infinite power in the image of oceans
englobed and suspended in space; by this swift illapse from landscape to a detached picture of the earth we are made newly aware of
the gravitational wonder which moulds the mobile and restless oceans
to the earth and gives them, seen from far enough away, the simple
shape of the sphere. But if a movement into space is suggested by
this first transition it is not continued; instead we are brought back
to an immediate contact with the air we breathe—this too is shown
to be a wonder. And we are then reminded that even the blueness
of the sky and the pleasure of our apprehension of it is a superadded
grace, not readily predictable from any quantitative view of the
world. By these quick shifts of suggestion Wordsworth persistently
dislocates our perceptions from their educated readiness to see the
universe as a Newtonian machine, and reminds us, by requiring a

quite different sort of focus at every point, that it is possible to organize perception of the universe in a different way, attuning our 'mind of man' to the sublimity of the heavens (rather than to the detail of their organization) and to the pathos of those human correspondences discoverable in sunset lights, blue skies and the ministrations of the living air, thus surrounding ourselves with a vibrant sense of wonder. If we are willing to see the world in this way, moreover, the remainder of the argument of 'Tintern Abbey' is given new backing, since the Wye Valley then becomes, not one place among others but a *central* place, where the existence of a human correspondence in nature is vividly impressed upon the receptive observer.

With this passage in his poem, Wordsworth reaches the stage in his career where he is most closely in Coleridge's orbit. Even here, however, he moves to a note of grandeur which Coleridge would not have chosen at this time. The final 'rolls through all things' gives to his 'something far more deeply interfused' not just the subtle and penetrative qualities of the primary consciousness but the majesty of a river. This is not an isolated example. Clutching for permanence, Wordsworth finds that the alternative universe which Coleridge is content to indicate by particular phenomena and particular states of consciousness is better seized by his own mind if it can be linked to the concept of a rolling stream. Coleridge uses the same general imagery of flowing water but in a more diffuse way, corresponding to his preference for springs over rivers. Wordsworth leans more heavily on his metaphor. In 'Tintern Abbey', in fact, it provides an axis for the whole poem, since the word 'rolls' (yet another verbal echo) refers back to the opening, with its

> waters, rolling from their mountain-springs
> With a sweet inland murmur.

By this echo the 'motion' and 'spirit' are made an actual presence in the landscape that he is surveying. The majesty of this movement in turn assists the force of a conclusion which, while addressed directly to Dorothy, can suggest a more universally available source of relief in a time of widespread despondency.

It is a feature of such resolutions in his poetry, however, that they are frequently more tentative than they may at first sight appear. So far as his immediate development is concerned, in fact, the crucial (and more vulnerable) passages in the poem are those which refer to the possibility that states of mind experienced in the midst of nature might be revelatory. Wordsworth was giving a good deal of thought to this question during 1798: there are a number of passages in the Alfoxden notebook which speak of such unusual states of consciousness. There were occasions, he says, when

> I lived without the knowledge that I lived
> Then by those beauteous forms brought back again
> To lose myself again as if my life
> Did ebb and flow with a strange mystery.

PW V 341

In a notebook containing a manuscript of Coleridge's 'Christabel' he goes further, speaking of states when

> things that are without
> Live in our minds as in their native home . . .

or when, after giving ourselves to nature, we have

> by aid
> Of the impressions which it left behind,
> Looked inward on ourselves, and learned, perhaps,
> Something of what we are . . .

PW V 344

or when

> the stirring and inquisitive mind
> Was laid asleep; the godlike senses gave
> Short impulses of life that seemed to tell
> Of our existence, and then passed away.

Ibid.

It was this train of thought, one concludes, that led him naturally back to recollection of similar states of mind in boyhood and what they might have revealed—recollections which were gradually to grow into the much broader fabric of *The Prelude*.

By the end of 1798 several of these remembered experiences had been written out in drafts corresponding very closely to the form that they would continue to have. To take them in the order in which Dorothy Wordsworth sent them to Coleridge in December 1798,[27] they begin with the description of skating in which he describes how, in the heat of his enjoyment, he 'wheeled about, / Proud and exulting like an untired horse, / That cares not for his home,' while the skaters around him seemed like the 'pack loud bellowing' of a hunt. The impressions that throng on eye and ears shade off into a sense of less pliable forms beyond, however—registered also by the excited consciousness:

> . . . far distant hills
> Into the tumult sent an alien sound
> Of melancholy, not unnoticed while the stars,
> Eastward, were sparkling clear, and in the west
> The orange sky of evening died away.
>
> WL(1787–1805)239

An implicit note of admonition (touched upon particularly in the metaphor of 'died') makes the peace of the paragraph's close a little uneasy; but Wordsworth now returns to the issues involved by a different route, describing occasional sorties of his own, when he would retire from the pack of skaters shouting their pleasure, and chase the reflection of a star, or, in the very height of movement, while the world was spinning past him, stop short, leaning back on his heels:

> . . . yet still the solitary cliffs
> Wheeled by me, even as if the earth had rolled
> With visible motion her diurnal round;
> Behind me did they stretch in solemn train
> Feebler and feebler, and I stood and watch'd
> Till all was tranquil as a summer sea.

Melancholy, in traditional eighteenth-century attitudes, was aligned with solitude; Wordsworth here implies, by contrast, that the individual consciousness is *less* subject to such visitations when it gives itself totally to its own individual experience in solitude than when it does so surrounded by its fellows. In the aftermath of his stopping short the 'diurnal round' of the universe is redeemed from the dreariness of mechanical process and caught into full and satisfying cadence.

The kind of experience described here is examined more closely in the episode of the stolen boat, the next passage to be transmitted by Dorothy in her December letter. Here we begin not with the innocent wild abandon of a common sport but with an 'act of stealth / And troubled pleasure.' Even as Wordsworth rows the shepherd's boat he hears mountain echoes and sees the moonlit circles left by his oar-blades turning themselves into 'one track / Of sparkling light'. He also fixes his eye intently on a rocky steep behind the point that he had left, to steer himself. Suddenly his prowess is interrupted by a startling effect of perspective, when

> from behind that rocky steep, till then
> The bound of the horizon, a huge cliff,
> As if with voluntary power instinct,
> Upreared its head : I struck and struck again,
> And, growing still in stature, the huge cliff
> Rose up between me and the stars, and still
> With measur'd motion like a living thing,
> Strode after me.

Ibid. 240

The vengeful presence which has intervened (and which one suspects had already been prepared for by his childhood reading of giants, in stories such as that of Jack and the Beanstalk) continues into subsequent days, temporarily obliterating, in this insistence, the more benevolent sights and sounds of everyday life:

> . . . for many days my brain
> Worked with a dim and undetermined sense
> Of unknown modes of being. In my thoughts
> There was a darkness, call it solitude
> Or blank desertion, no familiar shapes
> Of hourly objects, images of trees,
> Of sea, or sky, no colours of green fields
> But huge and mighty forms that do not live
> Like living men moved slowly through my mind
> By day, and were the trouble of my dreams.

Ibid. 241 and MS

This is the first hint in the drafts of a state of mind which seems to have oppressed Wordsworth from time to time—a melancholy which was not, like much eighteenth-century melancholy, slightly luxuriant in emotional overlay but terrifying by absence of *all* colouring and tone—a nightmare in which relationship with the world was removed, so that the external world was simply seen to exist, and no more.

William Empson has spoken of the mountains as a father-substitute for Wordsworth,[28] and F. W. Bateson has pointed out that since this incident took place at Patterdale, on his way home from school for the unhappy holidays with his guardian at Penrith, the disturbances described could be associated with his father's death.[29] If this is so, however, it could also be argued that the death is more relevant to the state of 'blank desertion' described here than to any subsequently induced sense of guilt. It is the deprivation that is then important, the sudden severance of the magnetizing link between parent and child which left the human being exposed to the blank forms of the world. The base of the experience, in other words, is not an event (his loss) but a more universal experience of alienation from the universe—an alienation which is for some human beings a permanent mode of life. To this his father's death had made him more vulnerable.

Yet while the experience makes the boy aware of alienation, he is also being rescued by a larger process. The huge forms may not move like living men, but they still move: the final nightmare of a totally static universe is avoided. Even in the moment of guilt and deathly terror, the forms give a *sense* of stately life. And the reference to 'unknown modes of being' is explained more fully when we return to the Alfoxden notebook, where he speaks of

> unknown modes of being which on earth,
> Or in the heavens or in the heavens and earth
> Exist by mighty combinations, bound
> Together by a link, and with a soul
> Which makes all one.
>
> PW V 340–1

In the 1799 *Prelude* this point is conveyed more indirectly. The majestic cadence ending 'and were the trouble of my dreams' is followed by a reassuring

> Ah not in vain ye beings of the hills
> And ye that walk the woods and open heaths
> By moon or starlight thus from my first dawn
> Of childhood did ye love to intertwine
> The passions,
> Not with the mean & vulgar works of man
> But with high objects with eternal things
> With life & nature . . .
>
> 1799 i 130–7

Springs

By the time that Wordsworth writes his first long version of *The Prelude* these beings are subdued into their underlying principle, a mode of benevolence that is also divine:

> Wisdom and Spirit of the universe!
> Thou Soul that art the Eternity of Thought!
> That giv'st to forms and images a breath
> And everlasting motion!

1805 i 428–31

In 1799, on the other hand, writing in a broader, more exploratory vein of the powers involved, he saw them less as 'Wisdom' and 'Spirit' than as 'powers' and 'Genii'. Taking a cue from Shakespeare, from Prospero's 'elves of the hills, brooks, standing lakes, and groves',[30] he continued:

> Ye Powers of earth, ye Genii of the springs!
> And ye that have your voices in the clouds
> And ye that are familiars of the lakes
> And standing pools, I may not think
> A vulgar hope was yours when ye employed
> Such ministry, when ye through many a year
> Thus by the agency of boyish sports
> On caves and trees, upon the woods and hills
> Impressed upon all forms the characters
> Of danger or desire, and thus did make
> The surface of the universal earth
> With meanings of delight, of hope, and fear
> Work like a sea.

1799 i 186–98

A passage such as this takes us to the core of Wordsworth's involvement with Coleridge at the time: the movement from evocation of magical powers to suggestion of vivifying interplay between the forms of nature and the mind of the growing boy is close to his friend's central themes. Wordsworth's own most characteristic concerns, on the other hand, were leading him in other directions. On the one hand he was impelled to ask the question which he had momentarily touched upon in writing 'Tintern Abbey': how far could any revelation in nature assist in the *moral* education of the child? From this point of view the crucial element in the episode of the stolen boat was that it was an act of guilt, committed in nature and subsequently admonished by forces of nature, acting in conjunction with innate powers of the mind itself. Pursuing this train of thought it was natural for him to continue with the episode entitled 'Nutting'[31] (the third and last passage transmitted to Coleridge in Dorothy's letter) in which he recalled an episode of boyhood ravage in the hazel-groves and continued,

> and unless I now
> Confound my present being with the past,
> Even then, when from the bower I turned away,
> Exulting, rich beyond the wealth of kings—
> I felt a sense of pain when I beheld
> The silent trees and the intruding sky . . .
>
> WL (1787–1805) 242

This attempt to suggest an even more direct moral intervention in the midst of nature is delivered hesitantly, however, and the episode (surprisingly at first sight) found no place in the completed *Prelude*. Wordsworth must soon have recognized that any attempt to argue that nature, acting directly upon a human consciousness, could build up a satisfactory code of moral behaviour must be of limited success. Instead he must work more indirectly—even in this passage. Just as he had moved quickly back from his suggestions about the origins of a man's best actions in 'Tintern Abbey' to the surer ground of nature's direct powers over the sensibility, so here he concludes 'Nutting' with the injunction

> move along these shades
> In gentleness of heart; with gentle hand
> Touch, for there is a spirit in the woods.

We are back with the cultivation of sensibility as central theme, and with the suggestion that that sensibility, at least, can, in propitious circumstances, make contact with a similar spirit in nature.

In order to pose the 'moral' question satisfactorily, therefore, Wordsworth was forced to circumvent the details of moral conduct and address himself to the central issue at stake. What (if anything at all) underpinned the relationship between the play of human spirits and the spirits of nature, between the outgoing sensibility and the informing 'sense' of the universe? Was there, in fact, a 'soul' at the heart of nature's 'spirits', a central and unified reality on which one could ultimately rely?

The question, which underlies much of the meditation in 'Tintern Abbey' was never far from Wordsworth's mind at this time: it re-emerges in a passage about his boyhood which he had transmitted to Coleridge even earlier than the ones just discussed: the account of the boy hooting to the owls until they replied, eventually setting up a 'wild scene / Of mirth & jocund din',[32] which he later commented on as follows:

> Guided by one of my own primary consciousnesses, I have represented a commutation and transfer of internal feelings, co-operating with external accidents, to plant, for immortality, images of sound and sight, in the celestial soil of the Imagination.[33]

Wordsworth, it will be noticed, speaks of 'primary consciousnesses' rather than a single 'primary consciousness': he seems to think in terms of visitations in time, rather than of a single central working in the consciousness itself. But his ultimate concern is not far from Coleridge's: he displays it further in his image of the 'celestial soil of the imagination', into which images can, under propitious circumstances, be 'planted'.

In the passage itself, that same concern is reflected in the assertion that the images of sight and sound were actually 'carried far into his heart': the whole passage becomes another—perhaps the central —exemplum of the process by which nature can sometimes speak to man in an answerable language. The interchange of life between boy and birds is overtaken by a subtler and more permanent mode in which nature herself speaks to the questing and self-exerting human spirit:

> ... And when it chanced
> That pauses of deep silence mockd my skill
> Then, often, in that silence while I hung
> Listening a sudden shock of mild surprize
> Would carry far into my heart the voice
> Of mountain torrents; or the visible scene
> Would enter unawares into my mind
> With all its solemn imagery its rocks
> Its woods, & that uncertain heaven received
> Into the bosom of the steady lake.

In a letter he sent on receiving the passage Coleridge said that if he had met those last lines running wild in the deserts of Arabia he would immediately have screamed out 'Wordsworth'.[34] When he himself wrote about mountains reflected in a lake, it was always as an incidental image, not a weighty conclusion. What Wordsworth had done in the passage miniatured his achievement in 'Tintern Abbey' and elsewhere, in fact: he had evoked a moment of Coleridgean wonder in the midst of the great impersonal permanences of nature, and shown how the wonder, and the permanence, could interact to educate a human being in the wisdom of the heart. At the end he leaves us contemplating the calm image which the boy himself saw, but though still, the scene is by no means static; its silence is a silence which is haunted and made resonant by the noises heard just before, when life called to life across the lake until the interplay of 'tremulous sobs, / And long halloos, & screams & echoes loud / Redoubled and redoubled' created an alternative universe to balance that still world, giving it a living quality of its own and negating the deathly threat that its permanence might otherwise have offered, by nourishing in the consciousness that perceived it a forceful, welling sense of its own immortality.

Genius and Mortality

When Wordsworth later came to recall the spring and summer of 1798 it was to find that they returned with unusual promptness and vividness—'in clearer view / Than any sweetest sight of yesterday.' He recalled that period to Coleridge's mind as a season

> when on Quantock's grassy Hills
> Far ranging, and among the sylvan Coombs,
> Thou in delicious words, with happy heart,
> Didst speak the Vision of that Ancient Man,
> The bright-eyed Mariner, and rueful woes
> Didst utter of the Lady Christabel;
> And I, associate in such labour, walk'd
> Murmuring of him who, joyous hap! was found,
> After the perils of his moonlight ride
> Near the loud Waterfall; or her who sate
> In misery near the miserable Thorn . . .
>
> 1805 xiii 386–96

The poems which he chose to name are among those which carry the greatest charge of mystery and supernatural power. An elegiac note is also lurking, however, both here and in the subsequent lines:

> Oh! yet a few short years of useful life,
> And all will be complete, thy race be run,
> Thy monument of glory will be raised.
>
> 1805 xiii 421–3

A retreat from the élan that marked the summer of 1798 had in fact begun shortly afterwards. It is to be dated, perhaps, to the point when Coleridge left the Wordsworths in Germany and went on to the more lively social scene of Ratzeburg. Left to themselves in a countryside which was not very hospitable to foreigners, the Wordsworths were less happy than they had hoped to be; Coleridge's withdrawal removed a presence which had been unobtrusively en-

livening their spirits during the preceding months. While Wordsworth was moved to write the powerful pieces on his boyhood just
examined, one is also aware of a change of atmosphere in his poetry,
a darkening of the setting against which human joy is seen to
flourish.

One concomitant of this alteration was a renewed awareness of
human death and its significance. In Coleridge's company, we may
assume, it was hard to resist seeing the world about one as a world
of life, full of forces springing up, renewing themselves—even, perhaps, communicating with one another at some subtle and subliminal level. In his absence, on the other hand, the opposite feature of
the dialectic reasserted itself; the energies of life gave way to the
still forms that dominated the natural scene. Whatever the status of
the 'universe of life' the fact remained that for each individual
human being in that universe death was waiting and that the sense
of loss, for those who were left alive, must remain bleak and
inexorable. During the subsequent period, in consequence, the sense
of life and genial power which had emerged so strongly in the first
volume of *Lyrical Ballads* was to be challenged constantly in Wordsworth's mind by a sense of mortality and inexorable fixities. A new
kind of poetry was the result.

The new tension is to be traced in the structure of many poems
in the subsequent period. It is stated, for instance, with bald directness in one of the earliest 'Lucy' poems, 'She dwelt among the
untrodden ways', sent in draft to Coleridge with the early *Prelude*
passages.[1] After describing the upbringing of a child who lived and
died close to nature, he concludes, barely, with the well-known
lines:

> But now she's in her grave, and Oh!
> The difference to me!

That puts the point simply and straightforwardly enough; it works
more subtly and dramatically in the accompanying poem (later to
become 'Strange fits of passion . . .') which sets out with precision
an effect corresponding to that which may be supposed to have been
brought into prominence by Coleridge's withdrawal. The pattern of
'There was a boy . . .' is repeated: a rapt mood of unusual intensity is followed by a sudden interruption which leaves the lover
(like the boy in the silence after the hooting of the owls) peculiarly
receptive to whatever is there to impress him. In this case, however,

the preceding activity has had an even more hypnotic effect. The lover, on his way to see his beloved, was lulled by the rhythm of his horse into a state of trance which was reinforced by the fact that his eyes were fixed on the moon (the possible magnetizing power of which had been explored in some of Coleridge's recent poems):

> In one of those sweet dreams I slept,
>   Kind nature's gentlest boon
> And all the while my eyes I kept
>   On the descending moon.
>
> My horse moved on; hoof after hoof
>   He rais'd and never stopped . . .

Regular motion while the eyes are fixed upon an attractive focus of light provides, in Coleridgean terms, a favourable hypnotic setting for the benevolent operation of primary consciousness, reinforcing all perception with a sustaining sense of life. A sudden break in that condition, on the other hand, is likely to precipitate human consciousness into its secondary condition—which is precisely what happens here:

> When down behind the cottage roof,
>   At once the planet dropp'd.
>
> Strange are the fancies that will slide
>   Into a lover's head;
> "O mercy" to myself I cried
>   "If Lucy should be dead!"

WL (1787–1805) 238

At one stroke the dipping moon removes the primary agent of light and hypnotic power and, in the act, restores the observer to a strictly Newtonian universe, where planets are governed by mechanistic laws in a system which is thought of as gradually but remorselessly running on towards death. This thought is immediately projected on to Lucy herself—not only is the narrator reminded of the possibility of her death, but the 'negative magic' generated by the trance's sudden cessation makes it disturbingly easy to believe that her death has actually taken place.

What has happened in this poem is, very literally and exactly, a 'fit of passion', therefore. After the hypnotic activity of riding under the moon, the break in the link turned his state from active to passive so sharply that the 'passion' leapt up as sudden fear.

In the manuscript version Wordsworth gave a further turn to the story by an additional stanza:

> I told her this; her laughter light
> Is ringing in my ears;
> And when I think upon that night
> My eyes are dim with tears.

PW II 29n

He was right to remove it from the published version, both because of its too-easy sentimentality and because it deadens the impact of ' "If Lucy should be dead!" '. It was better to leave the two states of consciousness suspended against one another, without further comment. Its very existence, however, suggests that the strange co-existence of joy and sorrow were a dominant theme in his mind at this time.

Similar juxtaposition of states of consciousness characterizes the most famous of the Lucy poems—also sent to Coleridge:

> A slumber did my spirit seal,
> I had no human fears:
> She seem'd a Thing, that could not feel
> The touch of earthly years.

> No motion has she now, no force;
> She neither hears nor sees,
> Mov'd round in Earth's diurnal course
> With rocks, & stones, and trees![2]

The two stanzas form a gnomic and reverberant statement, over which one might puzzle for ever, like a riddle of the Sphinx. Wordsworth has succeeded in making an iconic statement, where each reader may find his own poem. Without awareness of Wordsworth's ideas, indeed, it is hard to find a stable mode of interpretation. The logic of the other Lucy poems suggests one firm point, however—that for Wordsworth himself the two stanzas encapsulate, respectively, the 'entranced' and 'unentranced' states of consciousness which had been preoccupying him during these months.

At first sight the difference between the two states is overwhelming. In the original moment of entrancement all trappings of movement and development drop away, so that the poet is aware of the woman as a living essence which has no need to express itself in any earthly behaviour. He can even risk calling her a 'thing'. And the time of entrancement has the quality of eternity, so that even the process of time is barely imaginable. The second stanza presents the necessary converse—which is equally 'essential'. Time is a necessary part of all human experience, whereas the 'timeless moment' is not. Some human beings may have the experience of entrancement; all, without exception, must live in time. So Lucy must also be contemplated in the dreariness of her mortality. As a dead body she is indeed a thing (and one that cannot 'feel the touch of earthly years') but now as subject to an inexorable mechanical process. Deprived of self-initiating motion, devoid of the sense-experiences which the meanest living animal enjoys, her only force is that which is given her by the universe at large: an unspontaneous, joyless motion which rolls its predetermined course, one day exactly like another. She is one with all other 'objects of nature': rocks, stones and trees. The sublimity of the entrancement in the first stanza can do nothing to relieve the state described in the second; it merely intensifies its pathos.

That is the reading of the poem which is forced upon us at first by the bareness of the last phrase, 'rocks, & stones, and trees'. The only word which might give us pause is 'trees', placed rather unexpectedly at the end. This at least modifies the closing effect: had the poem been written to end in utter dreariness, the more uncompromising 'rocks' would have concluded it more appropriately. The final mention of even so limited an organism as a tree opens possibilities which one might have expected to find closed.

The extent of the loophole is indicated by Coleridge's comment on the poem, made just after it was composed:

Some months ago Wordsworth transmitted to me a most sublime Epitaph / whether it had any reality, I cannot say.—Most probably, in some gloomier moment he had fancied the moment in which his Sister might die.

CL I 479

Coleridge's unqualified use of the word 'sublime' here calls for comment, since it suggests that he was reading the poem in a manner more visionary than our first analysis would allow.

It is by no means impossible to do so. While the sense of bleakness is enforced by the bare images which conclude the poem and by the key word 'diurnal', the hard abstractness of which dehumanizes the stanza, rocks and trees—even the 'rolling round'—were elements in the imagery of 'Tintern Abbey', where they participated in a general movement from sensibility to sublimity. In such a context Lucy, 'roll'd round in earth's diurnal course',[3x] has become one with the 'motion', the 'spirit' that impels

> All thinking things, all objects of all thought,
> And rolls through all things.

Now, it might be argued, she really has no need of motion or of force, for she is one with the total motion of the universe. She cannot perceive, but the spirit with which she is united *is* everything, and the need for separate perceiving is therefore superseded. The whole universe enjoys the ecstasy apprehended by the poet's slumber-sealed spirit and so her death can be seen as having initiated her into the state shadowed by his trance.

If we read the poem against the background of 'Tintern Abbey' and of the many contemporary speculations which traced a principle of life in the whole universe, including rocks and stones, therefore, it is possible to see the last stanza as prefiguring a visionary transformation of the world of appearances. Rocks, stones and trees are all participants in the one Life: even the stars in their courses 'sing one song and it is audible'. Perhaps if human beings perceived fully, the harmony which is sometimes glimpsed in moments of entrancement would engulf the universe, showing the bewildering phenomena of life and death to be simply the flux and reflux of a larger cosmic animation. And the intimation is assisted by the majestic movement of the poem itself, which will not allow the objects of the last line to be totally static but carries them on in its sweep.

Coleridge's comment, made when he was still fresh from speculations with his friend concerning the 'active Universe' which were finding a place in Wordsworth's own early drafts for his long poem, suggests that he took the poem to end in this kind of esoteric sublimity. Nor is it possible to exclude this sense from the poem: there is too much in the last stanza, and particularly in the rhythm, which is working towards such an effect. It seems more likely that when Wordsworth wrote the poem the idea was working persuasively in his mind, but that it subsided relatively in later years: a hypothesis which may be supported by the fact that when he first published the poem he ended it with an exclamation mark, which he replaced in later editions by a simple full stop. It is possible to take that change as marking a retreat from sublime speculation and an indication that the irreconcilability of the two states of consciousness described was becoming the more compelling fact. When his imagination was most active it would continue to insist on making the universe visionary—yet if he lived too completely by such a vision the inhumanity of the world's forms and motions would undermine his love and the light would die into dreariness—until some further visitation of the imaginative power reversed the process again. If the effect is cyclical, however, it is not simply repetitious, for each turn of the cycle is greeted by a consciousness that comes to it with fresh perceptions of its own concerning the issues involved and therefore perceives the inherent patterns differently.

The riddle posed by such alternations may help to explain a passage which Wordsworth added to 'There was a boy . . .' before publishing it as a separate poem in the 1800 collection, and which, coming after the splendid image of the 'uncertain Heaven, receiv'd / Into the bosom of the steady Lake', has puzzled critics by its apparent flatness:

> This Boy was taken from his Mates, and died
> In childhood, ere he was full ten years old.
> —Fair are the woods, and beauteous is the spot,
> The Vale where he was born; the Churchyard hangs
> Upon a Slope above the Village School,
> And there, along that bank, when I have pass'd
> At evening, I believe that oftentimes
> A full half-hour together I have stood
> Mute—looking at the Grave in which he lies.

> 1805 v 414–22

After the preceding passage it is tempting to dismiss the lines, with one modern critic, as 'literary carpentry'.[4] They do not simply add a sentimental twist to the narrative, however, but provide a counterpart to the intimation of immortality in the preceding incident, so giving the whole process a further revolution through time. The boy may have felt more intensely alive as he hooted to the owls, but for the later observer what survives is the cold fact of his grave. In time, at least, his life has been negated—and Wordsworth's 'long half-hour' in front of the grave is a tribute in the same currency.

Yet paradox still hovers, in the words 'I believe that . . . I have stood'. Wordsworth, contemplating the grave and remembering the boy's life in these peaceful surroundings, has himself become entranced until he can no longer measure the passing of time. Once again, then, the alliance of time and death is not totally victorious.

Manuscript evidence has established that the 'Boy' was, in the original version Wordsworth himself;[5x] in one sense, therefore, he is to be seen as contemplating his own grave. To apply the fact too rigorously, however, is to miss the main point. The experience is one which he believes available to every boy brought up in such surroundings, and therefore a part of nature's universal work. So far from being a poem which is 'really' about his own boyhood and supposed death, it is a poem about everyone's imagination and everyone's death.

Despite this intellectual justification for the added lines, nevertheless, the literary critic is still driven to acknowledge a marked change of poetic intensity. Where the original lines possess a strong imaginative quality and originality, the added section might almost have been written by another poet. At the level of poetic quality, the term 'carpentry' is by no means inapposite, and one is left asking why this should be so.

One answer, I believe, is to be sought in an unexpected quarter, and concerns the fate of the two poets' speculations concerning hypnotism. One of Coleridge's main motives for going to Germany would seem to have been a desire to gain first-hand knowledge of recent work on the subject and its relation to physiology in general, in a leading European university. The fact that he was anxious to attend the lectures of Blumenbach at Göttingen lends credence to the supposition.[6] If so, however, his hopes must have received an unwelcome setback. So far from investigating it further and trying to throw more light on it, Blumenbach did not even believe in hypnotism *as a phenomenon*.[7] Since many of Coleridge's previous speculations had inevitably been tentative and intuitive, such an uncompromising attitude from one of Europe's leading physiologists must have had a stifling effect. And this, it may be suggested, is the reason for a noticeable discontinuity in his thinking on the subject. After his return from Germany he not only ceased to develop the 'magnetic' themes to be traced in poems such as 'The Nightingale', Part One of 'Christabel' and 'The Ancient Mariner', but deleted from the latter poem his most direct reference to hypnotic power. For the next fifteen years he maintained a silence on the subject, broken only by a scathing reference to 'animal magnetizers' in *The Friend*.[8] It was not until news came, some fifteen years later, that Blumenbach had changed his views and now believed in hypnotic phenomena, that he resumed his active interest.

At the same time, it seems, a positive way forward was discovered. The evidence of letters and notebooks suggests that, while now seting the specific issue of magnetism in the background, Coleridge continued to pursue certain related questions, concerning genius, poetic creation and the development of human perception. By wide reading, intense self-exploration and relevant scientific investigation, he would try to discover more evidence for his belief in the existence of a 'primary consciousness', independent of any theories of magnetism. In this enterprise, it would further seem, he was actively encouraged by Wordsworth, who believed the issues raised to be of major importance.[9]

Such an account is at least congruent with the course pursued by the two men during the following years. Coleridge's notebooks and letters give evidence of much speculation and self-experimentation on psychological matters connected with the theories we have mentioned, while the second part of *Christabel*, when composed, was characterized by a more analytic, probing tone than the first.[10] Wordsworth's poetry, meanwhile, was becoming correspondingly more down-to-earth. The resonance of passion which had marked his work at the height of his intimacy with Coleridge, is now more muted, and this may well be due to the latter's growing doubts concerning the validity of his ideas of magnetism, the suggestive power of which had offered an imaginative conception of the universe to counterpoint the starker version imposed by an eye that had kept watch on man's mortality.

A full account of Wordsworth's art during the subsequent years would dwell further on the growing element of sobriety, and the kind of truth-to-nature which that represents. Our present concern, however, is the continuing disturbance of his mind by the interest in unusual states of consciousness which, I have suggested, Coleridge's theories had set in motion and which could cause Wordsworth now to look back in delight on moods of 'excitation of the mind' in which, as he put it, 'all shades / Of Consciousness were ours'.[11] He could not, it seems, simply dismiss the powerful experiences which he had recently evoked, the more particularly since return to the Lake District revived some of them still more strongly. On a previous visit there he had written of the powerful links with the past which were created by return to its distinctive forms and sounds:

> Yet once again do I behold the forms
> Of these huge mountains, and yet once again,
> Standing beneath these elms, I hear thy voice,
> Beloved Derwent, that peculiar voice
> Heard in the stillness of the evening air,
> Half-heard and half-created.

PW V 340

Now, as he settled in Grasmere, the sense recurred, but in the context of his more recent disillusioned state. The most appropriate setting he could now find for his autobiographical reminiscences, therefore, was a context of self-deprecation and self-questioning. For one of his rhetorical models he took a trope that had often been used in English poetry but most memorably, perhaps, by Milton in *Samson Agonistes*, where Samson comments on the 'drooping' of his 'genial spirits' and his father asks despairingly,

> For this did the angel twice descend? for this
> Ordained thy nurture holy, as of a plant;
> Select, and sacred, glorious for a while,
> The miracle of men . . .?

ll. 361–4

Wordsworth, as John Woolford has pointed out,[12] seems to echo the tone as well as the form of this when he begins his new auto-biographical draft with the words:

> was it for this
> That one, the fairest of all rivers, loved
> To blend his murmurs with my nurse's song . . .?

and repeats the question, 'For this . . .?' in succeeding lines. The point which is now pressing home to him is the contrast between his remembered passionate experiences, with the growth that they had encouraged, and the comparative inadequacy of his current achievements.

If the idea that actual forces exist in nature, impressing themselves on the receptive human mind, had now lost some of its power for him, the idea that some kind of correspondence could be traced remained potent. His central point of focus now shifted, however, from the world outside to the human spirit and its development. In this respect, the harmonizing, ever-present note of the river in childhood, evoked in the opening lines, could furnish the clue to a potentially more satisfying significance in the whole process—hence his bold assertion just afterwards:

> The soul of man is fashioned & built up
> Just like a strain of music.
>
> 1799 i 67–8

It is equally germane to his cast of thought to argue that on a consciousness such as his own an education of the kind may need to act obliquely. His theory of how this might come about corresponds in certain ways to Coleridge's more melodramatic account, in 'The Destiny of Nations', of the way in which the energies of nature might be supposed sometimes to work in subtle ways to achieve the good:

> Some nurse the infant diamond in the mine;
> Some roll the genial juices through the oak;
> Some drive the mutinous clouds to clash in air,
> And rushing on the storm with whirlwind speed,
> Yoke the red lightnings to their volleying car.
> Thus these pursue their never-varying course,
> No eddy in their stream. Others, more wild,
> With complex interests weaving human fates,
> Duteous or proud, alike obedient all,
> Evolve the process of eternal good.
>
> CPW I 133

Wordsworth's account of 'favored beings' makes milder use of a similar distinction: some are seen to grow by a simple organic unfolding into good, others require a more complex fate. He aligns his own youthful experiences mainly with the latter mode:

> I believe
> That there are spirits, which, when they would form
> A favored being, from his very dawn
> Of infancy do open out the clouds
> As at the touch of lightning, seeking him
> With gentle visitation; quiet Powers!

Retired and seldom recognized, yet kind,
And to the very meanest not unknown;
With me, though rarely, in my boyish days
They communed: others too there are who use,
Yet haply aiming at the self-same end,
Severer interventions, ministry
More palpable, and of their school was I.

1799 i 68–80

That 'ministry more palpable' is partly to be identified with the
'ministry of fear' to which he refers later in the completed *Prelude*.
Read in the light of Coleridge's theory of 'primary consciousness',
the incidents which illustrate its working may be said to operate
through an 'opening of the clouds' less gentle than those known in
infancy, cutting an entry to the heart of consciousness by violent
spasms of fear, for example, which are all the more effective because the secondary processes by which the body normally engages
itself to the visible world cannot organize them into straightforward
perception. When the boy steals from a trap set by someone else, he
is pursued by

Low breathings coming after me and sounds
Of undistinguishable motion steps
Almost as silent as the turf they trod.

1799 i 47–9

His birdsnesting adventures are accompanied by disorientation of
the normal landscape, which thrusts itself on him as an alien
presence:

While on the perilous ridge I hung alone
With what strange utterance did the loud dry wind
Blow through my ears the sky seemd not a sky
Of earth, and with what motion moved the clouds

1799 i 63–6

A similar loss of bearings characterizes his experiences while skating
and (climactically) the episode of the stolen boat.

In all such ministries of fear it is to be supposed that the growing
boy was brought, through opening of his primary consciousness and
the consequent 'dim and undetermined sense / Of unknown modes
of being',[13] to a point where the universe impressed itself back upon

him in some way with unified grandeur. The larger workings of nature (otherwise liable to be disregarded) were thus gradually transformed into a permanent resource.

In the instances just cited, some unusual exertion or experience of fear was needed before the primary consciousness could resume communication with the 'spirits of nature'; but there had been a time, still earlier, when communication was immediate and absolute: 'With me, though rarely, in my boyish days / They communed . . .'. And while he was asking what purpose, if any, had been served in his own career by all these preparations, in terms of the actual situation in which he now found himself ('Was it for this . . .?') he could also, by turning aside from autobiography, explore his complementary sense that there were human beings who, growing up in close communion with the spirits of nature, needed no such fearful interventions, since they continued to be sought out with 'gentle visitations' by

> quiet Powers!
> Retired and seldom recognized, yet kind,
> And to the very meanest not unknown.

> 1799 i 73–5

Two poems of the time, 'Lucy Gray' and 'The Danish Boy', draw on this idea, together with the supposition that such a human being might in some sense haunt the place where he or she has lived (a supposition more readily explicable if we suppose that at its deepest level primal consciousness communicates subliminally between all organisms, human and non-human). 'Lucy Gray'[14] tells of a young child who set off to light her mother home from the town, only to be lost in a snowstorm. It is a crueller version of 'The Babes in the Wood'; Wordsworth points the contrast by drawing on a stanza which he much admired in that ballad ('These pretty Babes with hand in hand / Went wandering up and down . . .'[15]) to describe the lost child of his own poem:

> The storm came on before its time,
> She wander'd up and down,
> And many a hill did Lucy climb
> But never reach'd the Town.

Next morning her parents, who had searched for her all night, traced her footprints to a bridge over a stream, in the middle of which they were seen to cease. The effect is one of horror touched by pathos. This is not the end of the poem, however:

> —Yet some maintain that to this day
> She is a living Child,
> That you may see sweet Lucy Gray
> Upon the lonesome Wild.
>
> O'er rough and smooth she trips along,
> And never looks behind;
> And sings a solitary song
> That whistles in the wind.

This bare statement of a superstition is not perhaps exactly what Coleridge was looking for when he complained that Wordsworth paid too little attention to local superstitions,[16] but it does at least jolt any mind that is mechanized to follow conventional rules of sense-perception uncritically, by its hint that a living spirit might leave its impress on a place so powerfully that its image could in certain circumstances be picked up by other human beings. The note of mystery which these stanzas introduce is backed, moreover, by the opening of the poem,

> Oft had I heard of Lucy Gray,
> And when I cross'd the Wild,
> I chanc'd to see at break of day
> The solitary Child.

—where it is not clear whether the narrator saw her before or after the events of the poem, as child or as ghost. In his later note Wordsworth spoke of his 'spiritualizing of the character' here as an example of his imaginative treatment of common life, by comparison with, say, Crabbe;[17] and he told Crabb Robinson that 'his object was to exhibit poetically entire *solitude*', so that he 'represents his child as observing the day-*moon*, which no town or village girl would ever notice'.[18] The latter remark, which is backed up by his sub-title 'Solitude', suggests that he was trying to find some way of conveying the idea that a girl brought up away from any community larger than her own family might be more deeply attached to the forces of nature (as witnessed by her attention to the day-moon) and that, though the girl is betrayed to death in the snowstorm, this inner spirit, united in unconscious trust to the forces around her, is the spirit that lives on, to be sensed by other solitary wanderers.

The idea is extended to the animal creation in 'The Danish Boy',[19] a poem originally intended as an introduction to a longer ballad about a boy warrior who was killed for his valuables by a cottager who had sheltered him. The scene of the murder is shown as now devoid of life; no animals, birds or bees will make their shelter there. Meanwhile, however, animals nearby will sometimes betray a response to his sensed presence:

> And often, when no cause appears,
> The mountain-ponies prick their ears,
> They hear the Danish Boy,
> While in the dell he sings alone
> Beside the tree and corner-stone.

All trace of violence has disappeared from his songs of war: now they

> seem like songs of love,
> For calm and gentle is his mien;
> Like a dead Boy he is serene.

Wordsworth seems in the last line to be drawing upon the well-known fact that the faces of dead people sometimes exhibit an almost supernatural serenity.[20x] His poem extends the idea, half-voiced in 'Lucy Gray' and other poems, of tragedy subsumed, in time, into the harmony of nature. The implication that after the moment of tragedy the inner and vital impulse of the victim survives as an actual presence, sensed and respected by other living organisms around, is here presented more boldly than in the other poems, however.

Both poems contain experimental approaches to a tentative idea, authorized for Wordsworth by well-authenticated accounts of supernatural-seeming phenomena—the animals, for instance, who display signs of extra-sensory perception when passing places where some violent action has occurred. At the same time he is evidently anxious in each case to provide an alternative poem for those who do not share his preoccupation. The result is a slightly unhappy compromise, since the reader who does not respond to the more exploratory level may simply find the poems sentimental.

For the same reason Wordsworth was more successful at this time when he could present similar issues within the play of a more sophisticated and experienced consciousness, as in the poems about

'Matthew' the schoolmaster, based partly on the real-life William
Taylor who, shortly before his early death, had expressed himself
to Wordsworth in words, 'My head will soon lie low', which
distantly echo Samson's 'And I shall shortly be with them that
rest'.[21x] As an educated and aware man, Matthew can express the
interplay of his consciousnesses more openly and boldly than other
characters. The poems about him begin where 'There was a boy . . .'
left off, in fact, with Wordsworth looking at Matthew's name in
gilt letters on the school memorial board and commenting on the
total inadequacy of such a memorial to evoke the personality of the
man as he was.[22] As he tries to paint that personality in words, the
language which comes naturally to him is bound together by
imagery of pools, streams and fountains:

> Poor Matthew, all his frolics o'er,
> Is silent as a standing pool,
> Far from the chimney's merry roar,
> And murmur of the village school.
>
> The sighs which Matthew heav'd were sighs
> Of one tir'd out with fun and madness;
> The tears which came to Matthew's eyes
> Were tears of light, the oil of gladness.
>
> Yet sometimes when the secret cup
> Of still and serious thought went round,
> It seem'd as if he drank it up,
> He felt with spirit so profound.

The 'standing pool' image for Matthew in death is contrasted with
the images of continuing life in the torrent-like roar of the chimney
or the stream-like murmur of the village school at work. The living
Matthew is then pictured as a fountain reflecting an inner light, all
his activity relating back to an inward sense of joy. Finally, the
image of 'drinking' the 'secret cup / Of still and serious thought'
provides an image of calmness accompanied by satisfaction which
mediates between the static, dead 'standing pool' of the first lines
and the irresistible but also vulnerable fountain of his animal spirits.

In the following poem, 'The Two April Mornings',[23] the imagery,
as the title itself suggests, is that of the self-renewal of the earth in
spring. It is reinforced in the first line by the presence of the 'day-

spring' itself; for Matthew, however, the effect of the rising sun is
to reinforce his sense of loss:

> We walk'd along, while bright and red
> Uprose the morning sun,
> And Matthew stopp'd, he look'd, and said,
> "The will of God be done!"

The reason for his exclamation is Matthew's remembrance of
another spring, thirty years before, when on a similar April morning,
he had visited the grave of his nine-year-old daughter. As he turned
away he had met a child as beautiful as the one he had lost, 'whose
hair was wet / With points of morning dew':

> To see a Child so very fair,
> It was a pure delight!

He describes her with the imagery of fountain and sea-wave:

> No fountain from its rocky cave
> E'er tripp'd with foot so free,
> She seem'd as happy as a wave
> That dances on the sea.

But there is a dark undertow to both images. The cave in which the
fountain springs, the dark sea under the wave, both subtly indicate
the sense of mortality which was sharpened into exacerbation by the
sight of this girl:

> There came from me a sigh of pain
> Which I could ill confine;
> I look'd at her, and look'd again;
> —And did not wish her mine.

That last line is unexpected; it also rings with gnomic force.[24x] On
first impact it conveys an overwhelming sense of mortality which
cannot face the idea of re-entry into a relationship which in the past
brought such debilitating grief. Even the idea of the possibility of
loss which would be recreated by having another child like his own
is unfaceable. But it also suggests a contrasting feeling—coexistent,
perhaps, with the first. The experience of losing his daughter has
placed him altogether beyond the terms of family relationship:
after the first pang he can respond to a child like her with a delight

which knows nothing of any impulse to possess. The extraordinary coupling of emotions in the single statement is strengthened by our knowledge from the previous poem that Matthew was a man who impressed by his sense of life, and that his gravity always ran in conjunction with ebullience, so that the more bitter interpretation of the line would be out of character if it were not set off by some contact with his liveliness. In the last stanza of the poem, the contrast between mortality and self-renewal fuses into a single, magnificent image:

> Matthew is in his grave, yet now
> Methinks I see him stand,
> As at that moment, with his bough
> Of wilding in his hand.

One need not go to Virgil's golden bough to see the 'bough of wilding' as an emblem of self-perpetuating life; the sense is already there in the image itself. The month is April and the bough is in bud. If Matthew is, by his sense of loss, a figure of pathos, he also stands, bearing his wilding, as a man with untarnished faith in self-renewal. And, as in 'Tintern Abbey', the final work of the poem is carried out by the action of memory. In memory he is both known to be dead yet recreated as in life: in time at least, the unimaginable juxtaposition has been effortlessly accomplished, so that the link of life established between Matthew and the girl in the churchyard is seen to subsist at the core of the poem itself.

The sequence of poems is completed by 'The Fountain'.[25] As a young man, the poet rested with Matthew in a country place where the contrast between them was emblematized by the two most striking objects in the scene.

> We lay beneath a spreading oak,
> Beside a mossy seat,
> And from the turf a fountain broke,
> And gurgled at our feet.

The disorganized, characterless energy of the spring and the settled, rooted form of the oak might seem perfect emblems of the difference between the young man and the old—the one ebullient with a youth that is always jetting out into new forms, the other now compensated for the loss of youth by acquiring a strong settled countenance and manner.

But as in Eliot's *East Coker*, or Yeats's *The Tower*, the actuality of age is soon to be seen as different. When the young poet suggests that they should suit the occasion by singing a song, he is already breaking the mould—for if streams sing, trees do not: to ask an old man to sing is to suggest that he is still in continuity with the forces of his youth. Matthew does not reply to the young man's request directly, therefore, but lies in silence eyeing the spring. After a while he says:

> "Down to the vale this water steers,
> How merrily it goes!
> 'Twill murmur on a thousand years,
> And flow as now it flows.
>
> And here, on this delightful day,
> I cannot chuse but think
> How oft, a vigorous Man, I lay
> Beside this Fountain's brink.
>
> My eyes are dim with childish tears,
> My heart is idly stirr'd,
> For the same sound is in my ears
> Which in those days I heard."

The very scene about him emblematizes the contradictions of his existence. An old man is not simply a rooted tree: it is more as if a rooted tree were to know that it had once been a stream. And this paradox breeds others. Although one mourns from a sense of loss,

> "... the wiser mind
> Mourns less for what age takes away
> Than what it leaves behind."

What is 'left behind' is not a simple bared continuance of a permanent character, now stripped of some inessentials; it is a character which has been created by a fuller former existence, yet knows that the forces which fed that character are no longer available to maintain it:

> "But we are press'd by heavy laws;
> And often, glad no more,
> We wear a face of joy, because
> We have been glad of yore.

If there is one who need bemoan
His kindred laid in earth,
The household hearts that were his own,
It is the man of mirth."

When he goes on to say, finally, that through the loss of his kindred he is not now sufficiently beloved, the young man replies that
this is nonsense and that he will be a son to him. But Matthew,
while grasping his hands in warm recognition of the gesture, replies, 'Alas! that cannot be.' The old man is caught back into his
vegetal image of himself. The only love which could replace the
love that he has lost would be a love which had, like that, grown
through time—and this is impossible. As if in recognition of the
tragic paradox, the two friends leave the fountain and walk down
through the trees. But as they do so, Matthew gives a further twist
to the paradox, showing himself still to be a 'stream' by breaking
into song. And the song he sings is a final expression of his whole,
paradoxical condition. He sings not about a tree but about a church-
clock—an alternative emblem for his age, since although it has stood
for many years, it is artifice, not organism, and a perpetual reminder
of the time-process. Being artifice, however, it can do what a tree
cannot, and sing through time.

And, ere we came to Leonard's Rock,
He sang those witty rhymes
About the crazy old church-clock
And the bewilder'd chimes.

The reference to 'Leonard's rock', with its overtones of love and
death,[26x] should be enough to warn us against thinking of the clock
as like the impersonal bird-artifice of Yeats's 'Byzantium'. The crazi-
ness of its chimes belong rather to the world of Yeats's *Last Poems*.
In old age, Matthew's song is at one with Yeats's: 'Why should not
old men be mad?'[27] Behind the song, however, his eyes are as gay as
those of the sages in 'Lapis Lazuli'.[28] Like them, Matthew has learned
to enact the human paradox by keeping alive the fountain of ioy
without negating his consciousness of mortality.

In one respect, therefore, Wordsworth has now made his
with the Coleridgean universe of life. Matthew's gaiety provides an
acknowledgement that knowledge of mortality need not utterly quell

the fountain of genial spirits which is childhood's most valuable and essential resource. Once fully cultivated, rather, it will survive irresistibly into old age—even if, in the face of certain sorts of loss, its articulations will always sound like the accents of madness.

5

Possible Sublimities

It is not only in the 'Matthew' poems that Wordsworth expresses a feeling that as human beings we live a contradiction, mediated by different areas of our consciousness. The same sense pervades the early drafts of *The Prelude*, as we have seen; indeed, the very circumstances of his settlement at Grasmere involved a paradox of the kind. For the past few years he had lived a life with Dorothy which was unrooted—perhaps deliberately so. The long walking-tours, the tendency to take short tenancies as cheaply as possible, the frugality of their everyday living, all suggest an attempt at living in a new way, freed from the constraints imposed by domesticity and a high standard of living.

There was also a tentativeness about the venture, however. From time to time in his poetry Wordsworth speaks of 'homelessness' and 'houselessness' in an uncertain manner, as if he at once admires and is wary of the state. When he speaks of 'vagrant dwellers in the houseless woods' in 'Tintern Abbey', for example, there is an evident ambiguity of tone.

De Quincey describes Dorothy Wordsworth's life at the time as one of 'delightful wanderings—of what, to her more elevated friends, seemed little short of vagrancy'.[1] He also says that she was 'the very wildest (in the sense of the most natural) person I have ever known'; and records his first impression of her:

'Her face was of Egyptian brown'; rarely, in a woman of English birth, had I seen a more determinate gipsy tan.[2]

The very quotation used here is from Wordsworth's 'Beggars', with its indulgent note towards a family of vagrants encountered in Grasmere. The note of caution in Wordsworth's attitude, on the other hand, emerges in an early draft for 'Nutting' (addressed fairly clearly to Dorothy), in which he exclaims,

Possible Sublimities

If I had met thee here with that keen look
Half cruel in its eagerness, those cheeks
Thus flushed with a tempestuous bloom,
I might have almost deem'd that I had pass'd
A houseless being in a human shape,
An enemy of nature, hither sent
From regions far beyond the Indian hills . . .[3]

The coupling of an attraction to wildness with a fear of its purer form was emblematized in the settlement at Grasmere, a place which Wordsworth had first seen in boyhood from a vantage-point which was 'Not giddy yet aerial' and which had seemed to offer, even then, peace and excitement together:

> All that luxurious nature could desire,
> But stirring to the spirit . . .
>
> PW V 313

A similar sense of balance between opposing forms characterizes many of the descriptions in 'Home at Grasmere'. He finds the vale a spot of peace—so much so that he feels forced to justify himself for luxuriating in it:

> What if I floated down a pleasant stream
> And now am landed & the motion gone
> Shall I reprove myself ah no the stream
> Is flowing & will never cease to flow,
> And I shall float upon that stream again.
>
> Ibid.324 and MS

Having elaborated upon the peace which he can feel in such surroundings, he goes on to acknowledge that the human presences around him are not always contributory to that peace:

> An awful voice
> 'Tis true, I in my walks have often heard,
> Sent from the mountains or the sheltered fields
> Shout after shout reiterated whoop
> In manner of a bird that takes delight
> In answering to itself or like a hound
> Single at chace among the lonely woods,
> His yell repeating; yet was it in truth
> A human voice . . .

101

Such a voice, he continues,

> in some timid mood
> Of superstitious fancy might have seemed
> Awful as ever stray Demoniac uttered,
> His steps to govern in the Wilderness . . .

It was in fact, as he goes on to explain, that of some shepherd, his voice issuing

> An organ for the sounds articulate
> Of ribaldry impiety or wrath
> When shame hath ceased to check the noisy brawls
> Of some abused Festivity.

> Ibid. 325 and MS

Such evidences are seen as a sharp warning to him not to imagine that the sense of beauty which he feels in such surroundings is necessarily shared by the other human beings who live in the vale. This moralizing, down-to-earth note has, nevertheless, been surrounded by many echoes and resonances of a different kind, ministering to an underlying argument that for those who maintain a fully open human sensibility the combination of a central peacefulness with hints of a fearful wildness may keep alive, yet also reconcile, opposing but equally necessary forces in the psyche.

Further evidences of this subterranean preoccupation, scattered as they are among drafts and diversely arranged poems, and sometimes guarded by a staid diction and manner, can easily escape attention altogether. One of the most extraordinary pieces, for example, the poem 'To Joanna',[4] is included among *Poems on the Naming of Places*, and therefore liable to be considered as part of a different enterprise.

There are a number of strange features about this poem. It was written in 1800, well before his marriage to Joanna Hutchinson's sister Mary, and retails an incident in the Lakes at a time when Joanna is not known to have yet visited Grasmere. She is also addressed as having spent her early youth 'amid the smoke of cities'—which was not in fact the case. There is already much to indicate that the poem is less factually based than it might appear. The poem itself begins with an address to Joanna, suggesting that it is to be an affectionate conversational poem; it then proceeds (by way of an apology for doing so) with the record of an incident in which Wordsworth, as narrator, was interrupted by the local vicar while carving Joanna's name on a rock—and explained to his friend that he was doing so to commemorate an occasion when Joanna, catching sight of him while he was looking at a mountain in a moment of unguarded admiration, had been amused by his expression and laughed aloud. The sequel to her laugh was disproportionately dramatic:

> The rock, like something starting from a sleep,
> Took up the Lady's voice, and laugh'd again:
> That ancient Woman seated on Helm-crag
> Was ready with her cavern; Hammar-scar,
> And the tall Steep of Silver-How sent forth
> A noise of laughter; southern Loughrigg heard,
> And Fairfield answer'd with a mountain tone:
> Helvellyn far into the clear blue sky
> Carried the Lady's voice,—old Skiddaw blew
> His speaking-trumpet;—back out of the clouds
> Of Glaramara southward came the voice;
> And Kirkstone toss'd it from his misty head.

The incident is an extraordinary one, as the poem immediately acknowledges:

> Now whether, (said I to our cordial Friend
> Who in the hey-day of astonishment
> Smil'd in my face) this were in simple truth
> A work accomplish'd by the brotherhood
> Of ancient mountains, or my ear was touch'd
> With dreams and visionary impulses,
> Is not for me to tell; but sure I am
> That there was a loud uproar in the hills.
> And, while we both were listening, to my side
> The fair Joanna drew, as if she wish'd
> To shelter from some object of her fear.

Wordsworth's note on the incident to Miss Fenwick was, as usual, sober and factual: 'The effect of her laugh is an extravagance; though the effect of the reverberation of voices in some parts of the mountains is very striking. There is, in the Excursion, an allusion to the bleat of a lamb thus re-echoed, and described without any exaggeration, as I heard it, on the side of Stickle Tarn, from the precipice that stretches on to Langdale Pikes.'[5] Discussing the passage in the *Biographia Literaria*, on the other hand, Coleridge drew attention to a possible source in Drayton's *Polyolbion*:[6]

Which *Copland* scarce had spoke, but quickly every hill,
Upon her Verge that stands, the neighbouring Vallies fill;
Helvillon from his height, it through the Mountaines threw,
From whom as soone againe, the sound *Dunbalrase* drew . . . (etc.).

Reading this extract, and placing its mountain-echoes in the general
context of Drayton's 'humanized landscape', it is hard to believe that
Wordsworth's passage is as simply fanciful as the Fenwick note
might suggest. An earlier note in which he tried to describe the
method of the poem is less circumspect:

> The poem supposes that at the Rock something had taken place
> in my mind either then, or afterwards in thinking upon what
> then took place which, if related, will cause the Vicar to smile.
> For something like this you are prepared by the phrase 'Now by
> those dear immunities', *etc*. I begin to relate the story, meaning
> in a certain degree to divert or partly play upon the Vicar. I
> begin—my mind partly forgets its purpose, being softened by the
> images of beauty in the description of the rock, and the delicious
> morning, and when I come to the 2 lines 'The Rock like some-
> thing' *etc*., I am caught in the trap of my own imagination. I
> entirely lose sight of my first purpose. I take fire in the lines 'that
> ancient woman'. I go on in that strain of fancy 'Old Skiddaw' and
> terminate the description in tumult 'And Kirkstone' *etc*., describ-
> ing what for a moment I believed either actually took place at the
> time, or when I have been reflecting on what did take place I have
> had a temporary belief, in some fit of imagination, did really or
> might have taken place. When the description is closed, or per-
> haps partly before I waken from the dream and see that the Vicar
> thinks I have been extravagating, as I intended he should, I then
> tell the story as it happened really; and as the recollection of it
> exists permanently and regularly in my mind, mingling allusions
> suffused with humour, partly to the trance in which I have
> been, and partly to the trick I have been playing on the Vicar. The
> poem then concludes in a strain of deep tenderness.[7]

The interest of this note, written long before the other one, grows
under examination. The description is supposed to be of a trick
which he intended to play upon the vicar—and which succeeded:
'the Vicar thinks I have been extravagating, as I intended he should'.
But in spite of the affectionate tone of the whole note, this is not just

the story of a joke which turned out rather better than intended. When Wordsworth speaks of being 'caught in the trap of his imagination', or of a 'trance', his account is not lightly to be passed over. Once we stop listening to his suggestions about the interpretation of the incident and pay attention to what is being described, we see that centrally the poem is not about a mild practical joke but about the workings of the poetic imagination.

Daemonism is, after all, inherent in laughter, which, although usually thought of as a sign of affection, can also express an alienated mockery. Wordsworth is aware that the same opposing possibilities pervade all human relationships; from encounters between individuals to man's intercourse with nature herself. If nature can compel the observer to an entranced sense of harmony, she can also stand aloof in mockery of man's enterprises. And so when Wordsworth is in the grip of a delight in the total unity of nature,

> That intermixture of delicious hues,
> Along so vast a surface, all at once,
> In one impression, by connecting force
> Of their own beauty, imaged in the heart . . .

he is especially vulnerable to that side of nature which refuses to commune with the human heart. That other side finds a ready trigger in Joanna's laughter, which, directed at Wordsworth's rapt expression, carries a similar ambiguity. It is not surprising, then, that it should be taken up (or seem to be taken up) by the mountains, nor that their laughter should be equally ambiguous. As it is thrown about the mountain peaks it sounds less and less like human laughter, more and more like voices of infinity. The final succession of images—clear blue sky, speaking-trumpet, the clouds of Glaramara and the misty head of Kirkstone—are, in fact, close to Wordsworth's images of apocalypse.[8] They also have the final ambiguity of the apocalypse as Wordsworth sees it: it may portend the final revelation of infinity within the natural order, or it may simply prove that the whole human quest for meaning has been no more than a closet-drama played out against a void.

Because this is a passage about the relationship between the daemonism of laughter and the daemonism of the sublime, also, the incident with the vicar is more than a framing-device. Ostensibly this concerns a joke which nearly went too far: Wordsworth had intended to give an extravagant version of the incident which made

him carve Joanna's name in the rock, but was then so carried away
by his own imagination as almost to have convinced the vicar that
he was mad; he was therefore forced to recover himself quickly.
But this means that, at a deeper level, the joke is doubly on the
vicar. By starting his joke, Wordsworth begins to tap the resources of
his own daemonism, so that even as he comes to tell a story about
the way in which tender-heartedness may open the gates to daemonism, the daemonism of his own imagination steps in to reinforce the
second part of the incident and raise it to the sublime. The sublime
is still ambiguous; Wordsworth is forced to step sharply away from
the wheeling ascent of his daemonic power and back into rational
relationship with the vicar. In another sense, however, what has
happened mocks not only the vicar, but his rational religion as well.
What the vicar originally asked, with grave looks, was

> for what cause,
> Reviving obsolete Idolatry,
> I like a Runic Priest, in characters
> Of formidable size, had chisel'd out
> Some uncouth name upon the native rock,
> Above the Rotha, by the forest-side.

Wordsworth goes on to say that

> by those dear immunities of heart
> Engender'd betwixt malice and true love,
> I was not loth to be so catechiz'd . . .

If he had been in love with Joanna he would have been unwilling
to talk about her; equally so if he had disliked her; but his position
between the two emotions gives him an immunity of heart which
allows him positively to enjoy talking about the relationship. And
this feeling extends itself to the vicar. While he can honour Christianity for its own encouragement of human love and tenderness, he
feels a certain malice towards its rational dryness. For all his affection towards the vicar as pastor of the district he sees himself—to
this extent at least—as a rival, a Runic Priest keeping up secret rites
of propitiation to other powers. And what happens to him in telling his anecdote shows him to be justified. Nevertheless, the ambiguities of the daemonic *can* be maintained within a human whole,
as they were in Joanna's laughter. Somewhere between malice and
love there lies a condition of laughter which, while containing both,

is a preservative from the dangerous extremes of either. And the fact that this laughter humanizes the extremes might also be a key to nature herself: the apparently menacing echoes of the mountain might become rather a sound of harmony and joy—even a token (foreshadowed in Drayton's *Polyolbion*)[9x] that all nature is ultimately humanized, waiting only the apocalyptic moment of revelation to reveal the sum of things as a human harmony. Joanna's name on the rock is a memorial to that hint, fixing the ambiguities into the concord of a particular human relationship. So the poem can conclude in 'deep tenderness'.

What seems at first sight to be a rather simple private poem turns out, then, to be an extraordinary construction, spiralling back and forth between the banalities of village life, on the one hand, where a young man carves a name on a rock and the vicar pauses to comment, and the ambiguities of a universe which not only refuses to declare itself finally but is always reminding us of the fact, even by the process which is aroused in us when someone makes a joke.

Read in this fuller sense, 'To Joanna' is an important guide to Wordsworth's sense of himself as a poet. Hidden behind the palisades of matter-of-fact annotation which he has erected around the poem, lurking in the ambiguities, there is the ghost of a man who from early boyhood had regarded himself as a true priest of nature in some pagan, pre-Christian sense, communicating directly with the language of her wildness—a conception which must have had a strong appeal to a young man who had so felt the idomitability of his spirit as a child as to imagine that (whatever became of others) he would be translated (rather like Enoch and Elijah) to heaven.

To say this is to revert to a theme touched upon before. There are in the reminiscences of *The Prelude* persistent hints of a belief that the wildness of Wordsworth's upbringing had permanently initiated him into relationship with the more fearful aspects of nature, providing as bonus a sense of the 'one life' that inhabited all things. Yet the assertion immediately introduced a puzzle of its own. If Wordsworth was alone in his recognition, he was like a sane man among the mad—who is liable, on a general vote, to be accounted a madman among the sane. In order to communicate his experiences at this level, therefore, it was necessary to establish some kind of human universality for them—even if it were no more than the testimony of one other individual who, without possessing Wordsworth's long-term advantages, could be convincingly represented as having derived similar benefits from a life of solitude in nature.

It is for this reason among others, we may suggest, that figures such as that of the Pedlar in *The Excursion* were so important to him. It was essential to establish in authenticity a 'common man' who had come through natural means to a state in which the great vital processes of nature were imitated in his own mind. So the Pedlar, from the earliest version of the poem onwards,[10x] is pictured as having learned to read his Bible in a school which stood solitary on the edge of a mountain:

> ... From that bleak tenement
> He many an evening to his distant home
> In solitude returning saw the hills
> Grow larger in the darkness, all alone
> Beheld the stars come out above his head,
> And travelled through the wood, no comrade near,
> To whom he might confess the things he saw.
>
> Exc. i 125–31

This exposure to great and unfixable forms is an education in greatness of mind; and because experiences of fear were associated with them,

> deep feelings had impressed
> Great objects on his mind with portraiture
> And colour so distinct that on his mind
> They lay like substances, and almost seemed
> To haunt the bodily sense.

The force of impression becomes educative of the imaginative power, moreover; by comparing such images,

> And being still unsatisfied with aught
> Of dimmer character, he thence attained
> An *active* power to fasten images
> Upon his brain, and on their pictured lines
> Intensely brooded, even till they acquired
> The liveliness of dreams.

The same active power could then be brought to bear on nature, which was thereby seen not as blank and unchanging but as if it were itself the expression of the mind's activity in a face:

> ... many an hour in caves forlorn
> And in the hollow depths of naked crags
> He sate, and even in their fixed lineaments,
> Or from the power of a peculiar eye,
> Or by creative feeling overborne,
> Or by predominance of thought oppressed,
> Even in their fixed and steady lineaments
> He traced an ebbing and a flowing mind,
> Expression ever varying.
>
> Exc. i 154–62

It is in the nourishing of this active power of imagination that the power of romance is seen to have played its essential part:

> Romance of giants, chronicles of fiends,
> Profuse in garniture of wooden cuts
> Strange and uncouth, dire faces, figures dire
> Sharp-kneed, sharp-elbowed, and lean-ankled too,
> With long and ghostly shanks, forms which once seen
> Could never be forgotten—things though low,
> Though low and humble, not to be despised
> By such as have observed the curious links
> With which the perishable hours of life
> Are bound together, and the world of thought
> Exists and is sustained.
>
> Exc. i 180–5 and MS

These strange figures of old romance no doubt provided the images which had enabled Wordsworth, even as a boy, to look at a drowned man raised from the lake without traumatic effect. There is a still more important consequence: as the great forms of nature give a dimension of greatness to all that a man later sees, romance gives resonance to the organization of time, which is thus redeemed from being simply a succession of dead moments.

The growth of this active power in solitude is, finally, preparatory to the advent of love. For the Pedlar this comes when he goes out on the hills to tend his father's sheep and sees, with physical immediacy, the beauty of the universe. The experience is one of entering into a relationship with the visible universe so intense that all sense of his own identity disappears. The immediacy is emphasized by an imagery of 'drinking', 'melting', and 'swallowing':

> ... Sound needed none,
> Nor any voice of joy: his spirit drank
> The spectacle. Sensation, soul and form
> All melted into him. They swallowed up
> His animal being. In them did he live,
> And by them did he live. They were his life.

Exc. i 205-10

Many of these experiences, we know, corresponded to Wordsworth's own and were written down among drafts from which *The Prelude* was to be produced. In assigning them to this other character, therefore, Wordsworth was taking an artistic risk which would be justified to the extent that the poem's audience accepted the authenticity of the vicarious portrait. So far as he himself was concerned, the transference was justified by his recollection of similar characters whom he and others had known.

If human beings at large gave little evidence of equal susceptibilities this was not simply to be attributed to the inadequacy of their upbringing, moreover. That inadequacy was to be seen rather as accelerating the work of processes which in any case caused the human being's awareness of such forces gradually to wane. It was a process that Wordsworth could recognize as having occurred in his own experience and which forms the subject of the poem which many would regard as his greatest: the *Ode: Intimations of Immortality from Recollections of Early Childhood*.[11]

Despite the powerfulness of its language (Wordsworth comes closest here to a Shakespearean density and force) this is an enigmatic poem. One of the inherent puzzles comes into view as soon as one poses the elementary question appropriate to an ode: who or what is being invoked? The various addresses in the poem shade off into something more like simple exclamations:

> Thou Child of Joy,
> Shout round me, let me hear thy shouts, thou happy Shepherd-boy!

> O joy! that in our embers
> Is something that doth live ...

> Then sing, ye Birds, sing, sing a joyous song ...

> And O, ye Fountains, Meadows, Hills, and Groves ...

What common factor can be inferred from such a range of reference? Is this perhaps to be regarded as Wordsworth's Ode to Joy? Or his Ode to Nature? Neither idea quite fits all the instances, yet both seem to be involved. If Wordsworth had been called to the unwelcome task of identifying his purposes more closely, he would no doubt have been forced to say rather that he was invoking those elements in nature which gave evidence of joy. By addressing the happy shepherd-boys and the creatures of the spring, and by beginning even his last group of stiller natural presences with the word 'Fountains', he is paying his tribute to those unobtrusive vital forces in nature which keep alive the spirit of joy in the human observer. It is by the same token that he can link his whole argument about nature with 'intimations of immortality'.

Like the 'Lines written above Tintern Abbey', the *Ode* has a two-fold structure. It offers itself to the reader first as a narrative meditation upon the loss of a visionary power which was experienced overwhelmingly in childhood. Here, however, Wordsworth is moving back behind the passionate youthful relationship to nature or the earlier 'glad animal movements' of his boyhood in that poem, behind the earliest experiences described in *The Prelude*, even, to the time of a self-identification with nature which was unforced and totally unchallenged. Having described the gradual loss of that state, Wordsworth moves into an account of the forces in nature that helped reconcile him to the outer world and bring him to adult stability. But the poem may seem, on this basis, to peter out, losing the imaginatively eloquent utterance which characterized the earlier stanzas. It can achieve its fullest effect, in fact, only if the reader is responding to a second structure of subtler forces, working particularly through the imagery.

Here the central presence is that of the sun, the existence of the newborn child being primarily compared to the birth of a planet from it. The latter image has a direct counterpart in the physical realm. At birth the child is severed from a condition in which its heart is in direct communication with its mother's through the umbilical supply of food; his rising as a separate star from a source which was essentially fountainous is in that sense an accurate description of the birth process:

> The Soul that rises with us, our life's Star,
> Hath had elsewhere its setting,
> And cometh from afar:

> Not in entire forgetfulness,
> And not in utter nakedness,
> But trailing clouds of glory do we come
> From God, who is our home:
> Heaven lies about us in our infancy!

The daring of Wordsworth's theology in identifying God with the home from which the soul comes also deserves notice. Although the lines are sometimes held to express a belief that human beings existed before birth in Heaven (itself an unorthodox doctrine), what Wordsworth actually writes is that the child comes out of the creative God himself; it is the godlike radiance which it retains from the divine nature that transforms the world around it into 'Heaven'.

Wordsworth avoids total commitment to his planetary image. Instead, there are several suggestions at work: that of a planet becoming separated from the sun and gradually losing its self-generating radiance, or (following the imagery of home and palace) that of a being rising from an Atlantis that has been devastatingly submerged to find himself a castaway on the shores of the ocean. He is also drawing on the fact that any luminary, as it rises above the landscape, 'hath had elsewhere its setting'—while his picture of 'The Youth, who daily farther from the East/Must travel,' suggests a fixed earth, with the east always in one place. Despite these variant suggestions, however, the sense is not self-contradictory to the mind of the reader, who has no difficulty in making his way through the imagery and following the main sense. There is, indeed, a certain brilliance in the fact that while childhood vision is equated with something that human reason has discovered for itself (that the planets originally split off from the sun) the vision of the youth as travelling daily further from the East relies upon an illusion (that of the fixed earth) which is compelling only to the untutored mind. The 'commonsense' view of the world is thus disturbed and distanced.

It is only after this that the argument of the poem becomes slightly obscure. In the next section Wordsworth describes the process by which nature, having attracted to herself some of the child's outgoing power, is able to offer pleasures which, not being dependent upon the exercise of vision, can survive its loss. In this way he introduces his theme that the growth of the secondary consciousness is, in its first manifestations, a benevolent process. There follows a long description of the six-year-old child preparing himself for his future life by imitating all the forms that that life will take. This, however, is then followed abruptly by the famous apostrophe to the child as 'best Philosopher' and 'Eye among the blind', which, after the naturalism of the previous section, may seem out of place.

Examined more closely, on the other hand, that naturalism will be seen to involve the presence in the child of two supposed natural processes (once again attributable to the influence of Coleridge's theories[12]): the transmitted light that sustains growth, and the irritability that prompts the animal energy to experiment with other forms are mirrored with exactitude in Wordsworth's description of the young child in its family, at one and the same time drawing light from its parents' affection and driven to irritation by its mother's assaults of physical love:

> See, where mid work of his own hand he lies,
> Fretted by sallies of his Mother's kisses,
> With light upon him from his Father's eyes!

The imitative power thus set in motion is then seen to mime all the states of being that lie ahead of the child: weddings, funerals, business, love and strife—'As if his whole vocation / Were endless imitation'. And since it is sparked off by the interplay between the stream of affective light which assists the child's growth and the spring of free energy which enables it to imitate forms outside itself, this power is still bearing witness to the child's visionary origins. It is for this reason that Wordsworth finds it natural to take up his earlier imagery again in the next section:

> Thou, whose exterior semblance doth belie
> Thy Soul's immensity;
> Thou best Philosopher, who yet dost keep
> Thy heritage, thou Eye among the blind,
> That, deaf and silent, read'st the eternal deep,
> Haunted for ever by the eternal mind . . .

Much of the criticism that these lines have attracted is attributable to the abruptness of the transition and to the fact that, in the absence of precise meaning, the language may look over-grandiloquent and inflated, and therefore peculiarly inappropriate to a child.[13x] Occurring immediately after the description of an actual child surrounded by his toys it seems, indeed, at a first reading, slightly absurd. But part, at least, of the ground for criticism drops

113

away as one traces the counterpointing argument which has been running through the imagery, and which now issues in the implied image of a mountain-top view of the world by night. The child's vision is being compared to the moon which, shining over the dark abyss, seems totally detached from it, yet which, being 'haunted for for ever' by the sun, can by its light transform into unity everything beneath it. The imagery is highly compressed. The 'Eye' itself recalls the Platonists' belief that the eye could not see the light of the sun if it did not contain a sun-like element;[14x] the expression 'Eye among the blind' recalls the proverb that in the country of the blind the one-eyed man is king; while the image of a being that is devoid of hearing or speech, yet able to 'read' the deep, acts as a further bridge between moon and mind. The whole represents an attempt to render with precision the status of primary vision as it moves into contact with the world of human experience. It is not a mixed metaphor, therefore; the reader is called upon rather to respond to a serious and complex, but also compressed play of imagery. A similar vigilance is required in the succeeding lines:

> Thou, over whom thy Immortality
> Broods like the Day, a Master o'er a Slave,
> A Presence which is not to be put by . . .

While this continues the image of the child as moon, our attention is being transferred to the fact that the moon itself is a 'world', over which there broods a still more splendid light. The image takes up Coleridge's picture of the deep in 'The Ancient Mariner':

> Still as a slave before his lord,
> The ocean hath no blast;
> His great bright eye most silently
> Up to the Moon is cast—

and fulfils its emblematic quality by transferring the focus of our attention to the moon, haunted by the light of the great Dayspring itself. Under this powerful beam the deep is seen to hide a lost Atlantis and the mountains of the moon an Abyssinian paradise, where the condition of the child is one of aionic freedom, of a being dancing in liberty on a mountain-top:

> Thou little Child, yet glorious in the might
> Of untam'd pleasures, on thy Being's height . . .

The way is now clear for the rhapsodic passage which concludes the next section, where the light-fountain can appear, without effort or obtrusiveness, in the description of

> those first affections,
> Those shadowy recollections,
> Which, be they what they may,
> Are yet the fountain light of all our day,
> Are yet a master light of all our seeing . . .

The description of their power to

> make
> Our noisy years seem moments in the being
> Of the eternal Silence . . .

leads naturally into the culminating image of the 'immortal sea / Which brought us hither'.

By means of the double structure just examined, the *Immortality Ode* moves between two modes: the dramatization of loss and the imaginative affirmation of another persisting primal power. The first narrates Wordsworth's belief that primary consciousness is to be equated with a childhood power, the fading of which is necessary and irreversible, the second uses a mythic presentation of imagery to affirm the extent of its survival. Even the imitative power, for all its origins in processes connected to the original visionary power, is not that vision itself; indeed, the stages of life which it mimes will, when they actually arrive, prove to be modes of further solidification:

> Full soon thy Soul shall have her earthly freight,
> And custom lie upon thee with a weight,
> Heavy as frost, and deep almost as life!

This image of a man assuming the state of frozen vegetation, predictive of his body's death, may have prompted, in Wordsworth's mind, the complementary image of the 'burning bush' which could emblematize the energy and vision of childhood: if so, this helps explain his transition to the Phoenix image that opens the following section:

> O joy! that in our embers
> Is something that doth live . . .

and the open affirmation that, in spite of everything, vision survives. It is not the occasional experiences of restoration to that vision which are his final mainstay, however, since their charge of reality cannot by its very nature be carried over into the life of every day. What he now looks for is rather a range of experiences in which the fact of primal vision, and the fact of its loss in time, can be seen to be, in various ways, reconciled. When he writes 'We will grieve not, rather find / Strength in what remains behind', the examples which he gives all contain this quality:

> In the primal sympathy
> Which having been must ever be,
> In the soothing thoughts that spring
> Out of human suffering,
> In the faith that looks through death,
> In years that bring the philosophic mind.

The lines represent a recession from the vulnerable virtues of 'primary consciousness' to the more permanent value of 'primal sympathy', which is here established as Wordsworth's permanent resource.

In building his final stanza on the firmer basis of human sympathy, nevertheless, Wordsworth has still left room for the continued working of a visionary consciousness. The effect of the earlier stanzas cannot be negated; the maintenance of sympathy is further assisted therefore by the fact that

> in our embers
> Is something that doth live . . .

enlivening the feeling for other human beings, affording a sense of link with them through community of inward vision and encouraging fortitude by thwarted fear of mortality.

The process initiated in the *Ode* can, in fact, be seen to extend itself into the remainder of Wordsworth's career and works. While a combination of stoicism and affection will now provide him with a mainstay in both, his achievements in those modes will constantly be shot through with visitations from a deeper level of consciousness, normally triggered by some unusual phenomenon in the world of sense.

Unexpected radiances are their most frequent occasion. It is not for nothing that his unfailing response to sudden sight of a rainbow furnishes him with the opening of a famous poem or that that poem is used in turn as epigraph to the *Immortality Ode* itself. The experience of seeing a common sight illuminated by some unusual effect of light causes a no less delighted disturbance of steady expectation, reinitiating in his mind the old dialectic between the ability of death to impress form and the power of life to start a sense of infinity.

The light of the sun continues to provide the most vivid instances of the latter power. In 'Composed upon an Evening of Extraordinary Splendour and Beauty,'[15] written more than ten years later, he records the compulsive power of a long and beautiful sunset:

> Such hues from their celestial Urn
> Were wont to stream before mine eye,
> Where'er it wandered in the morn
> Of blissful infancy.
> This glimpse of glory, why renew'd?
> Nay, rather speak with gratitude;
> For if a vestige of those gleams
> Survived, 'twas only in my dreams.

After a somewhat pietistic reflection on the implications of this early light, and its temporary miraculous restitution,

> My soul, though yet confined to earth,
> Rejoices in a second birth!

the diurnal actuality of the universe infravenes:

> —'Tis past, the visionary splendour fades;
> And night approaches with her shades

Yet there is a contrary flow, assisted by the echo of *Paradise Lost*, where 'the shades of night' were explicitly associated with a defeated Satan, and the vision reverberates beyond the sobriety of the conclusion. As Wordsworth's note acknowledges, 'Allusions to the Ode entitled "Intimations of Immortality" pervade the last Stanza of the foregoing Poem.'[16] Since the power of visionary experience to continue its visitations has not declined over the years, the tentative, limited faith of the original *Ode* has once again been reinforced in time.

The phenomena involved are explored more intricately in 'Stepping Westward'.[17] Walking in a lonely part of Scotland, he and Dorothy were met by two women, one of whom greeted them with the words, 'What, you are stepping westward?':

The dewy ground was dark and cold;
Behind, all gloomy to behold;
And stepping westward seem'd to be
A kind of *heavenly* destiny:
I liked the greeting; 'twas a sound
Of something without place or bound;
And seem'd to give me spiritual right
To travel through that region bright.

The 'sound / Of something without place or bound' gives the traveller a sense of release from the finite in space; as not uncommonly happens in Wordsworth, this is followed by a release from the finite in time, which is achieved by the operation of the mind's ear, recreating the 'echo' of the voice. The echo is heard while he is still contemplating the glowing sky with its visionary gleams. There are touches which again remind the reader of *Paradise Lost*—the 'dewy eve' of Mulciber's fall, the evening of judgment in Eden and (above all) the evening of the expulsion when, to the west of the garden, the cherubim moved as an 'evening mist / Risen from a river o'er the marish glides'.[18] The last lines of the poem, in particular, recall Milton's description of his fallen beings, for whom 'The world was all before them' as they 'Through Eden took their solitary way':

... and while my eye
Was fixed upon the glowing sky,
The echo of the voice enwrought
A human sweetness with the thought
Of travelling through the world that lay
Before me in my endless way.

This is not Milton's paradise, however, or Adam's loss. Milton's pair might travel from glory to the light of common day but they knew what sort of universe they lived in and what rules they had violated. Wordsworth, stepping westward, has lost a different and more riddling paradise, imaged by the very sky in front of him. The question from the woman, uttered spontaneously when no necessity urged, has given her momentarily the aura of a supernatural messenger, reinforcing his sense that the attraction of the sunset light, eloquent for him of a possible visionary order beyond the immediate world, is perhaps obliquely acknowledged as such by all human beings:

If we, who thus together roam
In a strange Land, and far from home,
Were in this place the guests of Chance:
Yet who would stop, or fear to advance,
Though home or shelter he had none,
With such a Sky to lead him on?

The possibility which had been momentarily started into life by the sound of a resonant question, escaping the lips of a woman who emerged against the background of a glorious sunset, was one which reflected for Wordsworth on the phenomenon of human encounter generally. In all customary experience the rhetoric of encounter is of banality, of guarded utterances carefully restricted to the particular situation at hand, with allowance for limited overtones of kindliness and goodwill. If there is a hinterland of further consciousness in human beings one would hardly guess at it in the words which they let drop in their casual conversations with one another. Yet Wordsworth could never finally abandon the possibility that the awarenesses that had impressed themselves upon him in childhood and early youth were present, even if only vestigially, in all human beings. For this reason he gave immense weight to such rare encounters, in which words, however casually let slip, gave evidence of a possible mode of thinking, belonging to another order from that of the commonplace.

Perhaps even the rover encountered in the Wye Valley who had provided the stimulus for *Peter Bell* had by his 'wild stories' evinced something of the kind—if so, however, very obliquely. By far the most striking direct incident in this mode had been his meeting, many years earlier, with a discharged soldier which was to become a crucial incident in *The Prelude*.

In comparison with the sardonic, knowing wit of the rover, who was essentially a figure of the daytime, the soldier was a ghostly presence, encountered in an unearthly landscape. Wordsworth began writing his account (apparently with a separate poem in mind) at about the time when he was working on *Peter Bell*;[19x] once again the early drafts suggest the intricacy of his involvement with Coleridge at the time. He originally planned to set the scene for the episode by painting a haunted landscape of alienation, intimated by a dog that barked,

And every second moment rang a peal
Felt in my very heart. I could have thought
His wrath was bent on me—there was no noise
Nor any foot abroad—I do not know
What ail'd him but it seemed as if the dog
Howl'd to the murmur of the village stream . . .

Prel. 537

Another draft describes his feelings after he has met the man and looks down into the village, where he sees a landscape with no hint of human presence, only an omnipresent series of reflections from the moon:

. . . All were gone
To rest nor hearth nor taper-light appear'd
But every silent window to the moon
Shone with a yellow glitter . . .

These images both point to a similar element in the setting. The howling of the dog was taken from life, as Dorothy's journal records:

The manufacturer's dog makes a strange, uncouth howl, which it continues many minutes after there is no noise near it but that of the brook. It howls at the murmur of the village stream.

DWJ 27 Jan. 1798

A natural inference from this observation (and from more common phenomena such as that of dogs howling at the moon) would be that the sound of the stream was prompting an obscure response from some primitive force of being in the animal. Unearthly and disturbing as the howl might be to the human ear, it suggested an underground working of primal life. In the poem this effect is later reinforced by the hypnotic effect of a landscape in which windows are seen glittering silently to the moon: basically attractive, like the piece of glass which magnetized Wordsworth at the time of his deepest depression, they too give an obscure, half-threatening sense of permanent being.

In the event, these ideas were used most fully not by Wordsworth but by Coleridge—perhaps because they were felt to belong better in the more deliberately supernatural mode of poetry which the latter took as his sphere. The glitter of the moonlight was seen in the eyes of the dead men at the point when the Ancient Mariner was still under the spell of the moon and before the work of restoration had begun to show itself; and the howling of the dog was heard in the opening of *Christabel* (a manuscript version of which appears in the same notebook as Wordsworth's drafts). In her journal entry, Dorothy had previously described how the moon had emerged only once that evening:

> The withered leaves were coloured with a deeper yellow, a brighter gloss spotted the hollies; again her form became dimmer; the sky flat, unmarked by distances, a white thin cloud.
>
> DWJ 27 Jan. 1798

The thin white cloud also appears in the opening of *Christabel*, along with the 'mastiff bitch' howling not to the stream but to the time-bound chimes of the castle clock. Everything is contributing to a single effect: the forces of vitality subsist at their lowest ebb—yet for all that they do subsist, and in doing so tell us something about the nature of life itself.

This setting, with its underlying significance, offers an important clue to the way in which Wordsworth viewed the incident of the discharged soldier. In one sense, cut off as he was from all human relationship, he represented humanity at its lowest ebb. But just as the howling of the dog to the stream or the glitter of the windows to the moon both witness to something that is not finally alien to the human, rather a part of its own deepest being, the impersonal-sounding speech of the soldier turns into a surd proclamation of universal human truths.

Although Wordsworth suppressed the howling dog, he found an imagery which expressed the actuality of the original scene and rendered the symbolic sense at once unobtrusively and positively:

> ... I slowly mounted up a steep ascent
> Where the road's watery surface, to the ridge
> Of that sharp rising, glitter'd in the moon,
> And seem'd before my eyes another stream
> Creeping with silent lapse to join the brook
> That murmur'd in the valley.
>
> 1805 iv 370–5

The glittering of the moon on the silent, wet, serpentine road reinforces the peaceful sound of the brook itself, to produce a magnetism of light as well as of sound. In this landscape, where everything, moon, stream-like road and murmuring brook, evokes the subliminal, Wordsworth suddenly sees the figure of the soldier, which startles him enough to make him retire behind a hawthorn bush and observe him more closely:

> ... He was of stature tall,
> A foot above man's common measure tall,
> Stiff in his form, and upright, lank and lean;
> A man more meagre, as it seem'd to me,
> Was never seen abroad by night or day.
> His arms were long, and bare his hands; his mouth
> Shew'd ghastly in the moonlight: from behind
> A milestone propp'd him, and his figure seem'd
> Half-sitting, and half-standing. I could mark
> That he was clad in military garb,
> Though faded, yet entire. He was alone,
> Had no attendant, neither Dog, nor Staff,
> Nor knapsack; in his very dress appear'd
> A desolation, a simplicity
> That seem'd akin to solitude. Long time
> Did I peruse him with a mingled sense
> Of fear and sorrow. From his lips, meanwhile,
> There issued murmuring sounds, as if of pain
> Or of uneasy thought; yet still his form
> Kept the same steadiness; and at his feet
> His shadow lay, and mov'd not.
>
> 1805 iv 405-25

This figure makes a strange counterpoint to the scene. Against the 'peaceful voice' of the brook, 'murmuring sounds' of pain or restless thought issue from him; his dark shadow and 'steadiness' contrasts with the moonlight and is more like a mountain in shadow. Wordsworth, now feeling guilty and ashamed of his cowardice, hails him and hears his story:

> ... unmov'd,
> And with a quiet, uncomplaining voice,
> A stately air of mild indifference,
> He told, in simple words, a Soldier's tale,
> That in the Tropic Islands he had serv'd,
> Whence he had landed, scarcely ten days past,

That on his landing he had been dismiss'd,
And now was travelling to his native home.

1805 iv 442–9

The 'stately air of mild indifference' reinforces a suggestion which
was first evident in the contrast between the man's desolate figure
and the military dress which he was wearing; the 'now was travelling to his native home' by its elevated rhythm continues the sense
that the man's fading grandeur and lonely pathos may be not unlike
that of his fellow human beings in their pilgrimage towards the
earth from which they sprang. In the moonlight, indeed, he begins to
seem more like a supernatural visitant:

> . . . as it appear'd to me,
> He travell'd without pain, and I beheld
> With ill-suppress'd astonishment his tall
> And ghastly figure moving at my side;

1805 iv 465–8

And as they discuss his former hardships the contrast between possible grandeur and actual blankness (a contrast present also in the
moon that his face is reflecting) continues to impress itself:

> . . . solemn and sublime
> He might have seem'd, but that in all he said
> There was a strange half-absence, and a tone
> Of weakness and indifference, as of one
> Remembering the indifference of his theme
> But feeling it no longer.

1805 iv 473–8

When they finally reach a cottage and Wordsworth secures for
him a charitable lodging, he asks the man to ask in future 'for
timely furtherance and help' and not to 'linger in the public ways':

> . . . At this reproof,
> With the same ghastly mildness in his look
> He said 'my trust is in the God of Heaven
> And in the eye of him who passes me.'

1805 iv 492–5

It is small wonder that Wordsworth gives these words such emphasis and such an important position in Book Four of *The Prelude*.

They are finally expressive of the counterpoise between potential grandeur and actual simplicity which has marked everything about this man. In his firm pride and independence, refusing to voice his needs to anyone, in his accompanying quiet trust in God and in the sympathetic eye of his fellow man, he becomes for Wordsworth an absolute emblem of lonely human pathos—a pathos which the equally lonely sublimity of his independent pride can, in the end, only emphasize. The discharged soldier is the best example in Wordsworth's writings of what he means when he says that none of the horrors depicted by Milton

> can breed such fear and awe
> As fall upon us often when we look
> Into our Minds, into the Mind of Man . . .[20]

The significance of the encounter is intensified both by the sense of fear in the beholder and by the suggestion of lost grandeur in the object. The moment when Wordsworth, at night, and temporarily haloed by his own fear, meets the desolate soldier, still wearing the incongruous garb of his former state, is a perfect occasion of haunted pathos. And one could hardly find a better phrase to describe the effect than that which is used for the man's demeanour: 'ghastly mildness'; the fear and awe which surrounded the circumstances of the meeting continue to surround the link of human humility which the man's words establish and to give it resonance. The mildness redeems the fear and the fear makes the mildness impressive. By the fact of such interchange with another human being, moreover, the juxtaposition of sublimity with pathos which has characterized many of Wordsworth's boyhood experiences is here transposed into an enhancement of all human relationship; by the same token the event itself can remain more potent in the memory than any similar experience in total solitude would have been.

The episode so fully defines Wordsworth's growing attitude to the phenomenon of sublimity that it is not surprising to find him taking so much trouble over its expression. And when he concludes it (and the book of *The Prelude* in which it appears) with an account of how he saw the man safely lodged for the night and then after lingering briefly,

> . . . sought with quiet heart my distant home.

it is impossible to resist the echo of Milton's similar conclusion to *Paradise Regained*:

> . . . he unobserved
> Home to his mother's house private returned.

Just as Milton's hero needed to face an encounter with Satan in a wild place before he could properly proclaim the fatherhood of God, so the orphan Wordsworth had needed an encounter with an actual human being in a sublime place to gain his deepest awareness of the universal link between human beings.

If Wordsworth's urge to carve in a wild place the name of one for whom he felt a deep and resounding affection was that of a 'Runic priest', then, the cult to which he was devoted had many further ramifications. Unusual experiences in the wild places of nature were marked out for attention not merely for the sake of any Gothic pleasures which they might give, but because by their power to set in motion the full forces of the double consciousness by which all human beings ultimately lived they could render impressively the significance of those elements in human life which, however easily unrecognized and disregarded among the more pressing demands of everyday civilization, must be seen as central if human beings were to make sense of their twofold condition. The princely robes of childhood vision must inevitably become the faded uniform of everyday, perhaps, but the power that had invested that earlier state would survive so long as the strong affections that began then continued to flourish and develop. This for Wordsworth would be a permanent resource for the psyche against the omnipresent reminders of death in the world—since (as Coleridge once put it) 'all intense passions have faith in their own eternity'.[21] And to have met in the midst of wild nature a human being who, in the teeth of adverse circumstances, embodied a similar faith, helped to round the circle of his reassurance.

A Moving Permanence

The bare frontal impression created by Wordsworth's diction can often fall into light and shade once some ripple of disturbance in it is seen to be set up by its author's deeper emotional and intellectual preoccupations. Such transmissions, we have seen, may take place under various guises—through intricate play of the mind, as in 'To Joanna', through narrative argument backed by esoteric imagery, as in the *Immortality Ode*, or through presentation of symbolic event against a fitting background, as with the episode of the Discharged Soldier. Elsewhere—as we have also seen—it may be signalled obliquely, by the use of words with an unusual charge of meaning ('impulse', 'primal', 'infinite'); directly, through description of abnormal experiences in solitude; or, intermediately, by mention of the hauntings, radiances and aspirations that seized Wordsworth from time to time throughout life.

It is also the case, however, that some unyielding elements in the diction have a significance of their own. Throughout his poetry there is a recurring tendency for Wordsworth to be more dignified than he need be and to admire formality in the speech and behaviour of others, while also from time to time dwelling on details of everyday life in a manner that may strike a casual reader as banal or even absurd. For many readers the two factors war against one another; an apparently willed dignity is at such times undermined by bathos. Hence many of the most common criticisms of his work.

Coleridge himself was puzzled by some of the self-contradictions involved. He commented on them in the *Biographia*, where he cited among the defects in his friend's work 'a matter-of-factness in certain poems'.[1] He had criticized this feature as early as 1798, commenting to Hazlitt that Wordsworth

> . . . was not prone enough to believe in the traditional superstitions of the place, and that there was a something corporeal, a

matter-of-factness, a clinging to the palpable, or often to the petty, in his poetry, in consequence.[2]

Coleridge's disquiet has been echoed by some later critics. The Wordsworthian matter-of-factness is unappealing to those who like their poetry witty, imaginative and energetic; and those who find ample reason to praise it may still acknowledge how aptly Coleridge has caught a certain stone-faced sobriety in Wordsworth's diction, along with an occasional propensity for elevated consideration of objects such as swollen ankles and household tubs.

It is certainly not surprising that Wordsworth's matter-of-factness should have perplexed the Coleridge who, at least in times of inspiration, found it easy and natural to integrate his power of vision with his sense of the natural world—particularly as expressed through the sensitive motions of animate life. What he seems never to have seen, however, is that that tenacious hold on the factual might have been a necessary part of Wordsworth's defences, that he might have clung to it partly as protection against occasional but persistent fears of madness.

For obvious reasons, Wordsworth himself was reticent on the subject. It is from others that we hear about the evenings in the 1790s when his friends helped him to combat depression by incessant card-playing.[3] Yet a number of scattered references in his writings make it possible to glimpse the forms of the madness that sometimes approached and oppressed him.

The condition of his nightmare seems to have been twofold—exhibiting, in negative form, the polarities of his positive vision. In one mode, it was a total torpor of the mind, relapse into a sense of dreariness, where the external world was totally deadened and inert; in the other it was an inner and violent wildness, seizing and whirling him towards an endless abyss. Between the Scylla of rocky blankness and the Charybdis of manic possession, Wordsworth was sometimes forced to steer a delicate course. His feelings were, perhaps, like those of Samuel Johnson, related to an eighteenth-century belief that if human beings indulged imagination too far they might topple into insanity.[4] Hence the statement, repeated several times, that the power of his imagination in boyhood had sometimes been so overwhelming that he was forced to push against something that resisted, so as to be sure that there was anything outside him—to take hold of a wall or tree in order to recall himself from the 'abyss of idealism'.[5] The word 'abyss', a telling one, suggests a vertigo, a spinning out of control to destruction.

Although the period at Alfoxden served as a time of release from such fears, they did not altogether leave him. When, in the *Immortality Ode*, he writes of his gratitude for truths

> Which neither listlessness, nor mad endeavour,
>   Nor Man nor Boy,
> Nor all that is at enmity with joy,
> Can utterly abolish or destroy!

the terms 'listlessness' and 'mad endeavour' indicate the same two poles with precision. In 'Resolution and Independence', similarly, the manic-depressive alternation is both enacted in his plummeting dive from excess of joy to dejection, and characterized in the respective terms 'despondency and madness'.

This double-sided fear may help to explain certain episodes in Wordsworth's poetry which are at first sight puzzling. In 'We are Seven', for example, the narrator puts his point again and again to the small girl, exclaiming finally, 'But they are dead; those two are dead! / Their spirits are in heaven!' But, he goes on, 'The little Maid would have her will, / And said, "Nay, we are seven!"' In 'Resolution and Independence', likewise, the old man has no sooner finished telling of his livelihood than the poet asks him the same question again:

> —Perplexed, and longing to be comforted,
> My question eagerly did I renew,
> "How is it that you live, and what is it you do?"

—and the old man patiently repeats his story from the beginning.

This is not an inept narrative device; it reflects Wordsworth's own delight in encountering resistant identity. Although the two encounters are very different, the refusal of the little girl to be budged, the old man's calm acceptance of his way of life, each displays a welcome persistence. Coming from such unsophisticated characters, they are a support to his own, less assured sense of himself.

The trait marks him off sharply from Coleridge, who, less oppressed by such needs, could explain the girl's assurance simply by the fact that she 'felt her life in every limb'. Coleridge's sense of life was normally so vivid, in fact, that it helped to preserve Wordsworth himself from dejection, as the latter acknowledged in his 'Castle of Indolence' stanzas:

> Nor lacked his calmer hours device or toy
> To banish listlessness and irksome care ...

PW II 27

In a further tribute to Coleridge during his absence in Malta, Wordsworth was even more emphatic about the nature of his debt:

> My own delights do scarcely seem to me
> My own delights; the lordly Alps themselves,
> Those rosy Peaks, from which the Morning looks
> Abroad on many Nations, are not now
> Since thy migration and departure, Friend,
> The gladsome image in my memory
> Which they were used to be ...

1805 x 989–95

After John Wordsworth's death, Mary Lamb wrote, in perceptive doggerel,

> Why is he wandering on the sea?
> Coleridge should now with Wordsworth be.
> By slow degrees he'd steal away
> Their woe, and gently bring a ray
> (So happily he'd time relief)
> Of comfort from their very grief.[6]

Wordsworth possessed no equivalent inner resource. At best he could stave off depression by bouts of physical energy:

> Noisy he was, and gamesome as a boy;
> His limbs would toss about him with delight,
> Like branches when strong winds the trees annoy ...

PW II 26

or by attending to the equivalent phenomena in nature. The sound of trees filled with rushing wind was one which always attracted him—mediating, no doubt, between the stasis of the motionless tree and the totally unorganized energy of the wind so as to prompt, through the interlocking states, a correspondent state of controlled activation in his own psyche.[7] Such impulses from the outer world were capricious in visitation, however, and could not

E

129

be relied upon. For a more permanent defence against 'despondency and madness' he was forced to look in a different direction, concentrating upon the permanent in nature itself and linking that with human 'fortitude'.

It was no new preoccupation, of course. His various drafts for 'The Old Cumberland Beggar' show his admiration for this quality; in *Lyrical Ballads*, also, the Female Vagrant's concluding complaint was directed against the country 'Where my poor heart lost all its fortitude . . .'.[8x] The theme could be further traced in nature herself. On 19 March, Dorothy recorded in her journal that 'William wrote some lines describing a stunted thorn'; presumably these in the Alfoxden notebook:

> (On a) summit where the stormy gale
> Sweeps through the clouds from vale to vale,
> A thorn there is which like a stone
> With ragged lichens is o'ergrown,
> A thorn that wants its thorny points
> A toothless thorn with knotted joints;
> Not higher than a two years child
> It stands upon that spot so wild;
> Of leaves it has repaired its loss
> With hairy tufts of dark green moss
> Which from the ground in plenteous crop
> Creeps up and to its very top
> To bury it for evermore.

> PW II 240n and MS

A comparison with the lines 'A whirlblast from behind the hill', written the previous day after sheltering under a holly-bush in a hail-shower, suggests that during this period of almost daily meetings with Coleridge Wordsworth was thinking a great deal about the phenomena of 'death in life', as well as of 'life in death'. If the old thorn, its aged form buried under other life, was a good example of the first, the dance of the leaves in the hollies, roused not by a wind but by the movement of the hailstones, was a fine emblem of the second:

> As if with pipes and music rare
> Some Robin Good-fellow were there,
> And all those leaves, that jump and spring
> Were each a joyous, living thing.[9x]

But while this latter description is very close to the theme of 'the one life' in contemporary poems by Coleridge the description of the thorn reflected a preoccupation peculiar to Wordsworth. The sudden and spontaneous reappearance of new growth each spring might be one of the great mercies of the Newtonian world, but that world also contained another, complementary miracle, less spectacular, perhaps, but no less striking: the persistence of character when fertility had passed. That a tree brings forth new shoots each spring is one wonder; another is that through all its growth *it is gradually creating its permanent form*, so that when possibility of new growth has finally passed it will still stand, presenting its final character to the world. Old people have a similar sort of permanence. The bloom of their youth may be gone, they may no longer be beautiful, but what they are (as Wordsworth once observed[10]) is in one sense plainer. In old age, existing in the decline of physical vitality, yet still far from the skeletal fixity of death, a man may be more completely knowable than at any time since his childhood.

This may explain Wordsworth's fondness for tree imagery when describing old age. What was in humanity a source of fascination or humour, however, could be, when seen on an Alpine scale, overwhelmingly impressive. In the Simplon Pass,

> The immeasurable height
> Of woods decaying, never to be decayed
>
> 1805 vi 556–7

was one of the 'characters of the great Apocalypse'. And the same persistence of a form through the processes of decay and death could make even a stunted thorn memorable.

In the latter case, such persistence was seen under conditions of the greatest adversity. Having lost all its prickles and most of its distinctive form, the Quantock thorn was now partly dependent for its very shape on the lichens which had overwhelmed it.

None of these qualities was evident to Wordsworth at first. The thorn itself was noticed only when it appeared against the background of a stormy day: he had often passed it before in calm and bright weather without observing it. Recalling the fact in a later note Wordsworth goes on to describe his subsequent reflection:

131

I said to myself, 'Cannot I by some invention do as much to make
this Thorn permanently an impressive object as the storm has
made it to my eyes at this moment?'

PW II 511

The resulting poem, 'The Thorn', is one of the most experimental
in *Lyrical Ballads*. It is all the more striking, therefore, that the
'invention' which he decided upon should have been in line with a
habit which he soon afterwards satirized as characteristic of his
juvenile verse—that of associating tragic figures with lonely spots
in nature. In *The Prelude* he comments,

> Then, if a Widow, staggering with the blow
> Of her distress, was known to have made her way
> To the cold grave in which her Husband slept,
> One night, or haply more than one, through pain
> Or half-insensate impotence of mind
> The fact was caught at greedily, and there
> She was a Visitant the whole year through,
> Wetting the turf with never-ending tears,
> And all the storms of Heaven must beat on her.

1805 viii 532–40

In the same way, he recalls, if he saw a foxglove with only one bell
left, his fancy would immediately introduce a vagrant with her
babies, the flower drooping over her head in sympathy while her
children, unconcerned, played with the fallen cups on the ground.
Since this critical comment was written by 1805, it is rather surprising to find a poem of the same sort in a collection of 1798. By
that time, one would have thought, his poetic sophistication might
have rejected the old habit.

Stephen Parrish, who has also noticed this passage, along with
some others of the kind, finds the story of the woman in 'The Thorn'
so unconvincing that he has proposed a bold new reading of the
poem.[11] Her presence on the hillside, he suggests, is to be regarded
as a figment of the narrator's imagination: 'The Thorn', therefore, is
not a poem about a woman at all, but about a superstitious man and
a tree. No one mentioned in the poem, he points out, apart from the
narrator, claims to have actually seen the woman there, and he saw
her only on a day when visibility was bad. Clearly then, he came
across the thorn in a storm, thought he saw the figure of a woman

and heard a cry, and affixed these impressions to village gossip about events that had taken place in the village twenty years before. In all his comments on the poem, he further points out, Wordsworth dwells upon the narrator, his longest account of the matter concluding with the statement that his choice of such a character was made 'to exhibit the general laws by which superstition acts upon the mind.'

The hypothesis, though interesting, is open to various objections. Parrish consistently seems to overestimate the size of the tree, for example, speaking of the woman sitting *under* it, and of the 'creaking of its branches'; whereas Wordsworth is at pains to point out that it is 'not higher than a two years child'. Whatever it may have been twenty years ago, it is now small and stunted, and Wordsworth never says anything more than that she sits 'beside' it. This makes it less likely that the narrator could have mistaken it for a human being. If the narrator is simply making up a story to correspond with an illusion which he once suffered at the spot, moreover, it is not clear how this would fulfil Wordsworth's aim of making the thorn 'an impressive object'. The most cogent objection of all is to be found in a passage quoted earlier from *The Prelude*, where Wordsworth, speaking of his and Coleridge's poems in 1798, includes among them, alongside the Idiot Boy, 'her who sate / In misery near the miserable Thorn'.[12] Had he believed the woman to be an illusion he would surely have emphasized the role of the narrator at her expense.

What Wordsworth actually does say about the poem there, relating the misery of the woman to the miserableness of the thorn, points us more surely to the central theme of his poem, by suggesting that the woman, seeking to find some way of expressing her grief, finds it easier to sit by a stunted thorn than by any human being.

As de Selincourt and others have pointed out, there is a likely connection between this poem and the fragments of an old Scots ballad, copied into one of Wordsworth's notebooks,[13x] which associated the same plant with a deserted woman,

> And there she's lean'd her back to a thorn,
>   Oh, and alas-a-day ! Oh, and alas-a-day !
> And there she has her baby born,
>   Ten thousand times good night, and be wi' thee . . .

and which concluded,

> O look not sae sweet, my bonny babe,
> Oh, and alas-a-day ! Oh, and alas-a-day !
> Gin ze smyle sae ze'll smyle me dead;
> Ten thousand times good night and be wi' thee.

The parallel between the two poems should not be pressed too far, however. The open pathos of the Scots ballad is deliberately rejected as a mode of expression in 'The Thorn'. Where the woman of the ballad talks in connected snatches of allusive emotion, the woman who haunts Wordsworth's thorn can articulate only one phrase, repeated over and over again: 'O misery !'

The woman weeping for her dead child by the desolate thorn does not represent a simple juxtaposition of pathos and the picturesque, certainly. In the poem both elements are actually subdued. Instead, Wordsworth is associating the significance of the thorn with that of the bereaved mother at a deeper level. The thorn has by it a raised patch of coloured moss, representative of the new life which in the vegetable kingdom supervenes naturally upon the old. But the patch is also, by local repute, the grave of the woman's child; for her it must therefore signify not the infinity of life but the permanence of grief. Where in Wordsworth's earlier poetry the juxtaposing of the woman by a tree or flower would have been a work of sensibility, suggesting a sympathy between plant and human being which must be open to question, the relationship here works through counterpoint and is more profound. The moss which acts as a constant magnet to the woman underscores her own loss in a cruel manner: its form is eloquent of her loss, but its life and colour are enriched physically by the body of her child.

The key to the poem, in fact, is to be found in two lines from an earlier drama, *The Borderers*:

> Suffering is permanent, obscure and dark
> And shares the nature of infinity....[14x]

The thorn on the Quantocks was permanent, obscure and dark, but it did not for Wordsworth 'share the nature of infinity' until he saw it against the portentous darkness of a stormy sky, which presented it as an apocalyptic object. And such a sense could not be transmitted to a third person by any direct means: it could be communicated, if at all, only through a person who was, in herself, eloquent of the permanence and infinity which were brought together in loss and suffering. The mother repeats the same words again and again, since elaborate expression would bring no more relief. It is the act of expression, not the form of it, which relieves her heart—and even then so minimally that constant repetition is required. No lasting comfort is possible, since that would presuppose a consciousness existing in the mercy of time. It is of the nature of her grief that it opens her primary consciousness, yet since the *subject* of her grief is inexorably fastened to the irrevocability of the time-process, the sense of infinity which that consciousness brings is totally negative in effect, and her endless repetition, for all its inadequacy, is eloquent of the fact.

Although the limitations of language were finely exposed in the woman's barrenness of expression, Wordsworth's problem was not solved. He had interpreted the death in life of the thorn's existence by introducing a representative of the permanence and infinity which subsist together in human grief, but the woman's state of mind could not, by its very nature, be directly rendered through language. Any attempt to do so would falsify her inarticulacy.

Wordsworth's insistence on the particular character of his narrator, to which Parrish rightly draws attention, is, on this reading of the poem, not intended to indicate its true subject, but simply to assist the reader in his efforts to discover the nature of that subject. Since it is the whole point of the poem that the woman cannot express her grief, it follows that the poet cannot render it directly, either. Accordingly Wordsworth adapts Coleridge's method in 'The Ancient Mariner' (where he had tried to make the consciousness of a superstitious and repetitive seaman the appropriate medium for transmitting and suggesting a vision which could not adequately be rendered in direct form), and presents the woman through the eyes of another superstitious old seaman—an obtuse narrator who, while incapable of interpreting what he saw can, by the very energy of mind reflected in his garrulousness, betray his consciousness of a veiled significance. Looking at the thorn and the woman this narrator sees only an inexplicable persistence, yet his further subconscious awareness makes it hard for his mind to rest with that fact. He has clearly become obsessed by the woman and her dismal voice. He has also listened to all the village gossip—and all the village superstition—about her.

Yet all his observations and investigations leave the woman and the thorn inviolate. His primary consciousness is active enough to

A Moving Permanence

apprehend a significance, but not enlightened enough to comprehend its nature. This is particularly true when he approaches the elements of the scene which best express that nature. When he sees the thorn he describes it with all the trappings of a distancing pathos ('A wretched thing forlorn', 'This poor thorn'). He is even more obtuse when confronted by its companion in desolation: the self-renewing pool. Greeted by this example of fountanious infinity in a wild place, the only thing he can think of doing is to *measure* it:

> And to the left, three yards beyond,
> You see a little muddy pond
> Of water, never dry;
> I've measured it from side to side:
> 'Tis three feet long, and two feet wide.

LB (1798) 119

Since the narrator is blind both to the death in life of the thorn and to the infinity in the muddy pond, it is not surprising that he can enter no further into the nature of the emotion which draws the woman to visit this scene. Popular superstition, which also sees a significance in tree and pond, gives it form by supposing that the woman hanged her child from the one or drowned it in the other. But their real significance is that their respective permanence and infinity are twin emblems of the primal universe into which the woman's grief attracts her, drawing her back both to them and to the coloured mossy hill which, exhibiting the perpetual process of life in death, rivets her heart to itself still more surely.

In a collection of poems which we have seen to contain a strong esoteric element, 'The Thorn' is the most riddling poem of all. The existence of the obtuse narrator turns its statement into irony: the reader must recognize the presented narrative before he can appreciate its full statement. Yet the irony is not arrogant: after all, Wordsworth himself had often passed the original thorn and pond without noticing them. One point of the poem is that we are all, like the narrator, comfortably furnished with inadequate sympathies. When we are not suffering we forget the nature of grief, since we then exist in another area of consciousness—and this is no doubt a mercy as well as a tragic impediment.

Generations of readers have helped to confirm this point of the poem by laughing at the measuring of the pond. Wordsworth, who had explained, even in the 1798 preface, that the poem was not off-

ered in his own person, gave a long and considered account of the
narrator in 1800, as

> . . . a man, a Captain of a small trading vessel, for example, who
> being past the middle age of life, had retired upon an annuity
> or small independent income to some village or country town. . . .
> Such men, having little to do, become credulous and talkative
> from indolence; and from the same cause and other predisposing
> causes by which it is probable that such men may have been
> affected, they are prone to superstition. . . . Superstitious men
> are almost always men of slow faculties and deep feelings; their
> minds are not loose but adhesive; they have a reasonable share of
> imagination, by which word I mean the faculty which produces
> impressive effects out of simple elements, but they are utterly
> destitute of fancy, the power by which pleasure and surprise are
> excited by sudden varieties of situation and by accumulated imagery.
>
> PW II 512

The narrator of the poem, in other words, has kept his primary
consciousness open through his years of exposure to the sea, but
it functions only as an 'adhesive' quality, attracting him to particular objects and encouraging superstition; it does not endow him
with deeper knowledge. The reader must notice the narrator, but
also circumvent him if he wishes to see the full significance of the
poem. Wordsworth no doubt hoped that some, at least, of his readers
would do so; if most did not, on the other hand, that would simply
add point to the pathos of the poem for those who did. It was not
until 1820, after Coleridge had criticized the lines about measuring
the pond in his *Biographia*, that Wordsworth finally changed them.[15]

The scene of 'The Thorn' contains in small compass the three
qualities which Wordsworth would always ask of his surroundings.
He would not want to live far from great permanent objects, or from
objects which, like the sun or moving water, 'shared the nature of
infinity'; he would also require surroundings which kept alive the
magnetisms of his own heart.

This not only drew him to live in the country but coloured his
attitude to great cities. London had fascinated his boyhood imagination and the sense of its romance never quite left him. It was not
in its everyday life that the spell was found to be most potent, however, but at uncharacteristic moments. Sometimes at night its magic
as described by him foreshadows that of Yeats's Byzantium:

A Moving Permanence

> ... the peace
> Of night, for instance, the solemnity
> Of nature's intermediate hours of rest,
> When the great tide of human life stands still,
> The business of the day to come unborn,
> Of that gone by, lock'd up as in the grave;
> The calmness, beauty, of the spectacle,
> Sky, stillness, moonshine, empty streets, and sounds
> Unfrequent as in desarts . . .
>
> 1805 vii 628–36

Even Yeats's street-walkers have a place here, if only in the 'feeble salutation from the voice/Of some unhappy Woman' late on a winter evening 'when unwholesome rains/Are falling hard';[16] this too contributed to the mystery. And its nature was most vividly felt in the early morning, when the rising of the light-fountain and the flowing of the infinite river became dominant presences, hinting at a context to the 'heart' of the city which its busy inhabitants could hardly guess at.

So little awareness did they show, indeed, that Wordsworth was always more directly impressed by the threat of the city, the times when the mob could turn it into a raging whirlpool:

> ... when half the City shall break out
> Full of one passion, vengeance, rage, or fear,
> To executions, to a Street on fire,
> Mobs, riots, or rejoicings? . . .
>
> 1805 vii 646–9

At such times he was reminded of Paris after the Terror. And it was not only violence which frightened him. Bartholomew Fair, with its bedlam of confused spectacles, impressed him as a nightmare mill of humanity, drawing in and expelling people at every point. Wordsworth blends his twin intimations of nightmare in a single phrase, 'Oh, blank confusion!'; the multitude of impressions is so intense that they turn themselves into nullity, a picture of Man: 'his dullness, madness . . .'.[17] Only the observer whose vision had been nourished by the great forms of nature, he concludes, could contemplate such confusion without becoming perceptually disorganized and deadened.

The fair is a miniature in which the ultimate meaninglessness and illusory pleasures of the city are alike made manifest. The same point is made in the poem 'Star-gazers', where each person looking through the showman's telescope will, for whatever reason, 'slackly go away, as if dissatisfied'. The city as such is a false heart, which suggests its antitype only when the crowd is absent—at midnight, say, or on a winter morning after snowfall.[18] As David Ferry has pointed out, his devotion to such moments is a sign that Wordsworth's real metropolis is elsewhere.[19] Of the powerful emotional effect of drama in the London theatre, for example, he writes:

> . . . the storm
> Passed not beyond the suburbs of the mind
>
> 1850 vii 475–6

—a hint which is reinforced by his address to the prophetic spirit that

> dost possess
> A metropolitan temple in the hearts
> Of mighty Poets . . .
>
> PW V 5

For him London is no true metropolis; at best (and then in its uncharacteristic moments) it suggests what a true metropolis might be like. In the more characteristic life of the streets he finds his point of focus in the 'One Man, with a sickly babe outstretched' of *The Prelude*, whose love and concern to give it sun and air mark him as still, vestigially an inhabitant of the heart-nourishing world of nature, where 'the babe leaps up on the mother's arm'.

The confusion of London life, the disturbing alienation from even the simplest of natural resources, assisted Wordsworth's belief that human security was better sought in the rural community; even in the second edition of *Lyrical Ballads*, this belief was already an organizing idea. Wordsworth sent copies to several notable figures of the day, including Charles James Fox,[20] and stressed its social element:

> It appears to me that the most calamitous effect, which has followed the measures which have lately been pursued in this country, is a rapid decay of the domestic affections among the lower orders of society.

This effect, which Wordsworth blames on the spread of manufactures through the country, the heavy taxes on postage, workhouses,

Houses of Industry and Soup-shops, is linked in his mind with the loss of a spirit of independence. He relates how two of his neighbours, man and wife, have been threatened with being boarded out in the parish,

> . . . but she said, it was hard, having kept house together so long, to come to this, and she was sure that 'it would burst her heart'. I mention this fact to shew how deeply the spirit of independence is, even yet, rooted in some parts of the country. These people could not express themselves in this way without an almost sublime conviction of the blessings of independent domestic life.

In 'The Brothers' and 'Michael', Wordsworth continues,

> I have attempted to draw a picture of the domestic affections as I know they exist amongst a class of men who are now almost confined to the North of England. They are small independent *proprietors* of land here called statesmen, men of respectable education who daily labour on their own little properties . . . Their little tract of land serves as a kind of permanent rallying point for their domestic feelings, as a tablet upon which they are written which makes them objects of memory in a thousand instances when they would otherwise be forgotten. It is a fountain fitted to the nature of social man from which supplies of affection, as pure as his heart was intended for, are daily drawn.

In the last sentence psychological theorizing momentarily re-emerges. Affection is pictured as a stream, which links man both with his past and with other men. Ownership of a plot of land, however small, gives an outward and visible source for it in time and space, a continuous spring linking him physically with his own family, in past and future. For this reason it becomes for Wordsworth all the more important to preserve the way of life of such 'statesmen': they preserve a key to everything in human nature that he holds most important.

In 1802, the belief was still in process of formation: it was an assertion to be argued from plausible premises, a natural offshoot from a particular theory about the nature of human resources. As the years passed, however, this particular belief was to harden into received fact: everything that happened to Wordsworth strengthened his conviction that the things he most valued in his fellows were fragile and easily crushed. The only hope of maintaining them lay in a more thorough-going conservatism.

Two poems written in 1800, both about the life of a flower in wild country, witness to the early growth of the idea. In one,[21] the flower hangs by a waterfall which is only a trickle and pleads its right to exist alongside it. The poem ends, grimly:

> What more he said, I cannot tell.
> The stream came thundering down the dell
> And gallop'd loud and fast;
> I listened, nor aught else could hear,
> The Briar quak'd and much I fear,
> Those accents were his last.

In the other poem[22x] a flower is growing under a rock which has been temporarily lodged in a tree. The rock taunts it, pointing out how easily it could crush it; in this case, however, the tree is struck and it is the flower that survives:

> And in one hospitable Cleft
> The little careless Broom was left
> To live for many a day.

Although grouped among 'Poems of the Fancy', these poems do not negate one another, but combine into a complex statement. For the weak and sensitive the world is a cruel place; but they stand a better chance of surviving amid the rough justice of the existing order than they would against the release of pure energy. Somewhere in the clash of rough opposites that is involved in the human order as we know it, there are places where the humble and the weak survive; if the flood of passion or revolution takes over they may well have no hope at all.

What in 1800 could be treated as a matter for light disputation in a pair of contrasting poems was by 1802 a matter for more urgent concern, however, since Wordsworth's deliberations about marriage made him acutely conscious of the precariousness of trying to live by poetry alone. In 'Resolution and Independence', a poem of personal crisis, his various fears are openly voiced—including his fears of madness. And in that poem it is once again an experience of extraordinary survival in the midst of nature that offers an imagery and a memory to sustain him.

The leech-gatherer who came to his rescue was, however, something more than an object, such as the thorn. His primary appeal, one suspects, lay in the fact that he had actually realized the state of rootlessness to which Wordsworth had sometimes aspired and to the risk of which he always lay open. He appealed at once to the sense of motion and of permanence—a fact which seems also to be present in some of the experiences that gave rise to the poem. 'John who afterwards met him at Wythburn took him for a Jew', wrote Dorothy of his human prototype;[23] this was no doubt enough to set thoughts of the Wandering Jew at work in Wordsworth's mind. David Wright recently, retracing the walk on which Wordsworth experienced his original dejection, was startled to see, near a stagnant pool, a large rock which he at first took for a stooping man. It may be, he suggests, that Wordsworth was equally deceived—and in the process discovered an image.[24]

The special virtue of the leech-gatherer, however, was to be a man no longer magnetized to a particular landscape. He had gradually lost all the ties which Wordsworth in 1802 was about to assume: yet he had neither allowed himself to petrify in a particular place nor consented to be the sport of circumstance. He is compared to a rock—not an ordinary rock, but a rock on an eminence, which, by reason of its appearance in so surprising a place 'seems a thing endued with sense'. Or he is like a 'Sea-beast crawled forth, which on a shelf / Of rock or sand reposeth, there to sun itself,—transmitting a motionlessness so absolute that it appears eternal, even though the observer also believes it perfectly capable of movement. But the most characteristic image is the last one:

> Motionless as a Cloud the Old Man stood
> That heareth not the loud winds when they call;
> And moveth altogether, if it move at all.

The power of a cloud to remain itself in spite of its insubstantial fabric and its vulnerability to the elements, its ability to change shape without losing mass or unity, is for Wordsworth one of the most striking manifestations in nature, corresponding to the quality about the old man which makes the deepest impression: his impregnable identity, his unimpeachable fortitude.

By itself, however, this would not be enough to deliver Wordsworth from his fears, for pure permanence could be frightening. The final release comes as his intent observations and questionings begin to alternate with relapse into a state of trance. First the voice of the old man is 'like a stream / Scarce heard', then, when the old man has repeated his story,

> In my mind's eye I seem'd to see him pace
> About the weary moors continually,
> Wandering about alone and silently . . .

By his endless movement, the old man becomes a guardian against the alternative nightmare, in which the universe freezes into fixity. By his cheerfulness, his 'demeanour kind', and, above all, by his *stateliness*, he expresses the essential mercies of the ordinary universe of time and space.

Wordsworth never turned his back on the larger universe which frames the *Immortality Ode*, but he also needed a line of defence: and this his other poem provided. In his expansive moods he could dwell on the importance of vision and human affection as means of self-renewal, but he also needed the assurance that if he lost all the components of that world: family, friends, the known and familiar landscape, all would not, even then, be lost. The old man was a living witness to the possibility of living the life of a solitary wanderer and still surviving as an identifiable person.

In times of trouble, therefore, it was the philosophy of this poem, rather than that of the *Immortality Ode*, which would be his mainstay. In his 'Elegiac Stanzas', indeed, where he declared, 'A deep distress hath humanized my soul' he would go so far as to say that he had been forced to exchange a delusory form of permanence for an authentic one—that he must now identify himself not with the young, idealizing observer who in 1794 had been attracted by the glorious light surrounding Peile Castle's steady reflection, day after day, but with the castle itself, and develop a similar power of resistance:

> But welcome fortitude, and patient cheer,
> And frequent sights of what is to be borne !
> Such sights, or worse, as are before me here.—
> Not without hope we suffer and we mourn.

PW IV 260

His valediction to visionary power was not to be as absolute as this later poem might suggest. But the fact that he could accept, even for a time, so desperate a line of defence, suggest that fulfilment of his former ideals was now being envisaged largely in terms of a world more conventional than the one previously projected.

In one sense, indeed, he was to all intents and purposes settling down to an existence like that of thousands of his fellow-countrymen; his outward behaviour would henceforth be hardly distinguishable from theirs, apart from an occasional habit of going out into the garden or countryside and composing poetry aloud. What was important, however, was not so much the life he was leading but the steps by which he had reached it. The memory of these, working continuously in the mind, gave depth and resonance to his later domesticity.

The change in Wordsworth's ordering of the world may help to explain one of the most puzzling features of his career: the fact that, having already composed *The Prelude*, he left it in manuscript and did not publish it during his lifetime, yet went on to write another part of his projected epic, *The Excursion*, and published that without compunction.[25x] One reason, we may argue, was that he now felt many of the ideas in *The Prelude*, drawn from his long dialogue with Coleridge, to be of uncertain validity. Yet, since they were so intertwined with his own sense of himself as a poet, he could neither reject them, nor, by exposing them to public criticism, risk the sense of annihilation which might accompany sharp criticism or cold scorn. In *The Excursion*, on the other hand, he could avoid such exposure by resorting to a more conventional framework, allowing the weight of his poems to rest in a series of tales of ordinary life and working always within a context of received morality. The culminating speech of the completed poem is delivered, significantly, not by the Wanderer but by the more orthodox Pastor, who praises the milder dispensation of the Christian religion in relation to the heathen sacrifices of former times. The power of nature is thus given a strictly subordinate place and suggested mainly in the setting of the speech, delivered during a glorious sunset, when the clouds are

> giving back, and shedding each on each,
> With prodigal communion, the bright hues
> Which from the unapparent fount of glory
> They had imbibed, and ceased not to receive.
> That which the heavens displayed, the liquid deep
> Repeated; but with unity sublime !

Exc. ix 603–8

This glimpse of infinity, confirmed and reinforced by reflection from the lake, may be assisting the Pastor's transport, but it does not affect the matter of his utterance until the end, where in his own praise to the eternal Mind he affirms a relationship with the forms of nature:

> These barren rocks, your stern inheritance;
> These fertile fields, that recompense your pains;
> The shadowy vale, the sunny mountain-top;
> Woods waving in the wind their lofty heads,
> Or hushed; the roaring waters, and the still—
> They see the offering of my lifted hands,
> They hear my lips present their sacrifice,
> They know if I be silent, morn or even:
> For, though in whispers speaking, the full heart
> Will find a vent; and thought is praise to him,
> Audible praise, to thee, omniscient Mind,
> From whom all gifts descend, all blessings flow!

Exc. ix 743–54

A fuller examination of *The Excursion*, however, would show that its full structure is more complicated than the general weight of these passages might suggest. The poem was begun when Wordsworth was still working closely with Coleridge and there are passages, in Book Four for example, which make important claims about the relationship between nature and the human mind. While writing his poem, nevertheless, Wordsworth was moving to a more practical and conventional frame of mind, subordinating the contemplation of nature to an emphasis on right conduct and resorting to a shift of emphasis which may be traced even in small alterations to the text. A passage originally drafted as

> All things shall speak of Man, and we shall read
> Our duties in all forms, and general laws
> And local accidents shall tend alike
> To quicken and to rouze, and give the will
> And power which by a [   ] chain of good
> Shall link us to our kind.

PW V 401

becomes in the final version

> So shall they learn, while all things speak of man,
> Their duties from all forms; and general laws,
> And local accidents, shall tend alike
> To rouse, to urge; and with the will, confer
> The ability to spread the blessings wide
> Of true philanthropy.
>
> Exc. iv 1239–44

The idea that 'all things speak of Man' is now subordinated; the Coleridgean 'to quicken and to rouze' becomes the more manly 'to rouse, to urge'; the image of a power working through chain and links (with a vestigial implication, at least, of magnetism) is dropped in favour of advocating a more active philanthropy.

Alterations of this kind suggest a growing conviction (prompted partly, perhaps, by mindfulness of Coleridge's own fate) that belief in any natural magnetism, or other phenomena of the kind, might be morally debilitating. (In old age, he said that he was not disposed to reject without examination assertions with regard to the curative powers of mesmerism, but thought that clairvoyance ('supposing it for argument's sake to be true') would be 'an engine of enormous evil . . . shaking to the very foundations the belief in individual responsibility'.[26])

There is, at all events, a marked sobering of vision. The 'gravitation and the filial bond' assume a more prosaic form, in which nature, and the love which natural objects encourage for themselves, are respected because they give an abiding sense of law (leading to a natural sense of duty) and keep alive habits of affection which will in time be given to all humankind as well. So far as the theories which Wordsworth explored in company with Coleridge are still to be traced, they are guarded and related to the objectively verifiable. What was for Coleridge a miraculous dimension to the workings of the universe has now been largely identified with the wonder of gravitation in the normal sense; Coleridge's unifying spirit in all living things is centred by Wordsworth in the unambiguous processes of affection between man and nature and between man and his fellow human beings.

In allowing his beliefs to restrict themselves in this way, Wordsworth was both exposing his own, un-Coleridgean self to the bone and showing an uncannily prophetic sense of the coming era and its requirements. The strength of his later position lay in its concurrence with accepted beliefs and in its practical possibilities as a working 'philosophy of life'. The twin values of duty and affection were immune from the assaults of contemporary philosophic and scientific doubt: they preserved a continuity with the ideals of the eighteenth century while allowing for the intellectual events which had taken place in between. Men and women who had held an orthodox position of belief in the Bible (which had united eighteenth-century Christians, from Anglicans to Unitarians) and who might find that position undermined by the scholars who were producing evidence against the literal truth of the biblical record, could fall back on a Kantian belief in the absoluteness of moral duty and preserve a recognizable continuity with their former moral selves. The gentleman, equally, who in the previous century would have been a man of sensibility, delighting in the picturesque while preserving the established forms and distances of family life, could still, when such formalities were subverted by the events that followed the French Revolution, hope to keep his family life intact around a domestic affection associated with frequent contact with nature. In this way the scientifically-minded dilettante of the seventeenth and eighteenth centuries could re-emerge without too much strain as the Victorian family man, taking his children regularly to church and to the seashore. And even those intellectuals who found their beliefs more radically unsettled could find in Wordsworth a voice who spoke to their condition.

Wordsworth himself is not to be judged by the attitudes which some of his poems promoted, of course, but by the whole process of his own writing. At its best it continued to move between an erected structure of formal statement and a sense of subliminal reinforcement which gave it larger resonance. Even when his poetry moved away from the supreme achievements of The Prelude or the Immortality Ode, it could not altogether lose touch with what had gone before. Although further personal tragedies, such as the deaths of two of his children and Dorothy's sickness, coupled with a recognition that his contemporary civilization was going its own way of technological expansion and political expediency without much reference to the needs of the human heart, might make him move more towards established orthodoxy, greeting the Christian church as a bulwark for his own values, he could never finally allow himself to be delivered into the rigidity of total acceptance. To do so would have been to yield to one of the nightmares which he had been avoiding all his life.

Without embarking on any rash defence of Wordsworth's later poetry, therefore (the general decline of poetic power is obvious) one may suggest, for any reader who is willing to pursue the point that far, that even a poem too rigid to be readily defensible as poetry in the normal sense may contain some image or idea which bears the impress of Wordsworth's earlier processes, so that a conventional statement of beliefs will open to show another aspect. At the very moment when he seems to be accepting the rock of the law he may be seen to do so in the hope of striking a fountain from it. In the *Sonnets upon the Punishment of Death*, for example—poems which are, on a straightforward reading, justifiably repugnant to many modern readers—his reasons for supporting capital punishment include two which take the issue back to the health of the human heart. Life imprisonment, as an alternative to execution, is, he argues, itself inhumane:

> Ah, think how one compelled for life to abide
> Locked in a dungeon needs must eat the heart
> Out of his own humanity, and part
> With every hope that mutual cares provide . . .
>
> PW IV 139

And this reflection of his old fear of an imprisonment in a rocky cell which finally stifles the heart is accompanied by an assertion that the sudden knowledge of his own approaching death might act as a shock to the heart of the murderer and rehumanize it:

> Then mark him, him who could so long rebel
> The crime confessed, a kneeling Penitent
> Before the Altar, where the Sacrament
> Softens his heart, till from his eyes outwell
> Tears of salvation . . .
>
> PW IV 140

We are a long way now from the young Wordsworth who might have viewed such processes as a fitting prelude to release rather than to the gallows,[27x] but his ghost still walks in one respect: for better or worse, the health of the human heart is still a touchstone, and his hope for human improvement still lies in the process described (and Christianized) by Ellen, in *The Excursion*:

A Moving Permanence

'There was a stony region in my heart;
But He, at whose command the parched rock
Was smitten, and poured forth a quenching stream
Hath softened that obduracy, and made
Unlooked-for gladness in the desert place
To save the perishing . . .'

Exc. vi 918–23

This final duality in Wordsworth between duty and affection, the rock and the fountain, is seen as its most explicit in the last of the sonnets dedicated to Liberty and Order. Having rejected the contemporary fondness for 'casual boons and formal charities', and urged his fellows instead to 'seek the Sufferer in his darkest den', he voices his own duality of principle squarely:

Learn to be just, just through impartial law;
Far as ye may, erect and equalise;
And, what ye cannot reach by statute, draw
Each from his fountain of self-sacrifice !

PW IV 134

Inasmuch as the fountain is identified with the affectionate heart. the 'deadness' of the metaphor is, to that degree at least, redeemed. If a conviction of the weakness of humanity leads him to feel the need to protect it, similarly, he can invoke the image of a rock-face planted with flowers. The rock, like the law, is permanent, an abiding defence; but its ultimate justification lies in the fact that it protects the tender beauties of life which flourish in its shelter. Much of Wordsworth's later conservatism is explicable against that central imagery.

The last image is also a fair one to describe the face which Words-worth presented to the world in his later years—almost literally so. Haydon wrote that his head was 'like as if it was carved out of a mossy rock, created before the flood'; Henry Taylor wrote, more amusingly, of 'a rough grey face, full of rifts and clefts and fissures, out of which, some one said, you might expect lichens to grow'.[28] Neither of them, perhaps, knew that Wordsworth had used the same image for his own identity in *The Prelude*, where he wrote, in tribute to Dorothy:

149

A Moving Permanence

... but for thee, sweet Friend,
My soul, too reckless of mild grace, had been
Far longer what by Nature it was framed,
Longer retain'd its countenance severe,
A rock with torrents roaring, with the clouds
Familiar, and a favourite of the Stars:
But thou didst plant its crevices with flowers,
Hang it with shrubs that twinkle in the breeze,
And teach the little birds to build their nests
And warble in its chambers.

1805 xiii 220–9

Yet even as we examine Wordsworth's use of the image, we see that it is something more than an emblem for duty coexisting with affection. The significant addition is the phrase 'a rock with torrents roaring'. A simple rock-face, after all, however adorned with growing flowers, would still have a static existence. To rescue his image from the peril of paralysis, Wordsworth is forced to acknowledge the inadequacy of a concept which devises a dimension of infinity for it only by referring to the occasional life which nestles against it. He must go deeper, calling upon the energy of the fountain as well as its self-renewing, before the image will be fully adequate to his experience. Even if the sound of torrents hints at his alternative nightmare, therefore, it still indicates an essential resource.

This other side to Wordsworth's personality was (like his fears of madness) a hidden one, at least so far as explicit statement was concerned: but it could sometimes come to the fore when his status as a poet was in question. The gothic image of the poet as a man who chanted his verses in a savage place, drawing inspiration from his wild surroundings, was never entirely absent from his mind, and this necessarily presupposed the existence of a savage place in himself, corresponding to the wild energies of nature.

The hidden preoccupation emerges in a poem of 1814,[29] occasioned by memories of a visit to Dunkeld in 1803 which Dorothy described in her journal as follows:

The waterfall (which we came to see) warned us by a loud roaring that we must expect it; we were first, however, conducted into a small apartment, where the gardener desired us to look at a painting of the figure of Ossian, which, while he was telling us the story of the young artist who performed the work, dis-

appeared, parting in the middle, flying asunder as if by the touch
of magic, and lo! we are at the entrance of a splendid room,
which was almost dizzy and alive with waterfalls, that tumbled
in all directions—the great cascade, which was opposite to the
window that faced us, being reflected in innumerable mirrors
upon the ceiling and against the walls. We both laughed heartily,
which, no doubt, the gardener considered as high commendation;
for he was very eloquent in pointing out the beauties of the place.

DWJ (De Sel) 8 Sept 1803

Wordsworth, one suspects, had no great liking for practical jokes
against himself at the best of times, and whatever the nature of his
laughter on this occasion his poem shows that he was not altogether
amused. The use of Ossian as a mere painted device, to be whisked
aside as a picturesque scene exposed itself, was hardly flattering to
his idea of the poet's nature; he was further irritated by the fact
that the mirrors of the pleasure-house turned the controlling form
of the waterfall into total chaos:

> What pains to dazzle and confound!
> What strife of colour, shape and sound
> In this quaint medley, that might seem
> Devised out of a sick man's dream!
> Strange scene, fantastic and uneasy
> As ever made a maniac dizzy,
> When disenchanted from the mood
> That loves on sullen thoughts to brood!

The violence of the imagery suggests that Wordsworth was
offended not merely by bad taste but by a personal threat. To be
split and disappear, leaving an unorganized mass of surging waters,
was a dramatic version of one of his obsessive nightmares. That
this experience could be turned into a tourist attraction only exacerbated his annoyance. In the poem he moves first to a posture of fierce
defence; he recalls the effigy of a knight which he had seen by the
river Nid, and which, by contrast with the supine knight of the
conventional tomb, was portrayed trying to get his sword free in
order to defend the body of a hermit, whom the neighbouring monks
wished to remove from his favourite cell to their abbey.

A fitting monument to Ossian would not be cast quite in that
mould, however, he goes on—better a simple statue carved from

the rock of the place and left by the river, to watch over the local sanctities and act as tutelary genius to a nearby torrent, guarding its form:

> What though the Granite would deny
> All fervour to the sightless eye;
> And touch from rising suns in vain
> Solicit a Memnonian strain;
> Yet, in some fit of anger sharp,
> The wind might force the deep-grooved harp
> To utter melancholy moans
> Not unconnected with the tones
> Of soul-sick flesh and weary bones;
> While grove and river notes would lend,
> Less deeply sad, with these to blend!

If the simple image of a rock-face savoured too much of nightmare stasis a 'rock with torrents roaring', surrounded with the noise of winds or neighboured by running water, was closer to his sense of his own identity as a poet. The mature man must, in his eyes, suffer his human fate and become attentive to the sounds of human suffering and melancholy: the Coleridgean idea of the poet as an active harp or Memnon-statue, transmitting the harmony of the breeze, or the morning ray from the infinite sun-fountain, was by now a long-lost dream. But if in the loss of self-renewing creativity he had been forced to become a rock of fortitude, it was important for him as a poet that his permanence should still allow itself to be haunted by a sense of infinity—not the direct destructive infinity of the raging whirlpool, but the more contained sense of infinity which subsisted even in the melancholy notes of the wind, or the sustaining sounds of moving foliage and water.

7

The Haunted Places

There were some criticisms of Wordsworth which those who knew him personally did not make. Critics of his writings who had no direct knowledge of the man might suggest that he was sometimes feeble, or silly; those who knew him were conscious of a fuller power behind everything that he did. This, we have seen, was equally true of his fondness for the commonplace. Coleridge put his finger on an important truth when he commented,

> As proofs meet me in every part of the Excursion, that the Poet's genius has not flagged, I have sometimes fancied, that having by the conjoint operation of his own experiences, feelings, and reason *himself* convinced *himself* of Truths, which the generality of persons have either taken for granted from their Infancy, or at least adopted in early life, he has attached all their own depth and weight to doctrines and words, which come almost as Truisms or Common-place to others.[1]

A further reason for Wordsworth's matter-of-factness has emerged, however. His 'clinging to the palpable', we have argued, reflected a determination to retain a relationship with the objective world that would preserve him against the extreme workings of his own consciousness. Some of his more prosaic enterprises may be interpreted in a similar way—the more straightforward of his 'Poems on the Naming of Places', for example, organized his environment into an additional structure, related to his own most intimate human relationships. When he looked over towards Easedale he would be reminded of Dorothy; when he looked across to Bainriggs, of the Hutchinson sisters; when to Rydal, of the peaceful pool which he associated with Mary; when to the nearby grove, of John Wordsworth; and when north to Seat Sandal, of the fact that Dorothy had named it after himself. Thus the whole landscape became organized according to the circle of his intimate acquaintance. If in unpropitious times the scenery around Grasmere became threatening by reason of its indifference to human identity, the device provided a ready relief. His self-defence would be similar to that offered by Golding's Pincher Martin, as he proceeded to deal with the rock in the Atlantic on which he found himself by giving to its various parts familiar names such as 'High Street' and Leicester Square':

> 'I am busy surviving. I am netting down this rock with names and taming it. Some people would be incapable of understanding the importance of that. What is given a name is given a seal, a chain. If this rock tries to adapt me to its ways I will refuse and adapt it to mine. I will impose my routine on it, my geography. I will tie it down with names. If it tries to annihilate me with blotting paper, then I will speak in here where my words resound and significant sounds assure me of my identity.'[2]

There is a false side to Martin's enterprise, obviously. The names chosen by him are vulnerable, leading back to the dead values of a commercially-based civilization. In a somewhat similar way, even the familiar place-names of Grasmere were unreliable objects, as liable to solidify into blankness as any of the objects in nature which they signified. But the names of Wordsworth's most intimate relations could never betray him in this way, since they satisfied further psychic demands. While denoting a stable character, well known to him, they also indicated the underlying vitality or peacefulness of a living personality. So a stream surrounded by noises of joy is named after Dorothy, a calm spot of natural beauty hidden in the depths of wilderness after Mary, a track in the grove worn by the restless feet of his brother, 'the silent poet', after John, and two peaks where his wife and sister-in-law had often shown their delight in the prospect they opened out, after Mary and Sara. In each case, a wildness or a bareness is redeemed by some further quality, which in turn corresponds to the kind of resonance that attaches to the name of the associated person.

This was an ultimate resource, however. By their own qualities, in normal times, the great forms of the Lake District themselves guarded the poles of Wordsworth's consciousness, the value of their permanence in providing a focus of stability being matched by the ability of their wildness to answer his need for the sublime.

This last deserves further attention. Wordsworth had grown up in an age which was fascinated by records of Druids and Bards, primitive archaeological remains and the search for a true religion of nature. There were enough relics of former civilization in Cumberland and Westmorland to encourage his interest, and enough wildness in the countryside to make him conscious of forces that had nothing to do with the more comfortable presuppositions of eighteenth-century piety. We have already suggested that he cherished, sometimes consciously, the idea that a poet in his time must align himself with a tradition older than any recognized by his own Christian civilization. The case now to be put is that some of his most striking experiences in nature provided him, through their tenacious survival in the memory, with a resource even stronger than his identifications of permanency in individual human wanderers or particular places. By re-evoking and holding together in his consciousness their intimations of correspondence between certain forces in nature and the twofold working of the mind itself, they acted in a complex and dynamic manner to remind him continuously of the transforming power of imagination and of its consequent significance for his larger philosophy. Once the tensions they involved were wrought into poetry, moreover, their resources became even more unfailingly available.

From an early period, certainly, he had been aware of the role of the perceiving and transforming mind in his encounters with nature. It was not simply a matter of druidic and bardic traditions, but of the contemporary and more central instances. Akenside, for instance, ended his revised *Pleasures of the Imagination* with a picture of the poet as the supreme 'knower', drawing into one all contemporary knowledge. Such conceptions gave renewed significance to older and traditional images of the bard, charming the multitude into a fearful dance of rapture, or appearing on the mountain-top, radiant with the beams of a sun-god. From an early stage, however, Wordsworth's own sense of the sublime had begun to darken, in recognition of his own isolation. When he did place himself in the orthodox stance of sublimity, on a mountain-top (in *Descriptive Sketches*), there was little hint of radiance: his dominant emotions as he watched man braving mountainous dangers nearby were fear and awe:

> But now with other soul I stand alone
> Sublime upon this far-surveying cone,
> And watch from pike to pike amid the sky
> Small as a bird the chamois-chaser fly.

PW I 64

Fear enters many of his experiences of the sublime: on one occasion he actually uses the phrase 'sublimed by awe'.[3] And although
he occasionally uses the word to suggest its more normal contemporary sense of elevation and radiance, his more interesting usages
regularly carry connotations not of light, but of darkness, hollow-
ness and infinity. Sublimity is for him a dark power, experienced
more often by night than by day, less likely to inspire a human
being than to haunt him.

This sense had been present from his earliest years. One of the
first passages about his boyhood experiences (drafted even before
he had formulated the idea of writing *The Prelude*)[4x] described how

> I would stand
> Beneath some rock listening to sounds that are
> The ghostly language of the ancient earth
> Or make their dim abode in distant winds.
> Thence did I drink the visionary power.
> I deem not profitless these fleeting moods
> Of shadowy exaltation, not for this,
> That they are kindred to our purer mind
> And intellectual life, but that the soul
> Remembering how she felt, but what she felt
> Remembering not, retains an obscure sense
> Of possible sublimity . . .

1799 ii 356–67

This passage provides a key to many of the early passages in
The Prelude which describe the sense of an obscure leading or
guiding in childhood. During the vacation walking-tour of 1790, he
and his companion had planned to cross the Alps and no doubt
looked forward to the experience as one compared with which the
transit from one valley to another in the Lake District would pale
into insignificance. The episode turned to banality, however: while
they were following an upward path they realized that they had
lost their way and sought advice from a peasant, who, to their
bewilderment, directed them on a *downward* path:

> Hard of belief, we question'd him again,
> And all the answers which the Man return'd
> To our inquiries, in their sense and substance,

Translated by the feelings which we had
Ended in this; that we had cross'd the Alps.

1805 vi 520–4

It is not clear what they had expected. But there were enough accounts of Alpine sublimity available in writers such as Thomas Burnet (who wrote that a man who woke up unexpectedly on an Alpine peak 'wou'd think himself in an enchanted Country, or carried into another World'[5]) to encourage hopes of an emotion out of the ordinary. At the very least they must have expected an experience like the one described by Thomas Gray in a letter. Gray's party had been forced to pass directly over Mount Cenis, which he described in tones of rapture:

> It was six miles to the top, where a plain opens itself about as many more in breadth, covered perpetually with very deep snow, and in the midst of that a great lake of unfathomable depth, from whence a river takes its rise, and tumbles over monstrous rocks quite down the other side of the mountain. The descent is six miles more, but infinitely more steep than the going up. . . . The immensity of the precipices, the roaring of the river and torrents that run into it, the huge craggs covered with ice and snow, and the clouds below you and about you, are objects it is impossible to conceive without seeing them . . .[6]

Wordsworth, descending subsequently through the Simplon, might also have recalled passages such as a preceding description of Gray's, in which he described a way running through a deep valley by the side of the 'River Arc . . . which works itself a passage, with great difficulty and a mighty noise, among vast quantities of rocks, that have rolled down from the mountain tops', or another which describes their ascent to the Grand Chartreuse:

> . . . on one side the rock hanging over you, & on the other a monstrous precipice. In the bottom runs a torrent, called Les Guiers morts, that works its way among the rocks with a mighty noise, & frequent Falls. You here meet all the beauties so savage & horrid a place can present you with; Rocks of various & uncouth figures, Cascades pouring down from an immense height out of hanging Groves of Pine-Trees, & the solemn Sound of the Stream, that roars below, all concur to form one of the most poetical Scenes imaginable.[7]

While the elements of Wordsworth's description recall those in Gray, however, the Simplon scene was not witnessed by him with such simple and solemn pleasure. The range of his reactions was more complex and stretched far further, to assist at one of the great climaxes in his work:

> ... the brook and road
> Were fellow-travellers in this gloomy Pass,
> And with them did we journey several hours
> At a slow step. The immeasurable height
> Of woods decaying, never to be decay'd,
> The stationary blasts of water-falls,
> And every where along the hollow rent
> Winds thwarting winds, bewilder'd and forlorn,
> The torrents shooting from the clear blue sky,
> The rocks that mutter'd close upon our ears,
> Black drizzling crags that spake by the way-side
> As if a voice were in them, the sick sight
> And giddy prospect of the raving stream,
> The unfetter'd clouds, and region of the heavens,
> Tumult and peace, the darkness and the light
> Were all like workings of one mind, the features
> Of the same face, blossoms upon one tree,
> Characters of the great Apocalypse,
> The types and symbols of Eternity,
> Of first and last, and midst, and without end.
>
> 1805 vi 553–72

Although Wordsworth concludes by enunciating a sense of over-riding unity it is difficult to locate a unity of mood in the scene as described. Indeed, his own *Descriptive Sketches* of 1793 had described his reactions in different terms: the line 'Thy torrents shooting from the clear blue sky' appears in the earlier poem as part of the paradisal scene near Lake Como,[8] yet when in the same poem Wordsworth describes other elements which reappear in the *Prelude* passage, the mood is one of total desolation:

> By floods, that, thundering from their dizzy height,
> Swell more gigantic on the steadfast sight;
> Black drizzling craggs, that beaten by the din,
> Vibrate, as if a voice complain'd within;

Bare steeps, where Desolation stalks, afraid,
Unstedfast, by a blasted yew upstay'd . . .

PW I 56

In the *Prelude* description, moreover, there are further hints of disorder. The traveller finds at every point that his senses are progressively more dislocated. The 'immeasurable height of woods decaying, never to be decayed' presents him with the same spectacle as that of the Thorn : life is held between maturity and annihilation, confronting man with a permanent counterpart of his own paradoxical state. The waterfalls, known by separate reason to be demonstrating nature's movement at its most forceful, are seen as stationary.[9x] The winds (picking up the 'blasts' of the waterfalls) are utterly alien in the forlornness of their strife. If he looks up at the sky the traveller sees it as blue with torrents shooting trumpet-like from it, yet the sounds he hears around him are inescapable voices of muttering rock and drizzling crag. The very stream at his side becomes a 'sick sight / And giddy prospect', and is heard as 'raving'. (The brilliant subversion of Wordsworth's own stream-imagery conveys a total disorientation of the subconscious, an existential nausea). If in a last effort the traveller looks back to the sky, concentrating on that alone, he is now aware of clouds streaming across it anarchically, destroying even that suggestion of harmony. The scene is always offering to compose itself, always failing.

And yet, by the operation of a peculiar and inexplicable grace, there is a sense of unity in the scene. Even while the senses rebel, an underlying force in the human being comprehends the scene as a unity reconciling opposites. Not a unity which can be placed and ordered, as in an eighteenth-century landscape, but a unity which, imposing itself in the midst of tumult, is more valuable for that very reason, since it offers to hold in face of all possible discords. Such an operation of the imagination is more impressive than any looked-for visionary experience on the heights of the Alps might have been. It was one thing for the boy Wordsworth, when, standing on the hill at sunrise he 'beheld one life and knew that it was joy'; it was quite another for the young man to pass through this place of dislocation and to find his imagination able to recognize all the impossible contradictions of the scene yet still sense (it could not possibly define) a unity in all.

This working of the imagination *in extremis*, this power of the human being to apprehend a whole even when the physical senses are dislocated to the point of nausea, suggests that the true apocalypse of human experience may take place not in a stately sounding of trumpets from the heavens but in a moment when, against the calm of the heavens, blasts of warring powers of nature thwart one another—and yet are held together and understood in some unfigurable unity. Not a breaking of the present disorders and the creation of a new order, but the revelation of the whole natural universe as a unity within all its acknowledged dislocations—this would be for Wordsworth the final and only satisfying apocalypse.

Aldous Huxley was ill-advised to choose this passage as an illustration of Wordsworth's limitations, therefore.[10] For the situation is not (as Huxley seems to think) that of a staid Wordsworth reducing a wild natural scene to order through a facile sleight of intellect but that of a young Wordsworth surprised to find, against all his natural expectations, that his unity of imagination persists behind the most extraordinary dislocations.

The full poise of Wordsworth's attitude is made evident in the passage which he later inserted to introduce his description of the experience. In this, he describes the work of imagination in terms which have little to do with the radiant, sun-god imagery that Coleridge might have used on such an occasion. His whole emphasis is upon its negative, unknowable quality:

> Imagination ! lifting up itself
> Before the eye and progress of my Song
> Like an unfather'd vapour; here that Power,
> In all the might of its endowments, came
> Athwart me; I was lost as in a cloud,
> Halted, without a struggle to break through.
> And now recovering, to my Soul I say
> I recognise thy glory; in such strength
> Of usurpation, in such visitings
> Of awful promise, when the light of sense
> Goes out in flashes that have shewn to us
> The invisible world, doth Greatness make abode ...
>
> 1805 vi 525–36

An experience which was in itself a cloud, making impotent the hope of god-like artistic control, comes to be known only in retrospect as a deep and unshakable resource, the ultimate guarantee of a sense of greatness which use of the controlling and analytic eye would be more likely to dispel.

Once the limiting force of this view of imagination is grasped, the grandiloquence of the conclusion to the succeeding episode ('Of first and last, and midst, and without end'), which might otherwise help justify Huxley's distaste, is seen to be indulged within a larger control. It is a more hardly-won affirmation than its own rhythm might suggest.

It is further checked, also, by the description of the subsequent night. After their journey through the Simplon Pass, Wordsworth and his companion slept in a house which seemed still to be fully exposed to the cold, alienating powers that had oppressed them on their journey:

> That night our lodging was an Alpine House,
> An Inn, or Hospital, as they are named,
> Standing in that same valley by itself,
> And close upon the confluence of two Streams;
> A dreary Mansion, large beyond all need,
> With high and spacious rooms, deafen'd and stunn'd
> By noise of waters, making innocent Sleep
> Lie melancholy among weary bones.

> 1805 vi 573–80

Max Wildi, who has identified the house where they stayed, points out that the phrase 'deafen'd and stunn'd' may refer to an experience more overwhelming than appears at first sight. When Wordsworth returned to the scene with Dorothy nearly thirty years later he recalled the 'awful night' he had spent there and when she wished to go inside, refused to accompany her. As Wildi points out, this points to memories of a very alarming experience; he suggests that, exposed to the terrible 'sucking' sound of the torrent, Wordsworth may have suffered from a certain form of mountain-sickness, accompanied by hallucination, which sometimes attacks the sensitive.[11]

The suggestion is persuasive; if it is true, the night in the building can be seen as having wrought the sense of alienation in the Simplon Pass to nightmare—a nightmare not now of vortical dissolution, however, but of desolation. Yet it could also be climatic. Nausea, in Coleridgean terms, is one of the great rejecting forms of 'single touch';[11] it therefore brings the primary consciousness into play and so, negatively at least, assists the sufferer's sense of unity. It may not be accidental, therefore, that this night of dreary melancholy was followed next day by a strong sense of nature's harmony. By noon the travellers found that their stream was

magnified
Into a lordly River, broad and deep,
Dimpling along in silent majesty,
With mountains for its neighbours . . .

1805 vi 583–5

and soon they were spending whole days beside Locarno and Como. After the Alps, these calm lakes provided a welcome reversion to humanized nature:

. . . Ye have left
Your beauty with me, an impassion'd sight
Of colours and of forms, whose power is sweet
And gracious, almost might I dare to say,
As virtue is, or goodness, . . .

1805 vi 607–11

The return to familiar Wordsworthian territory corresponds with a letter to Dorothy at the time, in which he contrasted the 'repose' and 'complacency of Spirit' by Como with his feelings in the Alps, where he 'had not a thought of man, or a single created being' and thought only of the Creator.[12] We might be pardoned for supposing it to mark a decisive change of mood.

It was not quite the last of Wordsworth's Alpine experiences, however. As they left the shores of the lake and began to pass into the mountains again, the scene (even the lake itself, it seems) 'put on / A sterner character'. On the second night, misled by the local clocks, the companions rose up and started on their journey, imagining daybreak to be near, but found themselves lost, and sat on a rock to wait for the dawn:

An open place it was, and overlook'd,
From high, the sullen water underneath,
On which a dull red image of the moon
Lay bedded, changing oftentimes its form
Like an uneasy snake: long time we sate,
For scarcely more than one hour of the night,

162

The Haunted Places

Such was our error, had been gone, when we
Renew'd our journey. On the rock we lay
And wish'd to sleep but could not, for the stings
Of insects, which with noise like that of noon
Fill'd all the woods; the cry of unknown birds,
The mountains, more by darkness visible,
And their own size, than any outward light,
The breathless wilderness of clouds, the clock
That told with unintelligible voice
The widely-parted hours, the noise of streams
And sometimes rustling motions nigh at hand
Which did not leave us free from personal fear,
And lastly the withdrawing Moon, that set
Before us, while she still was high in heaven,
These were our food . . .

1805 vi 634–54

Although this is a less dislocated scene than that of the Simplon, it is also more subtly undermining. Dislocation of space can be dealt with so long as the body retains its own integrity of frame: even nausea is an act of the whole body. But dislocation of time is more sinister: bearings are more disturbingly lost, the nightmare sense more insidious. It is not now the sense of unity that is threatened, but that of intelligibility itself. The travellers move into a timeless state, where the lake is a sullen water embedding a sinister snake-like red moon and the mountains are perceived by the 'darkness visible' of Milton's Hell. If they try to sleep they are irritated back into wakefulness by insects; they cannot move on, since they are lost. They are thus suspended in unwilling wakefulness, able to hear only sounds which are as timeless as those of the unintelligible clock. As the rustlings threaten some physical attack and the withdrawing moon gives notice of total darkness, their fearful isolation intensifies.

Perhaps the striking feature of the account, however, is that there is no sequel of any kind. We are not told what happened to the travellers later that day, or afterwards; we do not know if dawn came quickly, or slowly, or what their final feelings were on restoration to the ordinary world. Wordsworth simply seals off the incident with a reference back to the 'pair of golden days' that had preceded it and the words, 'But here I must break off'. When he speaks of the travellers again they are returning home, seeing the armies of revolution—touched by them but feeling 'no intimate concern'.[13] If the manifestations of the struggle for liberty at this time find a place in their emotions, they simply fall into a general sense of universal joy. And the night when the young men gazed into the heart of fear is left hanging on the air—perhaps because it was not only unmanageable but also disconcertingly and riddlingly numinous.

Yet though dislocation in time is the worst of Wordsworth's nightmares, his language suggests that retrospectively those experiences too took on a positive power. 'These were our food', he comments—a statement which recalls the phrase 'feeding on infinity'. The two travellers in the forest, magnetized by the setting moon and fearful rustlings, were momentarily initiated into the very world of 'The Ancient Mariner': they were in one of the most fearful—and attractive—of Wordsworth's haunted places.

The only other passage in *The Prelude* which resembles this experience is the one, quoted earlier, recalling his night of fear in Paris, just after the September massacres, when he lay awake, his imagination conjuring up further images:

> 'The horse is taught his manage, and the wind
> Of heaven wheels round and treads in his own steps,
> Year follows year, the tide returns again,
> Day follows day, all things have second birth;
> The earthquake is not satisfied at once.'

1805 X 70–4

This strange passage (expanded in the later version) hardly seems at the beginning (with its echo of Shakespearean comedy[14]) to be frightening at all. What have horses being trained, or the wind of heaven wheeling round, to do with fear? But, as we saw earlier, it is the force of the circling imagery that is crucial here, revolving on and on into greater menace and threatening to become a vortex—

> Until I seem'd to hear a voice that cried,
> To the whole City, 'Sleep no more.'. . .

When the 'trance' was over, he recalls, the calmer voice of reason tried to talk him back into a state of calm,

> But at the best it seem'd a place of fear
> Unfit for the repose which night requires,
> Defenceless as a wood where tigers roam.

Despite Wordsworth's aspiring priesthood, moments such as this revealed a place of fear in nature—and in undisciplined human nature, for that matter—which might be necessary to his growth, but which he could not directly face. And this automatically excluded certain possibilities from his art: it was the subtle cause of a pervasive wariness. Such moments of extreme fear presented, in an absolute form, one pole of his recurring nightmare.

His retreat was by no means absolute, on the other hand. He might not in future court fearful enterprises, but experiences such as that in the Simplon helped him to recognize the value of his own upbringing in sustaining him through the experiences of fear he had later tried to face. He would therefore continue to encourage moderately dangerous adventures in the young. In 1816, for example, he addressed a poem[15] to a young lady who had climbed Helvellyn for the first time, and had found her first feeling of fear succeeded by confidence. He commented:

> Potent was the spell that bound thee
> Not unwilling to obey;
> For blue Ether's arms, flung round thee,
> Stilled the pantings of dismay.

PW II 286

The word 'Ether' is worth lingering over. If it looks at first like a relic of eighteenth-century poetic diction, a way of not saying 'sky' or 'mountain-air', examination of its appearances throughout Wordsworth's poetry suggests otherwise. Our experience of the air and sky is organized qualitatively as well as quantitatively. We know from our scientific education that the sky is an endless extent of space, yet our human perception insists on endowing it with substance. Although intellectually we know it to be nothing of the sort, we see it in the form of an arched vault. The blueness of the sky invites us to believe that it shares other qualities of coloured expanses, such as the sea, or green plains. When we look at the stars, similarly, we like to picture them in seas, or fields of space. The phenomenon is familiar enough; we tend to think of it, if we think of it at all, as an amiable foible of human perception. But

Coleridge, perpetually willing to ask 'what is the meaning of it?', had been ready to inquire whether such phenomena did not correspond to some important fact about the universe itself—and even whether, among other things, the ancient belief in a celestial ether might not in some form be true. Was it not possible that, subtly interconnected to the quantitative universe, some other, unmeasurable spirit remained at work, equally important for the sustenance of life, to which our more fugitive perceptions responded, even if our analytic intellect could not?[16x]

For all his native scepticism, Wordsworth was evidently drawn to a theory which would not only transform the universe into a magical place but explain some of his own unusual experiences in nature. And indications of such a fascination survive in his uses of the word 'ether', particularly in connection with magical experiences in nature. Phrases such as 'seas of ether', 'many a long blue field of ether', 'range the starry ether' or 'through ether steering'[17] convey a sense of the sky which would abolish its intimidating endlessness. When he addresses the lark as 'Ethereal minstrel! pilgrim of the sky!'[18] he is not indulging in repetition, but seeing the bird in two quite different lights. The lark, by its steady soaring, pays respect to the quantitative form of the element in which it lives; but it also expresses itself, through its song, in other and more absolute terms, which have no reference to time or space. In this respect its element is not air but ether, its song resembling the eternal song of Blake's bard, 'who present, past and future sees'.[19] The Coleridgean suggestion that this ethereal element might be the medium through which a link of universal human connection operates is also present, perhaps; a later poem includes the simile 'wide as ether her goodwill'.[20]

The central expression of this sense in Wordsworth is in the reference to

> something far more deeply interfused,
> Whose dwelling is the light of setting suns,
> And the round ocean and the living air,
> And the blue sky, and in the mind of man

in 'Tintern Abbey'. References elsewhere suggest that he felt this 'presence' to be particularly apparent in high, mountainous country. Reason alone would expect the climbing of a mountain to be an experience of increasing fear: the higher we climb the more conscious we should be of the drop beneath. Yet incremental vertigo is a rare condition; most people find that the experience gives growing pleasure. Far from feeling annihilated by the great forms of nature around, they feel more free. This suggests the working of a contrary, fear-annihilating principle in nature (similar perhaps to that which sustains a sleep-walker[21x]). Whether through the working of some actual 'ether', or through some subtle psychological effects operating at high altitudes—ministered perhaps through the very physical exertion involved—mountain-climbing can be a magical experience. In *The Prelude* Wordsworth pleads that the monastery of Chartreuse be spared, not only 'for the sake / Of conquest over sense, hourly achieved'[22] but also

> for humbler claim
> Of that imaginative impulse sent
> From these majestic floods—those shining cliffs,
> The untransmuted shapes of many worlds,
> Cerulean Ether's pure inhabitants,
> These forests unapproachable by death,
> That shall endure, as long as man endures
> To think, to hope, to worship and to feel,
> To struggle, to be lost within himself
> In trepidation, from the blank abyss
> To look with bodily eyes and be consoled.[23]

Once again, the sense of mountain-experience as taking place within an 'Ether' with power in some sense to preserve man from the 'blank abyss', is given dramatic expression.

Wordsworth could take that point still further, moreover. In his poem to the young lady he continues by declaring that her initiation on Helvellyn has made her free to enter on all the possibilities of mountain experience, from the Alps to the Andes. If we had not been alerted to the implications of the words 'spell' and 'Ether' in the earlier stanza, we might find the next stanzas disconcerting, since he now turns away from the mountains of contemporary travel to mountains of a more mythological significance:

> Thine are all the choral fountains
> Warbling in each sparry vault
> Of the untrodden lunar mountains;
> Listen to their songs!—or halt,

To Niphates' top invited,
Whither spiteful Satan steered;
Or descend where the ark alighted,
When the green earth reappeared;

For the power of hills is on thee . . .

PW II 287

What, one might ask, are mountains of the moon, or Milton's Niphates, or the Biblical Ararat, doing in this account of the delights awaiting a girl who has just performed the modest feat of climbing Helvellyn for the first time? And what, exactly, are the 'choral fountains'?

The answer seems to lie in a series of connections belonging rather with Wordsworth's earlier colloquies with Coleridge than with his more sober self of 1816. There are mountains on the moon, of course, but the reference to choral fountains hardly makes sense unless one also remembers another set of 'Mountains of the Moon', the range so called in Abyssinia. James Bruce, searching for the fountains of the Nile in 1770, had reached the river Abola, emerging from the valley between two ranges of mountains which he immediately identified as 'the Mountains of the Moon, or the *Montes Lunae* of antiquity, at the foot of which the Nile was said to rise'.[24] By a series of swift transitions Wordsworth has created a paradisal landscape, existing neither in the mountains of Abyssinia nor in the moon, but fusing the mysterious associations of both. In so doing he has followed the Egyptian myth which associated Isis, the goddess who sought to recreate the lost paradisal Osiris, both with the springs of the Nile in Abyssinia and with the waxing and waning of the moon. By her experience the young lady of the poem has been initiated into a similar mystery and revelation of the inward harmony of nature.

The invocation of such an image, however, even by suggestion, has called up the contrasting image of Milton's Satan, dancing in fury on Niphates as he recognizes his own loss of heaven's harmonic order; which in turn prompts an image corresponding to man's own forfeiture. When the original garden is flooded by the Deluge, the only hope for man is to find the green earth of a surviving place, a lonely Ararat from which he may begin to establish the limited pleasures of domestic life under the light of common day.

These rapid transitions recapitulate, in the course of eight lines, one characteristic pattern of Wordsworth's thought. Visionary themes are invoked, to be immediately followed by an assertion that our true home is with the more simple and domestic pleasures of the everyday. Yet this does not negate the sublime experience, which is seen as a necessary context for true appreciation of the common world.

The process throws light on many other celebrations of the commonplace in Wordsworth's poetry. Domesticity is held up as an important value, yet one likely to be fully appreciated only by those who have come at it through experiences of fear. In this respect, Coleridge's point that Wordsworth is attaching the depth and weight of his own experiences to truths which many have taken for granted from infancy is further validated.

It follows from this that many poems and passages in Wordsworth do not yield their full sense until they are looked at in their whole process. The extraordinary compression of allusion just examined suggests that the process may sometimes have been very elaborate, moreover—even that the full story of his esoteric priesthood was more extraordinary than has so far been indicated, reflecting a continuing exploration of the possibilities of correspondence between elements in the natural scenery and the life of the human being at all its levels. To examine this suggestion properly, however, we need to take another, more searching look at his central imagery of fountains, streams, rivers and the ocean.

Clouds from the Abyss

In his 'Essay on Epitaphs' Wordsworth speculates at some length about the relationship between outward nature and the human mind. He speaks, as elsewhere, of the sense of infinity which inhabits the imagination of the child and connects this with 'the early, obstinate, and unappeasable inquisitiveness of children upon the subject of origination.' Certain features of this inquisitiveness are, he claims, universal:

> Never did a child stand by the side of a running stream, pondering within himself what power was the feeder of the perpetual current, from what never-wearied sources the body of water was supplied, but he must have been inevitably propelled to follow this question by another: 'Towards what abyss is it in progress? What receptacle can contain the mighty influx?' And the spirit of the answer must have been, though the word might be sea or ocean, accompanied perhaps with an image gathered from a map, or from the real object in nature—these might have been the *letter*, but the *spirit* of the answer must have been *as* inevitably,— a receptacle without bounds or dimensions;—nothing less than infinity. We may, then, be justified in asserting, that the sense of immortality, if not a co-existent and twin birth with Reason, is among the earliest of her offspring: and we may further assert, that from these conjoined, and under their countenance, the human affections are gradually formed and opened out.[1]

The argument of this passage has, it will be seen, a close connection with that of the *Immortality Ode*. The childhood sense of infinity is closely linked to the childhood assurance of immortality, and this in turn is seen as source and sustainer of human affections. The larger image is of a child playing by a stream and learning to love the flowers that grow on its banks while nearby, only occasionally attended to, the stream impresses a steady sense of infinite energy.

Clouds from the Abyss

The childhood delight in following a stream down to the sea, or of tracing it further and further back into the hills until one finds its original spring, might suggest the operation of an unconscious wisdom, little regarded in a mechanical view of the universe:

> . . . for my own part, it is to me inconceivable, that the sympathies of love towards each other, which grow with our growth, could ever attain any new strength, or even preserve the old, after we had received from the outward senses the impression of death, and were in the habit of having that impression daily renewed and its accompanying feeling brought home to ourselves, and to those we love; if the same were not counteracted by those communications with our internal Being, which are anterior to all these experiences, and with which revelation coincides, and has through that coincidence alone (for otherwise it could not possess it) a power to affect us. I confess, with me the conviction is absolute, that, if the impression and sense of death were not thus counterbalanced, such a hollowness would pervade the whole system of things, such a want of correspondence and consistency, a disproportion so astounding betwixt means and ends, that there could be no repose, no joy. Were we to grow up unfostered by this genial warmth, a frost would chill the spirit, so penetrating and powerful, that there could be no motions of the life of love; and infinitely less could we have any wish to be remembered after we had passed away from a world in which each man had moved about like a shadow.[2]

In this passage Wordsworth moves as far as he ever did towards the Coleridgean position that the myths which grow up among mankind answer to permanent needs and therefore in some sense express great and lasting truths. In this light the child, asking where the stream comes from and flows to, and so gaining a sense of infinity, would be a surviving counterpart of those ancient Egyptians who created myths around their great river and its springs: their quest, it could be argued, was for a lost paradise not in Abyssinia but in themselves.[3x]

If the mythology of the Nile was geographically somewhat remote, moreover, another surviving myth had located itself nearer to Wordsworth's own native landscape. According to this tradition the area between England and America had once been a fertile plain, containing the city of Atlantis, which was submerged when the 'fountains of the deep' broke up. It is possible that this tradition helps to explain some of the imagery of immortality in Milton's 'Lycidas';[4] it was certainly a powerful element in the landscape of Blake's myths, where the submersion was made to correspond to the loss by man of his original, visionary perception of the world and his precipitation into a world dominated by space and time.[5]

For Wordsworth, obviously, the Atlantic had a commonplace existence as the ocean which washed the west coast of Cumberland and Westmorland near his birth-place. But it had also been known to his imagination in childhood as the 'abyss' which received the stream that flowed past his father's house. If, in later years, that same imagination explored legends of a lost Atlantis and wavered between wondering fascination and factual scepticism, his various experiences of the actual ocean, with its visionary beauty in sunlight and its sluggish roll in dull weather, can have done little to resolve the ambiguity.

Yet a connection between legendary tradition and the facts of ordinary human existence might be traced in the work of the Atlantic simply as a body of water. In fine weather or foul its operations were always, in one sense, a blessing. Even in overcast weather some of its waters were being drawn off by clouds to break on the nearby land-masses and replenish the streams there, providing human beings with one of their most essential needs.

The idea was not a new one. Shaftesbury, describing basic mercies in the universe such as Air, Water and Light, had written, of Water,

How vast are the Abysses of the *Sea*, where this soft Element is stor'd; and whence the Sun and Winds extracting, raise it into Clouds! These soon converted into Rain, water the thirsty Ground, and supply a-fresh the Springs and Rivers; the Comfort of the neighbouring Plains, and sweet Refreshment of all Animals.[6]

It received a new prominence, however, when juxtaposed with ancient myths of the clouded mountain paradise, the sacred river and the receptive sea, themselves viewed as counterparts to subconscious human processes. This ordinary work of the Atlantic could be seen as a more commonplace form of the work performed in the more absolute paradisal state and its self-renewing sunlit fountains; if it was less visionary it happened also to be an actual verifiable benefit, experienced in the world of fact—and corresponding, perhaps, to an inward potency of human nature itself.

There are some indications that Wordsworth, his attention focused as always, upon actual beneficences, was prompted by this recognition to invert tradition and invest his own 'ordinary' landscape with the numinousness accorded to mountains, springs and streams in ancient religions. In one poem, for example, he compared Skiddaw to the two-peaked Parnassus of Greek landscape and mythology:

> he shrouds
> His double front among Atlantic clouds,
> And pours forth streams more sweet than Castalie.

(elsewhere, significantly, he speaks of the 'Castalian fountain of the heart').[7] In the later version of *The Prelude* he addressed the same landscape directly:

> Moors, mountains, headlands, and ye hollow vales,
> Ye long deep channels for the Atlantic's voice,
> Powers of my native region!
>
> 1850 viii 216–8

The veiled sublimity which was conveyed by mountain-winds and by the roar of the sea could sometimes manifest itself more openly, as when the young Wordsworth saw the mountains shining, 'Grain-tinctured, drenched in empyrean light', at dawn or, some years later, mountains, clouds and sky mingling 'In one inseparable glory clad, / Creatures of one ethereal substance' over the Leven estuary.[8] During those periods of sunrise and sunset, indeed, the sun could be most readily thought of as a light-fountain. When Wordsworth writes admiringly of an eagle who

> Flew high above Atlantic waves, to draw
> Light from the fountain of the setting sun

in a later poem,[9] he is still drawing on a range of imagery, associating the visitations of the sun with the sense of immortality, which appears more explicitly in the 'Essay on Epitaphs':

As, in sailing upon the orb of this planet, a voyage towards the regions where the sun sets, conducts gradually to the quarter where we have been accustomed to behold it come forth at its

rising; and, in like manner, a voyage towards the east, the birth-
place in our imagination of the morning, leads finally to the
quarter where the sun is last seen when he departs from our eyes;
so the contemplative Soul, travelling in the direction of mortality,
advances to the country of everlasting life . . .[10]

The effect of the sun upon the ocean, temporarily touching it to
sublimity, provides a correspondence, in time and space, to the work
of human imagination in figuring a lost, sublime Atlantis, the
highest mountain-tops of which now survive only as forlorn rocks
in the ocean.

It is characteristic of the mature Wordsworth, however, that he
does not (and cannot) give a central place in his poetry to such
perceptions. For him their value is, once again, to touch the world
with possible sublimity, to give a depth to ordinary processes which
is more effective if *not* relied upon, or even considered too closely.

This complicated attitude to his native landscape is more compre-
hensible when viewed in the context of Wordsworth's early hopes
and aspirations, which had been over-ready to see the world in
visionary form. The poet who, with his young contemporaries, had
found the scene after the French Revolution more like that of a
'Country in Romance', feeling themselves to be

> . . . call'd upon to exercise their skill,
> Not in Utopia, subterraneous Fields,
> Or some secreted Island, Heaven knows where,
> But in the very world which is the world
> Of all of us, the place in which, in the end,
> We find our happiness, or not at all . . .

1805 x 722–7

had moved through disillusionment to a point where he could find
his original hopes realized—and then in a muted form—only
through contemplation of nature in seclusion. Prompted by the 'fear
and awe' which fell upon him when he looked

> Into our Minds, into the Mind of Man—
> My haunt, and the main region of my song

he could find there at least a force of beauty-making power which
transformed the ordinary universe:

174

Clouds from the Abyss

. . . Paradise, and groves
Elysian, Fortunate Fields—like those of old
Sought in the Atlantic Main—why should they be
A history only of departed things,
Or a mere fiction of what never was?
For the discerning intellect of Man,
When wedded to this goodly universe
In love and holy passion, shall find these
A simple produce of the common day.

PW V 4

It was the special virtue of such a philosophy that it could be maintained even when dull, cloudy weather, or the commonplaces of human living, might otherwise make it difficult to think of natural processes as symbolic of the ideal. At one and the same time it kept its point of focus in the link between the ordinary human being and the ordinary universe, yet reminded him that if he looked at these ordinary manifestations for long enough they lost their static drabness. A Lakeland mountain on a dull day is still honeycombed by springs and haunted by the noise of torrents from its sides; the ocean which heaves and rocks its dull body of death is still sustaining life in its depths and giving back water to be transformed into rain. Such phenomena renewed the link between the universe of commonplace experience and the universe of wonder which Wordsworth remembered from childhood, and had sometimes re-experienced in times of vision or trance.

This larger sense of mountains and ocean, of a permanent ministry which is also eloquent of potential sublimity, plays a part in some of Wordsworth's most characteristic poems and passages set in landscapes near the Atlantic, providing a necessary extension to his imagery of water flowing in streams and fountains. In the *Immortality Ode*, for example, the sight of water in lake or ocean under certain lights is one of the visionary experiences of nature which survives untouched as he grows up:

Waters on a starry night
Are beautiful and fair . . .

while on a spring morning the sense of power from the noise of torrents, and echoes among the mountains and the winds, coming 'from the fields of sleep' (a mysterious phrase, referring, perhaps, to the paradisal 'Fortunate Fields', which he seems to associate with Atlantis[11x], are positive forces to strengthen the sense of joy:

> The Cataracts blow their trumpets from the steep,
> No more shall grief of mine the season wrong;
> I hear the Echoes through the mountains throng,
> The Winds come to me from the fields of sleep,
> And all the earth is gay . . .
>
> 1807 II 148

However mysterious and ghostly they might be in other circumstances, they become, when caught up in the genial influence of a spring morning, auxiliary voices of its abundance and vitality.

In this poem, the more visionary sense of the ocean, as it shows itself during a splendid sunrise or sunset, is uppermost. The radiancy of light in clouds at sunrise (though not localized specifically in a seascape) is present in the phrase, 'Trailing clouds of glory do we come'; while the sense of the sea as a source of life-renewal lurks in a famous passage:

> Hence, in a season of calm weather,
> Though inland far we be,
> Our Souls have sight of that immortal sea
> Which brought us hither,
> Can in a moment travel thither,
> And see the Children sport upon the shore,
> And hear the mighty waters rolling evermore.
>
> Ibid. 156

Despite such visionary moments, however, the sight and sound in a landscape of waters running down to the sea must always be of ambiguous significance, their intimations of immortality growing more riddling as the years pass by. In the 'Lines, Composed at GRASMERE, during a walk, one Evening, after a stormy day, the Author having just read in a Newspaper that the dissolution of Mr. Fox was hourly expected',[12] it is the ambiguity itself which is felt and exploited. As in 'Resolution and Independence', the opening scene is filled by the music of waters after a storm:

> Loud is the Vale! the Voice is up
> With which she speaks when storms are gone,
> A mighty Unison of streams!
> Of all her Voices, One!

Clouds from the Abyss

Loud is the Vale;—this inland Depth
In peace is roaring like the Sea;
Yon Star upon the mountain-top
Is listening quietly.

The scene expresses a favourite Wordsworthian moment—a time of
activity between insufferable storm and lifeless quiet. It is therefore
a 'Comforter' to Wordsworth as he faces the approaching death of
Fox, and the subsequent grief of thousands who have regarded him
as their mainstay. Death itself is, as always, totally unknowable:

A Power is passing from the earth
To breathless Nature's dark abyss . . .

The brilliant use of 'breathless' expresses the ambiguity precisely:
death may be either, literally, a state of final inanimation or a supreme example of the stillness of body accompanying ecstatic vision
as the spirit is restored to its visionary source. Once deprived of the
mercy of breath Wordsworth does not know what man will find: it
may be the abyss of non-existence; it may on the other hand trans-
pire that instead of going down to a sunless sea, he will find himself caught up in a sublime process of perpetual renewal. And
even if the individual consciousness is simply snuffed out, a similar
renewal, imaged as it is by the ordinary processes that renew the
springs of Grasmere, will continue to be manifested more generally
in the world of life. These are the facts and possibilities of which the
Vale is eloquent, turning his despair towards comfort:

But when the Mighty pass away
What is it more than this,

That Man, who is from God sent forth,
Doth yet again to God return?—
Such ebb and flow must ever be,
Then wherefore should we mourn?

A similar imagery haunts the poem written when walking with
his daughter Caroline Vallon on the beach near Calais:

It is a beauteous Evening, calm and free;
The holy time is quiet as a Nun
Breathless with adoration . . .[18]

177

The sights and sounds which dominate this moment of trance are the sinking sun, the 'gentleness of heaven brooding over the Sea' and the sound of the sea itself:

> Listen ! the mighty Being is awake
> And doth with his eternal motion make
> A sound like thunder—everlastingly.

The reference to 'the mighty Being' is not simply poetic ornament, nor are the distant undertones of apocalypse accidental. For Wordsworth, it is a further irony of the situation that, according to his own beliefs, the young girl at his side who seems impervious to the scene, is, by very virtue of her child's imagination, possessed of a natural and unquestioning belief in immortality far more powerful and deep rooted than any intimation to be gained from a casual walk at sunset.

The implication of the poem is that whereas the child is possessor of an inly radiating sense which sets her in immediate communication with the creative power in the universe, the adult has lost that power but can still be haunted by it, and will therefore be all the more responsive to sights and sounds which remind him of its nature. When he is fascinated by the ebb and flow of the sea, for example, this is because his primary consciousness is responding to a flux and reflux which are characteristic of its own nature. This power, which can be fearful ('the tide retreats / But to return out of its hiding-place / In the great deep . . .'),[14] may also be a key to the nature of eternal being. Viewed in the context of passing time, the cycle of the seasons has a fatal inevitability:

> Summer ebbs;—each day that follows
> Is a reflux from on high,
> Tending to the darksome hollows
> Where the frosts of winter lie.[15]

The same is true of the processes of death in the individual, as with the wife of the Solitary in *The Excursion* after the death of her own children:

> . . . the immortal and divine
> Yielded to mortal reflux; her pure glory,
> As from the pinnacle of worldly state
> Wretched ambition drops astounded, fell

Into a gulf obscure of silent grief,
And keen heart-anguish . . .

Exc. iii 671–6

Yet behind these processes of life and mortality Wordsworth can believe in an eternal ebb and flow which (like the systole and diastole of the human heart) they may simply be prefiguring. In extremity, indeed, they emblematize it more intensely, as with the account of the Indian woman (mentioned earlier[16]) which Wordsworth called 'an attempt to follow the fluxes and refluxes of the mind when agitated by the great and simple affections of our nature'.

In view of the ambiguities involved, however, it is a crucial element in this belief that the ebb and flow of eternal being is thought to take place around a still centre—just as the child in *The Excursion* who holds a shell to his ear hears a sound which gives him a sense of

> . . . ebb and flow, and ever-during power;
> And central peace, subsisting at the heart
> Of endless agitation . . .

Exc. iv 1145–7

One of the features which he himself thought to be typical of *The White Doe* (and which he rebuked Lamb for not recognizing) was its exhibiting of 'fluxes and refluxes of the thoughts which may be made interesting by modest combination with the stiller actions of the bodily frame, or with the gentler movements and mild appearances of society and social intercourse, or the still more mild and gentle solicitations of irrational and inanimate nature'.[17x] It was a characteristic of the extraordinary creative power of the young visionary in *The Excursion* that his inner nature could actually impose the process upon inanimate objects:

> Even in their fixed and steady lineaments
> He traced an ebbing and a flowing mind,
> Expression ever varying.

Exc. i 160–2

While the motion of the sea, heard on a calm evening, or recaptured when holding a shell to the ear, might suggest a peace at the heart of motion, reconciling all the motions of the universe, nevertheless, total experience of the sea, in all seasons and weathers, must clearly remain ambiguous in signification. Logically, it was as easy (perhaps easier) to deduce from its workings that the heart of the universe was a total chaos, corresponding to the swirling and destructive turbulence of its waves in action. Any final attempt to come to terms with it would necessarily involve seeing it moving incessantly against the fixities of dry land, the rocks and mountains which stood in opposition to its flux, just as any attempt to come to terms with the primary consciousness must set it in relation to the 'secondary' structures of thought and observation by which adult men control their existence in a world of time and space.

It is for this reason that the dream of the rock and the shell in Book Five of *The Prelude* is of such central importance in Wordsworth's *œuvre*—presenting, indeed, the best model that Wordsworth ever achieved of his situation as an intellectual poet in the Romantic age. The passage comes immediately after one in which he laments the fact that nature and the human mind do not possess a firm point of correspondence—that the mind does not find any element in nature on which it can with certainty stamp its own image.

What cannot be conveyed by direct observation of the world can at least be conveyed through symbol, however. He proceeds to relate how once, sitting in a rocky cave by the seaside and reading *Don Quixote*, he (or, in the 1805 version, 'a friend')[18x] had fallen into a meditation on the fact that poetry and geometric truth alone had the privilege of permanence. This then passes into a dream. He finds himself sitting in the deserts of Arabia, alone, in distress of mind, and is joined by a Bedouin tribesman on a dromedary, who is carrying a lance, with a stone under one arm and 'in the opposite hand, a Shell / Of a surpassing brightness'. The tribesman explains that the stone is Euclid's *Elements* and the shell ('this Book') is 'something of more worth'. On holding it up to his ear, he

> ... heard that instant in an unknown Tongue,
> Which yet I understood, articulate sounds,
> A loud prophetic blast of harmony,
> An Ode, in passion utter'd, which foretold
> Destruction to the Children of the Earth,
> By deluge now at hand.

> 1805 v 94–9

The tribesman then says calmly that all is true that has been spoken and that he is on his way to bury the two books:

The one that held acquaintance with the stars,
And wedded man to man by purest bond
Of nature, undisturbed by space or time;
Th' other that was a God, yea many Gods,
Had voices more than all the winds, and was
A joy, a consolation, and a hope.

1805 v 104–9

Wordsworth pleads to be allowed to join him in his errand, but is not heeded; the man rides on, becoming more disturbed, and often looking backward to what is seen as a glittering light. When Wordsworth asks where it comes from,

'It is', said he, 'the waters of the deep
Gathering upon us,' quickening then his pace
He left me.

1805 v 130–2

He is last seen riding away over the sands, pursued by the waters of the deluge, and the dreamer wakes in terror.

The dream-figure of the Bedouin is a convincing projection of Wordsworth's own inner identity. The lance corresponds to his defensiveness in the world of social norms, while the stone and shell are, recognizably, the twin poles of his intellectual universe: the mathematical reason which dominated his scientific thinking and the poetry which awakened his sense of sublimity. There is also a correspondence, though not a straightforward one, with the twin extremes of his nightmare. In the case of the stone, its nightmare blankness as rock is redeemed as soon as it is known to be Euclid's *Elements*, for it is the mercy of geometry that it sets all fixed things in relationship and so becomes a paradigm for the bond that weds man both to his fellows and to the starry heavens. If pursued too exclusively, on the other hand, geometry would turn the universe into a machine; against this the nature of the shell offers a relief both by the beauty of its immediate visual form and by its inner voice when held up to the ear; it at once corresponds to the dual nature of poetry, in appealing to both eye and ear, and, at a further level, echo-reflects the nature of man himself, his surface character accompanied by haunting inner voices and radiancies.

The shell, however, is also ambiguous. Its form is, very literally, a form of death; even the whorled motion of its hardened characters, moreover, sets a stamp on Wordsworth's sense that passion is an

attractive force which, if unchecked, might become a devastating
vortex. And even when he holds it up to his ear, the ambiguity
continues. What he hears is 'a loud prophetic blast of harmony'; yet
the message conveyed through that harmony is one of imminent
destruction. The Bedouin's behaviour corresponds to the double
nature of the shell's voice; he describes it as a 'joy, a consolation, and
a hope' yet shortly afterwards he is fleeing from the deluge it por-
tends. And the deluge in turn has the same double nature: it appears first as a glittering light, the quality of water at its most
visionary, and is then known to be destructive.

In this complicated dream, therefore, Wordsworth is able to drama-
tize the warring elements of his vision. The stone gives us his permanent philosophy, which, clinging to the palpable, and relying
upon relationship, creates a universe of duty and affection, while
the shell suggests his enforced fascination with the facts of passion—
source of all that is beautiful in human life, yet revealing, if allowed
to race in total freedom, a vortical heart of nightmare.

In the dream, the climax of fear is merely another turn of that
cycle, for the flight of the Bedouin must be towards some rock, some
mountain in the desert, which will stand firm against the waters
and enable him to find a dry place above them, a rock in the ocean
where he can survive. It is a flight back to the world of the stone.

But although the dream is cyclical, the total actuality recorded in
the poem is not, for the terror is so fierce that it awakens the
dreamer—and in the same instant releases him from the world projected in his dream. In the moment of his awakening, the world
outside is seen as a redemption from nightmare, the 'fleet waters of
the drowning world' being replaced by the contained ebb and flow
of the Atlantic:

> the Sea before me; and the Book,
> In which I had been reading, at my side.

1805 v 138-9

The scene into which the dreamer has awoken is also one of rock
and shell, but with fear removed. The book at his side is not the
Euclidean rock of mathematical law but Cervantes' fiction, in which
the worlds of romance and realism are held together; the cave, the
shell in which he is sitting, is now no instrument of fearful prophecy
but a containing cell, into which the infinite noises of the sea are
brought and reconciled into harmony. The very elements which were

previously parts of a nightmare have become instruments of concord. The actual universe has come to Wordsworth's rescue, establishing itself as less nightmarish than the logic of his inner grapplings with it.

If one transfers this image, like the others, to a symbolic level, however, the conclusion is more puzzling. For Blake, one of the aptest images for the eighteenth-century attitudes which he opposed was that of a man sitting in a rocky cave, secure in his law-bound philosophy and reaping a vapid self-content by listening to echoes of his own sensibility. Wordsworth, who knew that the apparent assurance of the eighteenth-century psyche masked areas of unfaceable fear, must similarly have known that the security of the cave could be a false security, lasting only so long as the waters of the deep did not rise. How then could his awakening in a cavern by the sea come to be acceptable as an image of final relief from such a threat?

For an answer, we must look to his history in *The Prelude* as a whole. To wake up in an open cavern by the sea was for Wordsworth a relief at the level of his own symbolism only because his psyche, during its early exposure to the wildnesses of nature and the terrors of romance, had been brought to a further trust. From its experiences of the larger work of nature he had come to believe that its general processes were those of a continuous ebb and flow, corresponding to the movements of his own bloodstream, and surrounding a centre of calm. Thus nurtured he could outface—and by awareness of his own heart-work contain—the nightmare possibilities of deluge.

The dream of the rock and shell sums up one major theme of the earlier books of *The Prelude*, that of the growth of a sense of sublimity through early contacts with nature. Under Wordsworth's original conception of the poem, this demonstration would have concluded the poem, leaving him free to proceed with the presentation of a large-scale critique of man and society in *The Recluse*. The decision to extend it seems to have sprung from a recognition that the link between the lonely visionary experience of the boy and young man and the identity of the man who is addressing the reader in the mature poetry had not been made fully clear. It was important that the growth of feelings that connected him with his fellow men should be more fully explained.

No ready form offered itself for such a presentation. It was hard to leave behind the inspiration of the boy without suggesting a staid rockiness in the adult observer. Yet there was one device which presented itself to him, as it did to some other Romantic poets. Blake sometimes adopted the guise of the 'mental traveller', the visionary who moves through the world hardly recognized;[19] Browning later pictured the typical poet as the anonymous figure whom one 'saw go up and down Valladolid', remembered mainly for his scrutinizing eye and only later to be recognized as 'the town's true master if the town but knew'.[20] Such devices look back to an older romantic tradition, that of the king who travels disguised as a beggar.

For Wordsworth the role is slightly otherwise. For him the poet would be better characterized as the beggar who still wears the faded robes of some grander existence, like his own discharged soldier. And if his most characteristic image for his adult existence is that of a traveller, it is a traveller in a cloud.

The image recurs several times in his writings. The line 'I wandered lonely as a cloud' is so familiar that we see it there only with difficulty, but it also emerges in his comparison of the old Leech-gatherer's stillness to that of a cloud 'That heareth not the loud winds when they call; / And moveth all together, if it move at all,' and is an important image in his admiration for the old shepherd, Michael, **who**

> had been alone
> Amid the heart of many thousand mists
> That came to him and left him on the heights.
>
> LB II 202

The image of the cloud-wrapped man gives him a complex image for the progress of the adult man in a universe where he can never know the final truth: sometimes the cloud may open to reveal a landscape bathed in visionary light, sometimes it may enwrap him so completely as to threaten destruction. The dislocated sense of the phrase 'amid the heart' catches his insecurity finely. But the man who preserves his identity in this situation thereby increases his human stature: he is not unlike that other kind of shepherd-figure which Wordsworth sometimes glimpsed when bewildered by mist in his youthful walks, suddenly enlarged through the magnifying power of the mist itself to an eerie grandeur—

> In size a Giant, stalking through the fog,
> His Sheep like Greenland Bears . . .
>
> 1805 viii 401–2

Clouds from the Abyss

The cloud image has other relevances to Wordsworth's particular view of the universe. The cloudscape can, in some settings, touch a scene with visionary splendour; in others it reduces it to the light of common day. It is also the centre for the storm, where the energies of nature flash in pure freedom. On the occasion when Wordsworth adopts the image of the cloud-wrapped traveller most firmly for himself, this particular sense is in fact pressed home to describe the work of Imagination, that 'awful Power' which[21]

> rose from the mind's abyss
> Like an unfathered vapour that enwraps,
> At once, some lonely traveller.
>
> 1850 vi 594–6

There follows, at the heart of the cloud, a flash of lightning which reveals, in ultimate and unshakable conviction, the unified nature of his experience.

In all this there remains, hardly concealed, an implication of apocalypse. The thunder and lightning of the judgment day are familiar elements of Christian tradition, as is the ultimate moment when the clouds open to reveal the truth that has been hidden behind the processes of time. There is also, however, a sense in which Wordsworth endorses Christian tradition to the letter. When the heavens open in the Book of Revelation what is revealed, in the centre of the throne, the beasts and elders, is 'a lamb as it had been slain'. Removed from its conventional associations with the crucifixion of Christ and the doctrine of atonement and looked at purely as itself, the lamb may be seen as an emblem for the ultimate triumph of affectionate sensitivity. Like the ass on which Jesus rides into Jerusalem it can stand, divested of dogmatic reinforcement or distortion, as a prophetic symbol from the animal kingdom, an apotheosis of the open and vulnerable sensibility through which the growth of human understanding is advanced.

In Wordsworth's childhood the moments of apocalypse had more often been revelations of glory. In the Simplon Pass (one of the few occasions when the word 'apocalypse' is specifically mentioned) the revelation, though not glorious, had been of a unity beneath all the contradictory forces of the universe as they actually exist: this, however, was an unusual triumph. The apocalypses of his mature poetry are most frequently of a primal and reconciling mildness, ranging from the recollected 'ghastly mildness' of the discharged soldier to the 'eyes beaming courtesy and mild regard' of a shepherd which, along with other features, caused his face to strike the Wanderer as descended 'from a fount/Lost . . . in the obscurities of time.'[22]

The apocalypse described in the final book of *The Prelude* provides a climax to the theme of haunted mildness: it records the actual climbing of a mountain overlooking the Atlantic, an experience which included that of passing into clouds and out again above them. During his night-ascent of Snowdon, on a 'close, warm, breezeless summer night', the only noise which occasionally broke the silence was that of the guide's dog barking when he unearthed a hedgehog. The travellers climbed vigorously, and, gradually, their climbing became an experience almost out of time ('thus might we wear perhaps an hour away'); then there was a momentary disorientation, followed by the unexpected revelation as

> . . . at my feet the ground appear'd to brighten,
> And with a step or two seem'd brighter still;
> Nor had I time to ask the cause of this,
> For instantly a Light upon the turf
> Fell like a flash: I look'd about, and lo!
> The Moon stood naked in the Heavens, at height
> Immense above my head, and on the shore
> I found myself of a huge sea of mist,
> Which, meek and silent, rested at my feet:
> A hundred hills their dusky backs upheaved
> All over this still Ocean, and beyond,
> Far, far beyond, the vapours shot themselves,
> In headlands, tongues, and promontory shapes,
> Into the Sea, the real Sea, that seem'd
> To dwindle, and give up its majesty,
> Usurp'd upon as far as sight could reach.
>
> 1805 xiii 36–51

The whole scene, with even the sea—in the later version the 'main Atlantic'—dwarfed by the more immediate moon shining on the clouds, perfectly emblematizes the double nature of the universe as Wordsworth has come to see it. It is not a manifestation of perfect light and peace. The dwindling of the Atlantic's majesty does not diminish his sense of the abyss; on the contrary, that is emphasized both in the ethereal vault which is illuminated by the moon and in a 'fracture in the vapour', creating a hollow rift, and giving voice to

186

the roar of waters, which is specifically associated with 'Imagination':

> Meanwhile, the Moon look'd down upon this show
> In single glory, and we stood, the mist
> Touching our very feet; and from the shore
> At distance not the third part of a mile
> Was a blue chasm; a fracture in the vapour,
> A deep and gloomy breathing-place thro' which
> Mounted the roar of waters, torrents, streams
> Innumerable, roaring with one voice.
> The universal spectacle throughout
> Was shaped for admiration and delight,
> Grand in itself alone, but in that breach
> Through which the homeless voice of waters rose,
> That dark deep thoroughfare had Nature lodg'd
> The Soul, the Imagination of the whole.
>
> 1805 xiii 52–65

The ambiguity is almost absolute. To the visionary, this 'mountain of the moon' might appear like an unprinted photographic negative of that lost paradisal scene where the sun would illuminate a self-renewing fountain. To the scientific rationalist, on the other hand, it is an accident of the machine, the moon a delusive light in the dark abyss and the sound of streams a sombre model, in time and space, for the progress of human life to extinction in the gulf of death.

There can be no final answer. The paradoxes are left trembling in the air. But the scene impresses the observer with the importance of the question—to that extent its grandeur is conclusive. In one sense, indeed, the scene automatically validates itself as a counterpart to the mind that asks the question, and which *can* ask it only because it too is a moon-like intellect shining above the tumults of a passionate heart, listening to its many gods and voices, and striving to hear them as a harmony like that of the light which is striking it directly from an unseen sun:

> When into air had partially dissolved
> That vision, given to spirits of the night
> And three chance human wanderers, in calm thought
> Reflected, it appeared to me the type

187

Of a majestic intellect, its acts
And its possessions, what it has and craves,
What in itself it is, and would become.
There I beheld the emblem of a mind
That feeds upon infinity, that broods
Over the dark abyss, intent to hear
Its voices issuing forth to silent light
In one continuous stream; a mind sustained
By recognitions of transcendent power,
In sense conducting to ideal form,
In soul of more than mortal privilege.[23x]

The perception of this 'type' and 'emblem' had enabled Wordsworth to find an answer to one of the familiar archetypes of the eighteenth century, voiced memorably in the metaphorical language of Johnson. In 'The Vanity of Human Wishes',[24] the great man reared himself above the abyss to his own peril:

> For why did Wolsey near the steeps of fate,
> On weak foundations raise th' enormous weight?
> Why but to sink beneath misfortune's blow,
> With louder ruin to the gulphs below?

ll. 125–8

The utmost that Swedish Charles could achieve, for all his mighty forces and endeavours was

> a barren strand,
> A petty fortress, and a dubious hand . . .

ll. 221–2

And man, confronted by the ultimate question,

> Must helpless man, in ignorance sedate,
> Roll darkling down the torrent of his fate?

ll. 345–6

was left with only one course of action: a humble petitioning of Heaven for its merciful favours.

Wordsworth, on the other hand, standing on the barren strand of Snowdon by the steeps which lead to 'the gulphs below', listening to the sound of torrents, has actualized the scene which had, as imagery, troubled Johnson's fearful mind. By introducing the presence of the moon, moreover, he has added to the scene another element, equally actual, which suggests an alternative interpretation. If we knew the Snowdon scene, and only that, we should be intrigued by the mysterious luminary in the sky, but inclined to dismiss it. But from the rest of human experience we know that if we were actually standing on the surface of that blank circle above we should find ourselves in a sunlit landscape. Its finite light 'feeds upon infinity', in fact, and transmits the light and power of the sun, otherwise unbearable to the eye of man, as a still stream which human sight finds refreshing. The fact neither negates nor confirms the gloomy implications of the immediate landscape; it simply suggests an alternative pattern of interpretation, a different possible focus. But by so doing it liberates the observer, who need no longer feel himself absolutely enforced, like Johnson, into dependence upon the mercies of a law-bound universe. He is left free to face the prospects of total mortality or total immortality alike, resolute to balance the mortal knowledge of human experience in time against the immortal intimations of the human imagination and, while neglecting the claims of neither, to look for a way of seeing the world which would give an equal weight to both.

Such a pursuit, Wordsworth could feel, carried the privileges of the human mind to their highest level, while overcoming any fears of madness at taking on the contradictions of the world. A sense of the imagination simply as a transfiguring power within the human being would have emphasized his separation from the world and nudged him towards insanity, but the Snowdon scene, where imagination was located in the gloomy abyss which might yet turn out to be a milder version of the ether in which the sun shone, harmonizing and self-balanced, at once reconciled his varying senses of himself and externalized them into manageable landscape. Once again the biblical tradition of transfiguration on a clouded mountain has been developed into Wordsworth's image of the traveller and the cloud which, having risen from the abyss to enfold him, reveals, in a flash, the invisible world. On this occasion, however, the flash, too, is actual: it is the mild 'flash' at his feet by which the moon unobtrusively makes its presence known—and is in the same moment known to be always and unassertively there.

As soon as we allow our eye to revert to the figure of Wordsworth himself, of course—and a modesty both in the language and in what is revealed encourages us to do so—the difference between the mortal man below and the light above, permanent in spite of all its fluxes and refluxes, reasserts itself. Erasmus Darwin, on his ascent some years before, had been most impressed by the fact that even at this height, lichen still flourished;[25] the emotion which he felt readily transfers itself into one of intensified pathos at the thought of the long-dead Wordsworth standing there and identifying the mind of man with the lasting luminary above. If his self-identification *is* more than delusive fantasy, on the other hand, the pathos shifts again, this time to the whole body of humanity in the world below him who pass whole lives without ever becoming aware of the key to their existence which is given by the simplest operations of sun and moon above. Their voices, rising from the abyss 'to silent light / In one continuous stream' are truly a 'still sad music of humanity'.

The love of man which was to be true to such a sense of humanity was not simple: it could not have arisen without the prior work of imagination and awe. Although *The Prelude* ends with the praise of intellectual love, therefore, it is an essential feature of the argument that this cannot be reached without their interlocking ministries. Unless emotion is deepened by fear and reason illuminated by imagination, 'love' and 'intellect' remain no more than the combination of sentiment and reason which he deplored in his fashionable contemporaries. There are of course direct and natural manifestations of love in the world, as in the countryside in spring-time:

> . . . see that Pair, the Lamb
> And the Lamb's Mother, and their tender ways
> Shall touch thee to the heart . . .

> 1805 xiii 151–3

but it is only when this love has been set in a context of fear and passed beyond it that it will, in his view, become fully valid. The experience of fear is necessary, but even more so is the power of imagination, now finally symbolized by the ministry of water, in spring, stream and ocean:

> . . . we have traced the stream
> From darkness, and the very place of birth
> In its blind cavern, whence is faintly heard
> The sound of waters; follow'd it to light

And open day, accompanied its course
Among the ways of Nature, afterwards
Lost sight of it bewilder'd and engulph'd,
Then given it greeting, as it rose once more
With strength, reflecting in its solemn breast
The works of man and face of human life,
And lastly, from its progress have we drawn
The feeling of life endless, the great thought
By which we live, Infinity and God.

1805 xiii 165–77

In Coleridge's ideal vision, the stream of genius would ultimately return to its foundation and the abyss be replaced by an Abyssinian paradise. The poet and his genius are deified in the sun-like figure at the conclusion of 'Kubla Khan' who exerts a compulsive fascination on all who hear and see him. For Wordsworth, on the other hand, the divine element in the human being is more like a half-passive moon-god, at once brooding over the darkness like a dove or creative spirit, and drawing sustenance from an unseen fountain of light and power which it transmutes into a still stream of radiance. Yet despite this outstanding difference, he pays tribute to Coleridge for having given him a sense of 'pathetic truth' and, by finding his way into his 'heart of hearts', relaxed the grasp of fear, giving more rational proportions to 'thoughts and things / In the self-haunting spirit'.[26]

Coleridge's thought had acted so, we may infer, because his theory of primary consciousness had offered metaphysical explanation for experiences which might otherwise have been dismissed as abnormal, and so allowed them to be seen as parts of a larger process. He had turned Wordsworth's haunted places from places of fear into eloquent reliques of a lost paradise which, whether or not it had ever existed on earth, was still in some sense or other a potential key to man's nature. In this sense *The Prelude* is the last and greatest of Wordsworth's 'Poems on the Naming of Places': it gives to the whole universe an impress of the Coleridgean mind.

For that very reason, he could not finally know what he had done in writing the poem. The ambiguities remained, exacerbated by the failure of Coleridge's own promise and the deepening rift between the two men. In writing the later books of *The Prelude* he had firmly established his rôle as that of 'mental traveller', moving through the momentous events of his time, whether political or personal, and weighing their significance. The point to which he had come, on the other hand, might seem disappointingly similar to that from which he had started. The final stance of duty and affection which was his compromise between the old order of Law tempered by mercy that had characterized the eighteenth century and the new romantic order of love which he was not able to accept in all its implications had, in one sense at least, brought him full circle. To travel so was, perhaps, to travel only as a mountain could be said to travel. Yet one cannot say this without remembering that when he allowed Dorothy to name a mountain after him, it was, of those around Grasmere, 'The last that parleys with the setting sun' and where he had observed that 'the meteors make of it a favourite haunt'.[27] His later life in the Lake District, in fact, was eloquent of a need to live in a place which was responsive to muted lights and haunted at times by wild flashes. The necessary background to what must otherwise seem a rather prosaic set of attitudes was a country where moonlight on the waves of a lake, or waters 'murmuring from Glaramara's inmost caves', or even winds howling around mountain-rocks acted as perpetual reminders that infinity, for all its nightmare implications, might yet, out of time, reveal its heart not in an endlessness of space and of static being, nor as a consuming whirlpool in the abyss, but in a fuller revelation of the splendour and sublimity concealed in the simplicity of the light that insensibly feeds the vegetable creation, the mountain-spring at which a wild animal pauses to drink, or the breeze which unobtrusively reassures human beings with a sense of their bodily identity.

Between Eloquence and Subsequence

Time who makes war on temples till they fall
Towers till they waste away, though Nature love
Their mouldering ruins, cannot treat with words
Like an omnipotent . . .

Wordsworth, MS lines[ix]

After Coleridge's death in 1834, Wordsworth wrote to Henry Nelson Coleridge, 'though . . . I have seen little of him for the last twenty years, his mind has been habitually present with me . . .';[2] in the following period he tried on several occasions to express what it was that made his friend in retrospect 'wonderful'. By 1844 it was the image of a stream that came most naturally to his mind: the liveliest and truest image that he could give of Coleridge's conversation, he said, was

> that of a majestic river, the sound or sight of whose course you caught at intervals, which was sometimes concealed by forests, sometimes lost in sand, then came flashing out broad and distinct, then again took a turn which your eye could not follow, yet you knew and felt that it was the same river: so there was always a train, a stream, in Coleridge's discourse, always a connection between its parts in his own mind, though one not always perceptible to the minds of others.[3]

The imagery used at the time of his death was still more striking; when he describes Coleridge's power of 'throwing out in profusion grand central truths from which might be evolved the most comprehensive systems',[4] the image of a god-like figure casting forth living suns, each of which could be the heart of a new planetary system, looms momentarily, linking itself to the image, a few lines later, of Coleridge's mind as a 'widely fertilizing one', its seed 'lavishly sown'. Still more apposite is the image which he used a year later, in the 'Extempore Effusion on the Death of James Hogg':

> Nor has the rolling year twice measured,
> From sign to sign, its steadfast course,
> Since every mortal power of Coleridge
> Was frozen at its marvellous source.
>
> PW IV 277

The following of the large space-time setting by the metaphor of the frozen spring is eloquent of Wordsworth's debt to Coleridge for a sense of the eternal and the wonderful, self-renewing in the midst of nature's ordered cycle. And his phrase 'every mortal power' is a tribute to Coleridge's idea that even when all sign of life disappears a central spring may still survive beneath the ice, a mysterious Life in Death.

Although Wordsworth's stream image is fully appropriate to Coleridge's mind, his phrase 'majestic river' imports the bias of his own. Coleridge's ideas had internal consistency, but he had not the power to convert them into a major current. Wordsworth, by contrast, had that power on a scale which made his friend despair of his own poetic potentialities—so much so, in fact, that the sweep of the Wordsworthian current might blind us to the fact that the opposition between ice and spring was potent in his own mind, also, corresponding to the contradiction between his freezing sense of mortality and the attraction for him, as poet, of Coleridge's idea of genius.

That attraction was strengthened by the Coleridgean interpretation of animal energy. The idea of 'genial spirits' lent a new fascination to the sight of insects and birds, weaving communal patterns in their flight. After he and Dorothy settled in Grasmere he wrote some lines[5x] on water-fowl, and how, for no apparent reason other than their own pleasure, they shaped

> Orb after orb their course still round & round
> Above the circuit of the lake their own
> Adopted region girding it about
> In wanton repetition yet therewith
> With that large circle evermore renew'd
> Hundreds of curves & circlets high & low
> Backwards & forwards progress intricate

> As if one Spirit was in all & sway'd
> Their indefatigable flight . . .

There are many Miltonic echoes here, as De Selincourt has noted.[6] And as Wordsworth describes how they continue, against all expectation, to return, an unusual word enters his vocabulary. Their energy creates *temptation* :

> They tempt the sun to sport among their plumes
> They tempt the water and the gleaming ice
> To shew them a fair image 'tis themselves,
> Their own fair forms upon the glimmering plain
> Painted more soft & fair as they descend
> Almost to touch . . .

The use of the word 'tempt' is more than a piece of studied elegance. Wordsworth's other term for the water-fowl, 'feathered tenants of the flood', which looks like an example of the false diction attacked in the *Lyrical Ballads* preface, turns out on inspection to embody an exact meaning, in parallel with Wordsworth's wary attitude to homelessness. The paradox it encloses is that of a licence enjoyed by birds which are 'tenants', but tenants of the ever-changing 'flood'. In the same way the birds tempt the observer to the extremes of vision by the 'flash' of the sun on their wings or their still reflection on the water. Such modes of vision may be dangerous if cultivated in pure form, leading respectively to destruction or blankness. The human observer is better advised to focus on the birds themselves—delighting in (but not trying to emulate) the energy which takes them

> up again aloft,
> Up with a sally and a flash of speed,
> As if they scorn'd both resting place & rest !

The pure form of genial energy displayed by birds and butterflies can be rejoiced in by the human watcher but he, more than they, needs a place of repose, where his organic growth can be cultivated in peace. (The lines were written for the passage which was to be entitled 'Home at Grasmere'.)

Wordsworth had fewer reservations about Coleridge's idea of eloquence and its power, which helped justify his own poetic vocation. In 'Power of Music'[7] he describes a fiddler in Oxford Street as an 'Orpheus' who can charm the passers-by until the 'Coaches and Chariots', which 'roar on like a stream', are unheard; and in 'On the Power of Sound'[8] he writes at length of the ability of music to harmonize the passions, suggesting that it is related to a higher art:

> Pure modulations flowing from the heart
> Of divine Love . . .

Just as Coleridge's image, in 'Kubla Khan', of absolute genius creating a miraculous form carries a strong reminiscence of the sun-god Apollo building a temple for himself by his own music,[9] so Wordsworth's poem refers directly to a companion myth:

> The Gift to King Amphion
> That walled a city with its melody
> Was for belief no dream . . .

ll. 129–31

In the last stanza this belief is related back to the Hebrew story of Creation:

> A voice to Light gave Being;
> To Time, and Man its earth-born chronicler . . .

ll. 209–10

while at the end, a characteristic Wordsworthian image introduces his final tribute to the power of the word:

> O Silence! are Man's noisy years
> No more than moments of thy life?
> Is Harmony, blest queen of smiles and tears,
> With her smooth tones and discords just,
> Tempered into rapturous strife,
> Thy destined bond-slave? No! though earth be dust
> And vanish, though the heavens dissolve, her stay
> Is in the W O R D, that shall not pass away.

ll. 217–24

One is reminded of Coleridge's closing words in *Biographia Literaria*, addressed to the Word of God, 'whose choral echo is the universe'.[10] But although there is something of the same spirit in Wordsworth's conclusion, his 'Word that shall not pass away' has, by that token, a flinty, rocky quality, a permanence to which even music is

subject. It is the triumph of such an ideal Word that it satisfies
the demands of both ear and eye, the eloquence of its original utter-
ing falling immediately into the permanence of perpetually valid
statement.

In this respect Wordsworth is harking back to an older view of
language, one which takes as its ideal the making of statements
which will possess a biblical authority and permanence. The poet
who undertakes such a task is traditionally called to an austerity of
behaviour and a steady surveillance of human destiny which might
remind one of conventional representations of Father Time himself.
And Wordsworth evidently saw himself at times in such a role, his
lofty self-assurance combining with a desire to emulate those of his
own characters who could be seen moving closer and closer to a
stillness in nature that might consummate itself in death.

This latter, more secret affinity evidences itself not only in his
love of permanent forms such as rocks and mountains, but in the
kind of feeling that he evinces towards less permanent forms, such
as those of ice. In his description of skating the qualities of the
frozen water which emerge as impressive are its stillness, its resonance and its continuity with the more permanent forms beyond.
Coleridge, by contrast, is more fascinated by the processes of ice; its
modes of accretion, its power to mime the processes of organic life.
In 'Frost at Midnight' his awareness of its silent becoming provides
a fitting context within which to consider the future growth of his
own child.[11]

This is not to suggest that Wordsworth was indifferent to the
young and their growth. On the contrary, when on one occasion
he actually invoked, as the ultimate judge of all art, the figure of
Father Time himself, 'with his accustomed grey locks, his wrinkled
brow, his hour-glass in one hand—his destructive scythe in the
other', he was led on to suggest, tentatively, an addition to those
conventional trappings:

a sort of pilgrim's bottle attached to the Old Man's body from
which he might water in his progress such of the young plants
about him as he knows are destined for immortality.

PrW. III 315

The mode of the suggestion indicates its limitations, however.
Insofar as he himself adopts the role of Father Time, Wordsworth
can be indulgent to the promise of the young, but he finds it hard

to see in the processes of their growth any immediate relevance to the forms of his own art.

In this respect he seems to be moving against a development in human culture that had been taking place since the eighteenth century. For the one fact that was becoming evident in the expansion of human knowledge was that there are no permanent words, no ultimate statements, which can be set before the whole of mankind as commanding universal acceptance. To anyone who has considered the full range of human civilizations, Forster's suggestion that if one were to utter the 'permanent' truths of Christianity in an Indian cave, 'all its divine words, from "Let there be Light" to "It is finished" ' would resonate only as a dull and meaningless echo,[12] has the compelling force of negative vision.

Although it would be tempting on these terms to allow Wordsworth finally to fall into the stance suggested by some of the later portraits—that of an authoritative figure worn down by time who yet preserves a sad kindliness towards the world—it is wise to bear in mind his own picture of the poet in *The Prelude*:

> The Poet, gentle creature as he is,
> Hath, like the Lover, his unruly times;
> His fits when he is neither sick nor well,
> Though no distress be near him but his own
> Unmanageable thoughts. The mind itself
> The meditative mind, best pleased, perhaps,
> While she, as duteous as the Mother Dove,
> Sits brooding, lives not always to that end,
> But hath less quiet instincts, goadings on
> That drive her as in trouble through the groves.

1805 i 145–56

Any picture of Wordsworth as a statuesque, indulgent figure receives a check from lines like these—and from the recorded impressions of his contemporaries throughout his life. Hazlitt wrote that in addition to 'a severe, worn pressure of thought about his temples' there was 'a fire in his eye (as if he saw something in objects more than the outward appearance)', and—most unexpected of all to the general reader—'a convulsive inclination to laughter about the mouth, a good deal at variance with the solemn, stately expression of the rest of his face'.[13] Leigh Hunt described his eyes as 'like fires, half burning, half smouldering, with a sort of acrid fixture of regard';[14] even in his sixties R. P. Graves declared of him, 'I never met a mind which to me seemed to work constantly with so much vigour, or with feelings so constantly in a state of fervour.'[15]

It is the tension between fixity and burning, mentioned by both Hazlitt and Hunt, that is crucial. Some writers have been intent to write out of their own emotions; others have bent their art towards a faithful rendering of the objective world; Wordsworth, as man and as poet, was always most aroused at the points where the two modes met and challenged one another's existence, for then his powers of passionate utterance and calm, appraising intellect were both potently engaged. His 'official' picture of himself as a statuesque, haunted figure, yearning towards central love and peace, has its own truth, but he was closer to accuracy about his total achievement when he projected his dream-picture of the figure, half Quixote, half Arab, who galloped off across the sands to find a safe hiding-place for the rock and the shell.

The whole Wordsworthian enterprise: the wanderlust, the ability to inspire intense devotion, the tendency to 'see something in objects more than the outward appearance' contains a good deal that is recognizably chivalric. For the modern reader, however, the most fascinating element in his poetry lies in continual hints of something further still—of a daemonic presence in the statue, an Arabian energy behind the Quixotic gesture.

Wordsworth's acknowledgement of such a force in himself is often askance or subterranean. It can be traced as early as *The Borderers*, the final version of which climaxes in an image of statuesque suffering. As he tells her of her father's death, Marmaduke says to Alvina

> Conflict must cease, and in thy frozen heart,
> The extremes of suffering meet in absolute peace.
>
> ll. 2215–16

while for himself he rejects all possibility of leadership and can accept existence only as a haunted, driven man. There is another side to the play, however, represented in everything that relates to the villain, Oswald / Rivers. Wordsworth's early psychological essay shows him to be a focus for his own preoccupation with the force of imaginative energy, including his fears of its misuse:

The *mild* effusions of thought, the milk of human reason, are unknown to him. His imagination is powerful, being strengthened by the habit of picturing possible forms of society where his crimes would be no longer crimes, and he would enjoy that estimation to which, from his intellectual achievements, he deems himself entitled. The nicer shades of manners he disregards, but whenever, upon looking back upon past ages, or in surveying the practices of different countries in the age in which he lives, he finds such contrarieties as seem to affect the principles of *morals*, he exults over his discovery, and applies it to his heart as the dearest of his consolations. Such a mind cannot but discover some truths, but he is unable to profit by them, and in his hands they become instruments of evil.

PrW I 77

'Such a mind cannot but discover some truths': what Wordsworth sensed throughout his career was that the very process of exercising energy, whether imaginatively or through action, could bring one to a state where truths impressed themselves, of their own accord, with compelling yet effortless power.

This larger discovery of Wordsworth's is also his most crucial mode of deliverance from time: it corresponds in form to the two figures of *kairos* and *aion*, Opportunity and Eternity, which we saw at the outset to have been the two major figures by which time was represented in classical art. We claimed earlier that they involved a sense of time which was quite other than the sense of chronological progression. We also saw that they involved a sense of man as being in an immediately direct and intricate relationship, whether active or passive, with the time-process. The active mode comes to its climax when man reaches out and meets the particular occasion fully, seizing time by the forelock. The passive mode reaches its apogee as man opens himself completely to the sense of an eternity which is not an event at the end of time but an active and renovating force within nature herself, impressing its power upon the individual.

What Wordsworth had discovered in youth was that the two modes of deliverance could complement one another in actual sequence; that the timeless moment of ultimate exertion in action, when the body did its utmost to fit itself to nature was often followed, in the period of relaxation after such exertion, by a timeless experience of infinite perception, when the phenomena of nature

transformed themselves into a harmony that impressed itself directly
on the senses. *Kairos*, opportunely seized, would then change naturally into *aion*; the great permanencies of nature could cease to be
dreary objects in a diurnal round, presenting themselves instead as
objects of wonder—'an inexhaustible treasure' (as Coleridge once put
it, describing Wordsworth's aim as a poet),

> but for which, in consequence of the film of familiarity and
> selfish solicitude we have eyes, yet see not, ears that hear not,
> and hearts that neither feel nor understand.

CBL II 6

This preoccupation with the relationship between image and excitement in the workings of genial creativity, which recurs throughout *The Prelude*, emerges into its most explicit statement in the last
but one book, where, having declared that Nature's power to give
both emotion and moods of calmness is the 'sun and shower' of her
bounties, he goes on

> Hence it is,
> That Genius which exists by interchange
> Of peace and excitation, finds in her
> His best and purest Friend . . .

1805 xii 7–10

The final lines of *The Prelude* are predictably peaceful and advoca-
tive of love; but the means by which this love is declared to be
generated and sustained is through the mind's realization of its own
nature:

> In beauty exalted, as it is itself
> Of substance and of fabric more divine.

And this in turn directs us back to the processes by which such
learning has been acquired in the poem—processes which are, again
and again, 'interchanges of peace and excitation'—notably in the
revelatory moments which give point to its successive themes. Most
of these follow a similar pattern. An unusually intense exercise of
energy is followed by a cessation, during which some external appearance of nature or man registers itself with unusual clarity,
impressing upon the observer a sense of quiet passion interfused with
infinity. Typical instances are the experience of skating and stopping short; the boy's hooting to the owls, followed by sudden silence;
the night of dancing and gaiety followed by revelation during the

morning sunrise and common dawn; and the evening walk followed
by the meeting with the discharged soldier. The two most characteristic and climactic examples are the crossing of the Alps, where the
unwitting crossing, undertaken in expectant energy, is followed
(after a pang of disillusion) by the walk through the Simplon during
which, as we have seen, the actual landscape itself takes on the
nature of an apprehensible infinity, and the final ascent of Snowdon,
where Wordsworth, climbing energetically ahead of his companions—

> . . . With forehead bent
> Earthward, as if in opposition set
> Against an enemy, I panted up
> With eager pace, and no less eager thoughts . . .
>
> 1805 xiii 29–32

is interrupted by the unexpected sight of the moon, impressing
itself at this moment of interrupted energy as a valid emblem of
the human intellect itself.

The process suggested one way in which the human organism
might be opened to visionary experience without resort to drugs or
stimulants. Wordsworth, who had seen the melancholy effects of
opium and spirits upon Coleridge, was necessarily aware of the
dangers of such artificial methods, yet he could not easily dismiss
Coleridge's belief in the importance of the primary consciousness to
which they might afford access. Instead he concentrated on his own
awareness that the same level of consciousness might be wakened
into activity by the simple exercise of animal energy. A putting
forth of effort could be followed by the apprehension of an influx or
impulse from the heart of nature herself, impressing her own images
of mildness and stability with visionary power.

In spite of the constant recurrence of this pattern in *The Prelude*,
it is natural to ask what evidence there is that Wordsworth himself
laid so much significance upon it. As it happens, however, a surviving anecdote by De Quincey shows that he not only appreciated
it, but sometimes half-courted its effects as an adult. De Quincey
describes how he once walked up to Dunmail Raise with him,
hoping to intercept a carrier with newspapers containing critical
news of the Peninsular War, and waited until midnight before
giving up hope. While they waited Wordsworth had occasionally
put his ear, Indian-fashion, to the ground;

At intervals, Wordsworth had stretched himself at length on the high road, applying his ear to the ground, so as to catch any sound of wheels that might be groaning along at a distance. Once, when he was slowly rising from this effort, his eye caught a bright star that was glittering between the brow of Seat Sandal and of the mighty Helvellyn. He gazed upon it for a minute or so; and then upon turning away to descend into Grasmere, he made the following explanation: —'I have remarked, from my earliest days, that, if under any circumstances, the attention is energetically braced up to an act of steady expectation, then, if this intense condition of vigilance should suddenly relax, at that moment any beautiful, any impressive visual object, or collection of objects, falling upon the eye is carried to the heart with a power not known under other circumstances. Just now, my ear was placed upon the stretch, in order to catch any sound of wheels that might come down upon the lake of Wythburn from the Keswick road; at the very instant when I raised my head from the ground, in final abandonment of hope for this night, at the very instant when the organs of attention were all at once relaxing from their tension, the bright star hanging in the air above those outlines of massy blackness fell suddenly upon my eye, and penetrated my capacity of apprehension with a pathos and a sense of the infinite, that would not have arrested me under other circumstances.' He then went on to illustrate the same psychological principle from another instance; it was an instance derived from that exquisite poem, in which he describes a mountain boy planting himself at twilight on the margin of some solitary bay of Windermere, and provoking the owls to a contest with himself, by 'mimic hootings' blown through his hands. . . . Afterwards, the poem goes on to describe the boy as waiting amidst 'the pauses of his skill', for the answers of the birds—waiting with intensity of expectation—and then at length, when, after waiting to no purpose, his attention began to relax—that is, in other words, under the giving way of one exclusive direction of his senses, began suddenly to allow an admission to other objects—then, in that instant, the scene actually before him, the visible scene, would enter unawares

'with all its solemn imagery'.
This complex scenery was—What?
'was carried far into his heart'.[16]

Wordsworth seems also to have associated this process with the build-up of electricity in clouds or the increase of temperature in a fever. In his poem *The Waggoner* he describes the atmosphere just before a storm:

> The air, as in a lion's den,
> Is close and hot;—and now and then
> Comes a tired and sultry breeze
> With a haunting and a panting,
> Like the stifling of disease . . .

i 15–19 (PW II 178)

The imagery is of growing crisis, as in a fever—as if the mind, passing into a delirium of 'haunting and panting', were opening more and more to its own primary processes until the climax. The oppressive atmosphere around the Waggoner is having the same effect: so that when he hears an appeal from a woman by the wayside, amid darkness and thunder, and then her sobs followed by a flash of lightning, his impatient kindness is like a corresponding discharge from the heart. In Wordsworth's more searching accounts, the equivalent experience is usually succeeded by something more like a 'negative flash'—a flash which impresses not by blinding brightness but by gentle mildness. The 'flash of mild surprise' of the old Leech-gatherer, or daffodils 'flashing' on the inward eye, are simple examples of the phenomenon, while in *The Prelude*, the work of the imagination between the experience of disillusionment and the visionary experience in the Simplon Pass is described as a moment

> when the light of sense
> Goes out in flashes that have shewn to us
> The invisible world . . .

1805 vi 534–6

and the ascent of Snowdon is interrupted when 'a Light upon the turf / Fell like a flash', revealing the moon. Coleridge was fond of the image (which occurs in Boehme); in an early poem he used the phenomenon of flowers supposedly 'flashing' in the evening as an image for lovers meeting.[17] It was probably he who introduced Wordsworth to it as an image for a revelation in the heart. Wordsworth's transformation of it into a 'mild apocalypse' is, on the other hand, characteristically his own. In this form, his mode of 'negative genius' was again presented: not this time, however, as perfected image but as verifiable process. The reader might or might not share his belief in the transcendence of affectionate love; but he could empirically test for himself whether or not the exercise of energy sometimes offered a point of transit into intensified vision.

The activities which precede the visionary moments in *The Prelude* are not always straightforward bouts of animal energy. As in the crossing of the Alps, simple *expectation* may be a potent factor; and on at least one occasion it was the main one. Towards the end of a later book Wordsworth returns briefly to his childhood with memory of two further experiences. At the end of one school term he had climbed impatiently up to a crag from which he could see two highways, along either of which the horses to bring him home might be coming. Before he had been home ten days his father died; and reflection on this event led him to look on it (with the 'trite' morality of childhood) as a divine correction of his desires. In memory of it he often revisited the place:

> And afterwards, the wind and sleety rain
> And all the business of the elements,
> The single sheep, and the one blasted tree,
> And the bleak music of that old stone wall,
> The noise of wood and water, and the mist
> Which on the line of each of those two Roads
> Advanced in such indisputable shapes,
> All these were spectacles and sounds to which
> I often would repair and thence would drink,
> As at a fountain . . .
>
> 1805 xi 376–85

It would have been easy to dismiss his youthful emotions as a luxuriating in his own grief, an illegitimate supplement to callow moralizing; but Wordsworth's later view sees through the soft shell of youthful sentimentality to a real value. If the time of expectation on the crag intensified the pathos of his father's death, it also performed a negative work of genius by giving it a dimension of spring-like infinity and so making it bearable. So his frequent revisitations of the place became in turn a way of 'feeding on infinity': the image of the fountain is tellingly invoked. And Wordsworth goes on to maintain that the experience has continued to work in his imagination—that even now when he sits listening to a storm and rain, or walks in a grove in summer and hears high trees rocking in a strong wind overhead, the sensation which he then derived returns. In the 1850 version, he goes further and connects it (though now with restraint and elegance) to the power of redeeming mental energy from vortex, and stagnant consciousness from stasis:

> . . . some working of the spirit,
> Some inward agitations thence are brought,
> Whate'er their office, whether to beguile
> Thoughts over busy in the course they took,
> Or animate an hour of vacant ease.
>
> 1850 xii 331–5

I suspect that his reason for separating this incident from his other childhood experiences and placing it later in the poem was that (like Golding's three events 'set apart, exceptional and out of the straight line altogether') it presented the visionary element in his experience with a central purity. Other episodes could be associated with high animal spirits and the pursuit of pleasure; this one was associated with deep suffering. Its revelatory quality could not be explained away simply as a delusory overflow from youthful pleasure.

The same is true of the other childhood episode which is reserved for this late point in the poem. In episodes like those of the stolen boat and birds nesting, guilty pleasure was followed by visionary alienation and fear; on this occasion he had been visited by fear in a very pure form. During a childhood excursion on horseback near Penrith Beacon he had been separated from the servant who was accompanying him. Becoming frightened, he dismounted and led his horse on. As he did so, he says, he reached a spot where a murderer had been hanged in iron chains, and where his name, cut in the grass and preserved by local custom, still survived. Going up again to the bare common he caught sight of the beacon and also saw a girl with a pitcher on her head, forcing her steps against the wind.

> It was, in truth,
> An ordinary sight; but I should need
> Colours and words that are unknown to man
> To paint the visionary dreariness
> Which, while I look'd all round for my lost guide,
> Did at that time invest the naked Pool,
> The Beacon on the lonely Eminence,
> The Woman, and her garments vex'd and toss'd
> By the strong wind.
>
> 1805 xi 308–16

206

When, later, he revisited these scenes with Dorothy and the Hutchinson sisters, the pleasure which he felt owed something, he thought, to the power of the earlier experience.

Here again it is the total lack of pleasure in the original experience which invests it with unusual value. It was an early form of the experience in the Simplon Pass: even more than that, it was an 'apocalypse of the actual'. The landscape itself was seen without hint of glamour and in a context of fear, yet the imagination's power imprinted itself—to make it indelibly dreary, but not totally blank. And the whole affair, though pleasureless, seemed to bear vitally upon the grounds of pleasure. An experience which might be regarded by a modern clinical psychologist purely in terms of trauma is seen by Wordsworth as having had a value of its own; the onflowing current of energy from his own fear enabled the boy to hold the scene before him in an aura of vision which redeemed it from total horror.

In *The Prelude* as a whole, this occasional 'ministry of fear' supplements the pervasive work of energy. To be terrified is also to know the extreme of passivity; yet through experiences like the one at Penrith Beacon Wordsworth discovered that in the depths of fear in nature, where he might have expected to find himself engulfed between uncontrollable vortex within and blankness of scene without, he was conscious of an active power which could seize even dreariness and make it visionary. Perhaps the same active power was always, though less obtrusively, at work, redeeming the contraries and so allowing human beings to greet the universe.

He had felt that active form of power most positively, perhaps, during his youthful participation in Lakeland sports, when the pleasure of performing well was backed by a common enjoyment and an excitement shared by all. In the years of disillusionment after the Revolution, on the other hand, he had found himself forced to the opposite extreme—searching for those points where the 'one human heart' had succeeded in finding a lasting form for its workings, without laying itself open to the disenchanting effects of later, contradictory events.

It was for this reason, no doubt, that he found himself, throughout life, fascinated by the extraordinary prevalence, in all times and regions, of the human epitaph. He wrote three memorable essays on the subject,[18] and concluded the last with an epitaph of his own in which the very man he chose to commemorate was a man of unusually literal passiveness, a man (still alive when he wrote[19]) who might seem to have been excluded from the entire world figured in 'On the Power of Sound' by his physical deafness:

> When stormy winds
> Were working the broad bosom of the lake
> Into a thousand thousand sparkling waves,
> Rocking the trees, or driving cloud on cloud
> Along the sharp edge of yon lofty crags,
> The agitated scene before his eye
> Was silent as a picture . . .

Exc. vii 409–15

Yet although his disability might seem to undermine Wordsworth's belief in a universally available sense of resonance, a further look at his life helped to confirm it. What the man could not hear directly in nature he learnt through his own inward mind:

> The dark winter night,
> The stormy day, had each its own resource;
> Song of the muses, sage historic tale,
> Science severe, or word of Holy Writ
> Announcing immortality and joy
> To the assembled spirits of the just
> From imperfection and decay secure . . .

The counterbalancing of scientific truth and biblical imagination, together with further ballasting from a life of active service in the fields, made this man more, not less, an exemplar of human possibilities:

> . . . evermore
> Were all things silent, wheresoe'er he moved.
> Yet, by the solace of his own calm thoughts
> Upheld, he duteously pursued the round
> Of rural labours . . .

At the end of the epitaph the reader is invited to contemplate his grave, hearing over it, as he does so, the sound of a nearby pine-tree which the dead man himself never heard. The pathos of the dead man is intensified here—but only momentarily, since the total work of the poem indicates that although the man did not hear the sound of the tree he knew the more important inner power which such sights and sounds figure. Pathos is thus overtaken by sublimity;

and this very process enforces Wordsworth's point: it is of pathos and sublimity that he writes, elsewhere,

> . . . without the exertion of a co-operating *power* in the mind of the Reader, there can be no adequate sympathy with either of these emotions: without this auxiliary impulse, elevated or profound passion cannot exist.

He goes on,

> Passion, it must be observed, is derived from a word which signifies *suffering*; but the connection which suffering has with effort, with exertion, and *action*, is immediate and inseparable.[20]

Silent contemplation can never, for Wordsworth, be a virtuous activity in itself. The silence which he values is the one that supervenes on energy and carries over its power, so making us aware, in a single experience, of the full universe figured by that flux and reflux:

> Energy, stillness, grandeur, tenderness, those feelings which are the pure emanations of nature, those thoughts which have the infinitude of truth, and those expressions which are not what the garb is to body but what the body is to the soul, themselves a constituent part and power or function in the thought . . .
>
> PrW II 84

And this is nowhere more true than in the case of the written language, where the alternation of energy and stillness (which participates in the very process of the spoken word) must be matched by some equivalent interplay of activity and passivity in the reader's mind if the successive characters before him are not to relapse into dead cyphers.

In his ultimate insistence upon the importance of the active power, Wordsworth not only encourages a convergence between Coleridge's 'primary consciousness' and his own native delight in sturdy, independent human effort, but foreshadows a link with the Victorians more central than his official legacy of duty and affection. His successors in this vein are not simply the Wordsworthians who delighted in climbing mountains and enjoying a liberating sense of unified vision at the summit, but all those Victorians who, like Carlyle, believed in the importance of exerting the will energetically and who by-passed the doubts and confusions of the age by committing themselves to action—whether they took the advice of the ageing Coleridge and committed themselves to Christianity in the assurance that they would by that very activity come to 'know the doctrine',[21] or whether they set themselves to further the great technical enterprises of the age by building cities of steam or defending the outlying posts of a trading empire.

Our admiration of Victorian achievements has long been accompanied by misgivings at the inadequate idea of human nature which caused many of them to gear their energies to a faith in the indomitability of human will. It is not simply the slums and industrial waste that affront us, but the incalculable personal damage inflicted by a one-sided stress upon the importance of 'character'. However much one warms to the debates, the good causes, the broad amusements, one is conscious of a spontaneity uncultivated and a life-force channelled and thwarted. Their many monuments to affection take on a corresponding pathos.

From this reprehension Wordsworth himself is, like the more perceptive of his Victorian followers, largely exempt. What he had learned from nature preserved him from prostration before the machine; and even if, like many of his successors, he put too much weight on the workings of the heart, his sense of its contradictions, assisted by the long dialogue with Coleridge, kept him from ever regarding it as a servile adjunct to the single-thrusting force of mechanical will. Whatever the merits of the fountain as an image for the operations of the heart, it was at least a better model than the piston. So long as he continued to use it he was continually reminded of a basic fact which was to escape many of his Victorian successors: that unless a human being keeps alive a free play of spontaneous energy, to which his more direct purposes are continually related, his 'character' must inevitably harden towards deadness.

It is to Wordsworth's dealings with his own energy, then, that we may finally look for a key to the active element in his writing and to his powers of survival as a poet. His own stream of energy—physical and mental—was firmly channelled, but it was not dammed against the unconscious. The apparent calmness of its products was therefore deceptive. When urged to the intense activity of bringing together the contradictions of the human heart and resolving them into a stately flow of words, it called for a similar stress and reflux from the reader if it was to achieve its full effect. When drawn to alteration of the visible landscape, its aim—to remind a perceptive observer of the unity of the human heart—would be best realized by those who came to it aware of the contraries of human experience. Its most characteristic *physical* discharge was in walking by road or fell, an exercise which left no mark on nature, but alternated the activity of travel with moments of passive exposure to whatever language nature might speak.

He also continued to enjoy skating. His neighbours might deplore his absence from their more indulgent pleasures, such as their toffee-feasts in winter and cherry-feasts in summer,[22] but they were forced to admit his prowess in the one sport he shared with them. As a skater he was champion of the neighbourhood—indeed, many had learned their skill from him in youth. In this activity, one suspects, he could preserve a link with his earlier, more passionate self, recovering (if only vestigially) the republican community which he had glimpsed more recklessly as he galloped with his school-mates across the Leven sands and which had seemed for a time finally disclosed as he walked through the fêted villages of revolutionary France. In the more limited sphere of Rydal Water, the gravitating figure of the ageing poet could still enjoy, among the genial company of his fellow-skaters, a sense of filial bond. Not a man speaking to men perhaps ('He was not a man as folks could crack wi' '[23]) but a man among men, nevertheless, who could feel a link of common energy encouraging the skill in which he demonstrated his pre-eminence.

But it is when we press ourselves to the point of trying to imagine that stretch of frozen water in the evening, after the skaters had left it to a stillness and darkness broken only by the sound of distant torrents or the visiting light of the moon, and ask ourselves what image or mark of his presence could have survived *then* ('Hundreds of curves and circlets', only, perhaps?), that the paradoxes and near-contradictions which have proliferated in this study finally come together to intertwine and reverberate. For it is the local inhabitants themselves who have left the answer to our question. When they looked back on their austere neighbour in later years, and warmed to the memory of his skating exploits, there was one *tour de force* which they particularly liked to recall.[24] They would mention the skill and quiet absorption with which he would sometimes write a poem on the ice—or simply trace, year after year, in its seasonally recurring, seasonally vanishing substance, the cursive lineaments (*alias* the successive characters) of his own name.

Notes

The suffix 'x' to a note indicator in the text signifies that the note contains further information, as opposed to simple references and cross-references. Place of publication is London, except where otherwise indicated.

CHAPTER 1

1. Letter to Southey, 14 August 1803. CL II 977.
2. Quoted, Moorman I 114.
3. 1805 iv 91–120.
4. A. N. Whitehead, *Science and the Modern World*, Cambridge 1926, p. 117.
5. Ibid., p. 116.
6. 'Mescal: a new artificial paradise', *Ann. Rep. Smithsonian Institute*, 1897, 537–48 (cited by J. R. Smythies in *Biology and Personality* (ed. Ramsey) Oxford 1965, p. 156).
7. Fenwick note of 1843: PW IV 463. See also below, pp. 32, 127–8.
8x. C. C. Southey, *Life and Correspondence of Robert Southey*, 1849, I 63. For a good discussion of the whole question, see J. C. Smith, *A Study of Wordsworth*, Edinburgh 1944, pp. 10–12.
9x. 1805 xii 272; xiii 71 (var.); i 1: 63. In his note on 'underpresence' (1805 xiii 71) de Selincourt gives several other examples of this formation, such as 'under-thirst' and 'under-countenance', and comments on its significance.
10. *Selected Essays*, 1934, pp. 283–8.
11. See below, pp. 127–9.

CHAPTER 2

1. (1921.) Republished, T. S. Eliot, *Selected Essays*, 1932, p. 289.
2x. In addition to those to be mentioned in this chapter, two long studies of the subjectivity of time may be found in H. Meyerhoff, *Time in Literature*, Berkeley and Los Angeles 1953, and Madeleine B. Stern, 'Counterclockwise', *Sewanee Review*, XLIV, 1936, 338–65.
3. William Golding, *Free Fall*, 1959, p. 6.
4. Frank Kermode, *The Sense of an Ending*, 1967, pp. 46–52, etc.

5x. The term *kairos* seems to owe its currency in theological thinking to idiosyncratic use by Paul Tillich, for whom it played an important part in the formulation of his 'theology of crisis'. It was later developed by Oscar Cullman, (*Christus und die Zeit*, Zurich 1945, Eng. tr. 1951) and John Marsh (*The Fullness of Time*, 1952). As Frank Kermode also points out, however, these usages have been criticized by James Barr who, in *Biblical Words for Time* (1962) argues that, however useful such appropriations might be for pursuing current theological preoccupations, they do not correspond to the demonstrable biblical usages of those words.

6. E. Panofsky, *Studies in Iconology*, New York 1939, pp. 71–2.

7. Ibid., pp. 72–3.

8. Fenwick note, PW IV 463.

9. Pope, *Essay on Man*, IV 383–6; Cowper, 'A Comparison', l. 1.

10x. Thus John Logan, writing of the 'movement of the whole society', says 'All that Legislators . . . can do, is to give direction to that stream which is forever flowing' (*Elements of the Philosophy of History*, Pt. i, 1781, p. 16) and William Russell writes that he does not give an extended account of mediaeval society, since it is like looking for the springs of the Nile when one could contemplate the 'accumulated majesty of that river' as it flows through the rich and fertile plain. (*History of Modern Europe*, 1788, II, 205–6). Both quoted in T. P. Peardon, *The Transition in English Historical Writing*, New York 1933, pp. 53, 66.

11x. Dryden, 'To my Dear Friend Mr Congreve', quoted W. J. Bate, *The Burden of the Past and the English Poet*, 1970, pp. 26–7. Although Bate argues that Dryden's praise of Congreve is no more than 'conventional compliment', however, it should be noted that it is conceived in the same imagery and is not necessarily ironic:

> Firm Doric pillars found your solid base,
> The fair Corinthian crowns the higher space;
> Thus all below is strength, and all above is grace.

Dryden also claims that Congreve has the 'genius' which previous writers had lacked.

12. Quoted, but with uncertain reference, by H. Ben Israel, *English Historians on the French Revolution*, Cambridge 1968, p. 12.

13. H. T. Parker, *The Cult of Antiquity and the French Revolutionaries*, Chicago, Ill. 1937, ch. ii.

14x. Ibid. pp. 62–4. Parker mentions in particular Manon Philipon, Brissot and Robespierre.

15x. 'Regular circular motion is above all else the measure, because the number of this is the best known.' Aristotle, *Physics* IV, 223b–4a. Tr. R. C. Hardie and R. K. Gaye in W. D. Ross (ed.) *The Works of Aristotle*, VIII, Oxford 1930. Quoted, J. G. A. Pocock, *The Machiavellian Moment*, Princeton N.J. 1975, pp. 5–6.

16x. St Augustine, with his deep knowledge of the classical philosophers, knew well that the Stoics had held a philosophy which saw time as running in circles and devoted several chapters of *The City of God* to a refutation of the idea, particularly where it involved the idea of the world being from time to time dissolved and renewed (XII xi–xx).

17. See Herschel Baker, *The Race of Time*, Toronto 1967, p. 62 and, for a fuller account, Frank Manuel, *Shapes of Philosophical History*, 1965, pp. 50–64.

18x. George Hakewill, *An Apologia or declaration of the power and providence of God in the government of the world. Consisting in an examination and censure of the common errour touching natures perpetuall and universall decay*, 1627. Discussed, Baker, op. cit. pp. 61–2. Since including this quotation I have noticed that Wordsworth used it himself in a note to his 1815 'Essay, Supplementary to the Preface' (PW II 415).

19. See *Oxford English Dictionary*, s.v. Revolution 8.

20. Op. cit. (note 17 above).

21. Frank Manuel, op. cit., pp. 96–101.

22. Chorus from 'Hellas'. *Poetical Works* (ed. T. Hutchinson, corrected G. M. Matthews), Oxford 1970, p. 477.

23. 'Great spirits . . .', Keats, *Poems* (ed. M. Allott) 1970, pp. 67–8.

24. S. Daniel, 'Musophilus', ll. 189–90, Dedication to *Philotas*, ll. 25–30; *Cleopatra*, ll. 348–58 (Cited Baker, op. cit., p.62).

25. See, e.g. Chaucer, *Knight's Tale*, 925, *Monk's Tale*, 3587, 3636, etc., etc.; Shakespeare, *Hamlet*, II ii 517, *Lear*, II ii 180, etc., etc.

26. WL (1787–1805) 56 (letter of 3 August 1791).

27. 1805 iii 56–9.

28. Ibid. v 568–607, and vi 80–109.

29. Unidentified reviewer of *An Evening Walk* in *The Gentleman's Magazine*, 1794, LXIV, p. 257.

30. 'I grieved for Buonaparte . . .' PW III 110.

31. 'Festivals have I seen . . .' PW III 111.

32. PrW I 33–4. (See also my 'The Revolutionary Youth of Wordsworth and Coleridge: another view', *Critical Quarterly*, Summer 1977, XIX, pp. 79–87).

33. Milton, 'On the New Forcers of Conscience under the Long Parliament', l. 20.

34. See Moorman I 178–87.

35. Preface to 'Guilt and Sorrow', PW I 94–5.

36x. PW I 94–127. For full text and discussion see *The Salisbury Plain Poems of William Wordsworth* (ed. Stephen Gill), Ithaca, N.Y. and Hassocks, Sussex 1975.

37. Stanza 58, ll. 519–22.

38. Stanza 61, ll. 547–9.

39. Chronology 145–6 and n.

40x. 1805 x 914–7. The last line should be compared with Coleridge's handling of the same image in *Christabel* (cf my *Coleridge the Visionary*, 1959, pp. 183–4).

41. *The Notebooks of William Blake* (ed. D. V. Erdman), Oxford 1973, p. 28 (and Emblem 55 (quoting *The progresse of the Soul*, st. 4)).

42. 'A Vision of the Last Judgment', BW 614; 'Ah! Sun-Flower', BW 215.
43. *Europe*, 14:23 (BW 244); *Marriage of Heaven and Hell*, 151.
44. Plates 13 and 14; BW 768–9.

CHAPTER 3

1. PrW (Gr) III 469 (cf. 492).
2. 'Reflections on having left a Place of Retirement', CPW I 107; 'Tintern Abbey' ll. 95–9 (PW II 259–63).
3. 'This Lime Tree Bower . . .', CPW I 178–81; 'Tintern Abbey', ll. 14–16.
4. A good account on these lines is given by M. Rader, *Wordsworth: a Philosophical Approach*, Oxford 1967.
5. Mainly in my *Coleridge's Poetic Intelligence* (1977), but also in parts of *Coleridge the Visionary* (1959) and my contributions to *Coleridge's Variety* (ed. Beer, 1975).
6. See *Coleridge's Poetic Intelligence*, ch. ii, etc.
7x. For an apparent origin of this phrase in Boehme see ibid., pp. 125–6.
8. For the eighteenth-century iconography of Newton see A. Blunt, 'Blake's "Ancient of Days" ', *Journal of the Warburg Institute*, 1938, II, pp. 53–63; M. K. Nurmi, article in *The Divine Vision* (ed. V. de Sola Pinto) 1957, pp. 207–16.
9. Southey's translation of the Ode is reprinted in my *Coleridge the Visionary* (1959), pp. 297–300, and discussed, pp. 74–5.
10. Letter of 18 September 1794. CL I 103.
11. See *Coleridge's Poetic Intelligence*, ch. iv.
12. See above, p. 49.
13. Ibid., ch. iii.
14. H. W. Piper, *The Active Universe*, 1962.
15. Ibid., pp. 24–5, translating Diderot, *Rêve d'Alembert* (Œuvres, Paris 1875–7, i, pp. 139–40).
16. Ibid., p. 24, translating Robinet, *Considérations Philosophiques, etc.*, Paris 1768, pp. 8–10.
17x. PW I 58. The text of all quotations from the *Lyrical Ballads* is taken from the first published version.
18. For the first, see Wordsworth's *Immortality Ode*, l. 112 (PW IV 282); for the second, Coleridge's 'Fable of the Maddening Rain' in *Lectures 1795* (CC 215) and *The Friend* 1818 (CC I 7–9).
19. CPW I 285–92.
20. For Wordsworth's account, see Fenwick note to 'We are Seven'. PW I 360–1.
21. See *Coleridge's Poetic Intelligence*, ch. vii.
22. PW II 386.
23. See *Coleridge's Poetic Intelligence*, pp. 42–3 (quoting Hucks's *Pedestrian Tour*, 1795, pp. 29–31) and cf. CBL II 32.
24. Stanza 26 (cf *Salisbury Plain Poems* (ed. S. Gill) 1975, p. 73).

25x. LB (1798) 180–2 (PW I 41). In 1798 the next line read 'Such heart did once the Poet bless', changed afterwards to 'Such as did . . .'.

26. 'Expostulation and Reply'; 'The Tables Turned'; 'Lines written at a small distance . . .'; LB (1798) 184, 187, 97 (PW IV 56, 57, 59).

27. The first two passages, revised, are in *The Prelude* (1805) at i 452–89 and 372–427.

28. W. Empson, *Seven Types of Ambiguity*, 2nd ed., 1947, p.20.

29. F. W. Bateson, *Wordsworth: a Re-Interpretation*, 2nd ed., 1956, p.55.

30. *The Tempest*, V i 33.

31. PW II 211–12.

32. 'There was a boy . . .' LB II 14–15. PW II 206 (text from MS JJ). Cf. 1805 v 389–422 (1850 v 364–97); and see below, pp. 85–6 and n.

33. Preface to 1815 *Poems* (PrW III 35n; PW II 440n var.).

34. Letter to Wordsworth, 10 December 1798, CL I 452–3.

CHAPTER 4

1. WL (1787–1805) 237 (cf. PW II 30).

2. CL I 480 (cf. PW II 216).

3x. This is the wording adopted for the 1800 edition of *Lyrical Ballads* (II 53).

4. F. W. Bateson, *Wordsworth: A Re-Interpretation*, pp. 21–4.

5x. The conclusive evidence is MS JJ of *The Prelude*, first published in an appendix to de Selincourt's edition in 1932 (pp. 639–40). Aldous Huxley had already come to the same conclusion before this, however (*Texts and Pretexts*, 1932, p.156, cited Bateson, op. cit., 22n).

6. See my *Coleridge's Poetic Intelligence*, 1977, p.193.

7. Friend (CC) I 59n.

8. ll. 364–5 (PW II 1040) Cf. *Coleridge's Poetic Intelligence*, 158; Friend (CC) II 51 (cf. I 59 and nn).

9. *Coleridge's Poetic Intelligence*, 225–30.

10. Ibid., 233–8.

11. PW V 344.

12. Letter to *Times Literary Supplement*, 6 June 1975, p. 627.

13. 1805 i 419–20 (See above pp. 73–4).

14. LB II 64; PW I 234.

15. See his 1800 Preface : PW II 402.

16. 'My First Acquaintance with Poets', HW XVII 117.

17. Fenwick note, PW I 360.

18. HCR I 190 (11 September 1816), quoted ibid.

19. LB II 171 ('A Fragment'); PW II 156–8.

20x. Cf. his sonnets 'Methought I saw the footsteps of a throne' and 'Even so for me a Vision sanctified' (written on the death of Sara Hutchinson), PW III 16–17.

21x. 1805 x 501–2; *Samson Agonistes*, l. 598. There is also a reference to Gray's *Elegy*.

22. LB II 120; PW IV 69.

23. LB II 123; PW IV 69.
24x. We may compare Wordsworth's later admiration for the Duke of Ormond's statement 'that he preferred his dead Son to any living Son in Christendom'. This, says Wordsworth, has 'the infinitude of truth'— though its sublimity 'consists in its being the secret possession of the Father' (PrW II 88).
25. LB II 127; PW IV 71.
26x. See 'The Brothers', ll. 356–82 (LB II 19–41; PW II 1–13) and my *Wordsworth and the Human Heart*, 1978, ch. iv.
27. W. B. Yeats, *Collected Poems*, 2nd ed. 1950, p. 388.
28. Ibid., p. 338.

CHAPTER 5

1. De Quincey, 'William Wordsworth', in *Recollections of the Lakes and the Lake Poets*, DQW II 160.
2. Ibid., II 134.
3. PW II 505.
4. LB II 182–7; PW II 112–14.
5. Note of 1843, PW II 486–7.
6. Drayton, *Poly-Olbion*, Song xxx, ll. 155–8 (*Works*, ed. J. W. Hebel, Oxford 1933, IV, 575). Quoted variatim, CBL II 82.
7. PW II, 487, quoting a notebook devoted largely to *Peter Bell*, MS 2.
8. See below, pp. 158ff.
9x. See, e.g., title-page to *Poly-Olbion* (1612), which shows the landscape in a human form (reproduced as fig. 52 in my *Blake's Humanism*, Manchester 1968).
10x. See Jonathan Wordsworth, *The Music of Humanity* 1969, pp. 172–83. My references are to *The Excursion* (PW V), but the quotations are taken from the earlier text (which almost completely agrees with it at these points).
11. PW IV 279–85.
12. See above, pp. 60–1 and n.
13x. This was Coleridge's criticism (CBL II 111–2). Coleridge's attitude to Wordsworth's poetry requires further discussion elsewhere.
14x. This doctrine, which Coleridge cites in a notebook of 1804, derives originally from Plotinus, but was also quoted by John Smith in his *Select Discourses*. See CN II 2164 and n.
15. PW IV 10.
16. Ibid., 13.
17. PW III 76.
18. *Paradise Lost*, xii, 629–30.
19x. See Prel. 536–9 for an account of the drafts quoted. A brief examination of the drafts suggests that Wordsworth may originally have thought of writing a separate poem about this encounter.
20. Preface to *The Excursion* (1814), ll. 38–40. PW V 4.
21. Note of March 1811, CN III 4056. See my *Coleridge's Poetic Intelligence*, 1977, pp. 225–6.

CHAPTER 6

1. CBL II 101ff.
2. Hazlitt, 'My First Acquaintance with Poets', HW XVII 117.
3. De Quincey, 'William Wordsworth', *Recollections of the . . . Lake Poets*, DQW II 194.
4. See, e.g., the account of Samuel Johnson by W. B. C. Watkins, *Perilous Balance*, Princeton, N.J. 1939, pp. 88–92.
5. Reminiscence to Professor Bonamy Price (PW IV 467) and Fenwick note (PW IV 463), cited above, p. 22.
6. Cited Moorman II 39.
7. See below, p. 206.
8x. This line first appears in the second version of 'Salisbury Plain'.
9x. 'A whirl-blast from behind the hill . . .', LB II 96–7; PW II 127–8, app. cr. The 1815 reading of the last line quoted, 'were dancing to the minstrelsy' recalls the 'choral minstrelsy' of Coleridge's *The Nightingale*, composed in the following month of 1798 (CPW I 266). For 'death in life', see my essay in *Coleridge's Variety*, 1975, pp. 67–72 and *Coleridge's Poetic Intelligence*, 1977, pp. 122–8.
10. Cf. his remarks to R. P. Graves on the subject. C. Wordsworth Jr., *Memoirs of William Wordsworth*, 1851, II, 481.
11. S. Parrish, *The Art of the 'Lyrical Ballads,'* Cambridge, Mass. 1973, pp. 95–114.
12. 1805 xiii 402–3. See above, p. 79.
13x. D. Herd, *Ancient and Modern Scottish Songs*, Edinburgh 1776, II, 237–8. For the version in Wordsworth's commonplace-book (though transcribed somewhat misleadingly in form by comparison with the original MS) see PW II 514.
14x. Lines 1,543–4; PW I 188. The importance for Wordsworth of these lines is demonstrated by his use of them as part of his epigraph to 'The White Doe of Rylstone' (PW III 283). (In original MS 'shares'= 'has'.)
15. See CBL II 36 and nn; PW II 241 app. cr.
16. 1805 vii 637–40.
17. Ibid., 696, 716.
18. 'Star-gazers', 1807 II 87–9 (PW II 219); and see, e.g., 'St Paul's', PW IV 374.
19. D. Ferry, *The Limits of Mortality*, Middletown, Conn. 1959, pp. 132–4 etc.
20. Letter to Charles James Fox, 14 January 1801. WL (1787–1805) 312–5.
21. 'The Waterfall and the Eglantine', LB II 54–7; PW II 128–30.
22x. 'The Oak and the Broom', LB II 58–63; PW II 130–4. Mary Moorman points out (Moorman I 101) that these poems resemble some of Langhorne's *Fables of Flora*.
23. 3 October 1800. DWJ 42.
24. *The Sunday Times Colour Supplement*, 29 March 1970, p. 14.

25x. Wordsworth gave as his reason for not publishing the poem the unsatisfactory Copyright Acts, and his desire to leave some property for his heirs (see Moorman II 551). There would also have been some gain in publishing early and investing the proceeds for his heirs, however, and I cannot help feeling that this account helped to rationalize certain personal misgivings, suggested in my discussion. David Ferry's theory (op. cit., note 19 above, ch. iv) that *The Prelude* turned out to be a more inhuman poem than he had meant it to be should also be considered in this context.

26. Memoir (1845) by Lady Richardson; PrW (Gr) III 450.

27x. It is debatable whether Wordsworth's deeply-rooted legal sympathies would ever have allowed him to support the remission of punishment for murder, however, even if the murderer were totally repentant. The need for the law to take its course seems to be accepted even in 'Salisbury Plain'. The nearest he comes to a different view is in 'The Convict' in the *Lyrical Ballads* of 1798 (PW I 312–4); and this poem was never afterwards reprinted.

28. B. Haydon, *Diary* (ed. W. B. Pope) Cambridge, Mass. 1960, II, 148; H. Taylor, *Autobiography*, 1885, I, 181. Cited variatim, D. Perkins, *Wordsworth and the Poetry of Sincerity*, Cambridge, Mass. 1954, p. 26.

29. 'Effusion in the Pleasure-ground on the banks of the Bran, near Dunkeld', PW III 102–5.

CHAPTER 7

1. Letter to Lady Beaumont, 3 April 1815, CL IV 564.
2. William Golding, *Pincher Martin*, 1960, pp. 85–87.
3. 1850 vii 153.
4x. Two third-person drafts are in the Alfoxden notebook. See Prel. 523.
5. T. Burnet, *Sacred Theory of the Earth*, I, xi (1722, I, 191).
6. 7 November 1739. Gray, *Correspondence* (ed. P. Toynbee and L. Whibley) Oxford 1935, I, 126.
7. Ibid., 122n (from journal). The letter version was available in Wordsworth's time.
8. l. 130:PW I 50.
9x. Wordsworth once spoke to De Quincey of a cataract being 'frozen by distance'. 'Lake Reminiscences', *Tait's Edinburgh Magazine*, VI, N.S. Cf. his delight in the torrent at Aquapendente which 'hangs, or seems to hang, in air' ('Musings near Aquapendente', ll. 10–16, PW III 203).
10. *Do What you Will*, 1929, pp. 118–19 (*Collected Essays*, 1960, p. 4).
11. M. Wildi, 'Wordsworth and the Simplon Pass', *English Studies*, XL, Amsterdam 1959, pp. 2–9. Cf my *Coleridge's Poetic Intelligence*, p. 257.
12. Letter of 6–16 September 1790, WL (1787–1805) 34.
13. 1805 vi 696 (1850 vi 769).
14. 'His horses are bred better; for, besides that they are fair with their feeding, they are taught their manage.' (*As You Like it*, I i 13).

15. 'To —— on her first ascent of Helvellyn' : PW II 286–7.
16x. See my *Coleridge's Poetic Intelligence*, pp. 60, 71–2, etc. Coleridge, while drawn to the belief, was unwilling to ascribe to aether a *material* existence. See his note to Southey's *Joan of Arc* (taken largely from Andrew Baxter), CPW II 1112–13.
17. PW II 320; 332 (*Peter Bell* 33); III 354 ('Alfred); IV 203.
18. PW II 266.
19. 'Hear the voice of the Bard !' BW 210.
20. 'The Triad', l. 164 (PW II 296).
21x. Wordsworth's interest is shown in 'The Brothers' (PW II 1–13), where a sleep-walking incident is central to the poem's action. (For Coleridge's possible part in this see CN I 540 fols. 35v–35 and n.) Wordsworth returned to the general theme about 1827 in 'The Somnambulist' (PW IV 49–54).
22. 1850 vi 457–8.
23. MS A² of *The Prelude* (Prel. 200); cf 1850 vi 461–71.
24. James Bruce, *Travels to Discover the Source of the Nile, in the years 1768, 1769, 1770, 1771, 1772 and 1773*, Edinburgh 1790, III 582–83. Quoted J. L. Lowes, *Road to Xanadu*, 1927, p. 373.

CHAPTER 8

1. PrW II 51; cf. Friend (CC) II 337–8 (22 February 1810).
2. PrW II 51-2; cf. Friend (CC) II 338 (22 February 1810).
3x. For a fuller development of this point with reference to contemporary knowledge of Egyptian myth, see my article, 'Blake, Coleridge, and Wordsworth, some Cross-Currents and Parallels, 1789–1805' in *William Blake: Essays in Honour of Sir Geoffrey Keynes* (ed. M. D. Paley and M. Phillips), Oxford 1973, esp. pp. 246–257.
4. *Lycidas*, ll. 155–64; cf. my comments in 'Milton, Lost and Regained' : *Proceedings of the British Academy*, 1964, pp. 153–5.
5. See my *Blake's Humanism*, Manchester 1968, pp. 116, 227; and *Blake's Visionary Universe*, Manchester, 1969, pp. 99–100, 110.
6. Shaftesbury, 'The Moralists', iii, 1 : *Characteristicks*, 1723, II 378–9.
7. 'Pelion and Ossa flourish side by side . . .', PW III 3–4; 'Why, Minstrel, these untuneful murmurings . . .?', Ibid., 6–7.
8. 1805 iv 335; x 474–83 and see above, p. 46 and below, pp. 201–2.
9. 'Eagles', PW III 268.
10. PrW II 53; Friend (CC) II 339 (variatim).
11x. See the lines, 'Fortunate Fields—like those of old / Sought in the Atlantic Main', just quoted. In one MS, Wordsworth wrote 'fortunate islands'—the phrase commonly found in the classics; his change of phrase suggests a deliberate allusion to the Atlantis myth, therefore. If we take this in conjunction with his phrase 'the celestial soil of the Imagination' (see above, p. 77), the sense of the line in the *Ode* would seem to be that, on a bright spring morning, the winds blowing from the Atlantic are so gentle as to be indistinguishable from the

'paradisal' sense of a pleasurable dream. In other words, there is an implicit correlation between the *total* activity of the human mind (compared with its paradisal state in times of pleasurable dream and trance), on the one hand, and the *total* activity of the Atlantic (by contrast with its suggestion of a lost Atlantis in times of calm weather), on the other. See G. Whalley, 'The Fields of Sleep', *Review of English Studies*, 1958, N.S. IX, 49–53.

12. 1807 II 139–40; PW IV 266–7.

13. 1807 I 123; PW III 17.

14. 1850 x 81–3; and see above, pp. 41, 164.

15. 'The Longest Day' : PW I 249–51.

16. See above, p. 66, and my *Wordsworth and the Human Heart*, 1978, ch. iii.

17x. Letter to Coleridge, 19 April 1808, WL (1806–11) 223. Cf. also the mystical experience described in some notebook lines which end 'as if my life / Did ebb and flow with a strange mystery'. PW V 341.

18x. In the 1805 version the incident is related as having happened to a friend. De Selincourt, discussing the question, (Prel. 539–40) draws attention to a similar dream in Descartes and concludes that the dream might originally have been Coleridge's. Since the poem is addressed to Coleridge himself, however, this seems unlikely. Wordsworth's general tendency seems to be away from self-identification (as in 'There was a boy . . .') rather than towards it, moreover. It is impossible to reach certainty on the point, but I have assumed for the purposes of this discussion that the dream really was Wordsworth's : he certainly endorsed it surprisingly late, if not.

19. See his poem of that name and cf., e.g., his 'Ah ! Sun-Flower', and *Milton*, 15 : 21–35. (BW 424, 215, 497).

20. 'How it strikes a Contemporary' : *Men and Women*, 1855, I, 177–83.

21. For 1805 version see p. 160 above.

22. Exc. v 786–7.

23x. This later version (1850 xiv 63–77) should be compared with the 1805 version (xiii 66–84); there the work of the mind is related back to the work of the spirit of nature, on which more stress is laid. In that version he also states that the meditation rose in him 'that night'. It is less likely that it was articulated in all its ramifications at that time, than that the image of the moon and 'breathing-place' as like a human presence first struck him then, to be developed and refined much later. His omission of the words 'that night' in later versions may reflect a recognition that his first version had been open to misunderstanding and that the total evolution of the concept had lasted over several years.

24. Samuel Johnson, *The Vanity of Human Wishes*, ll. 125–8, 221–2, 345–6. *Poems* (ed. D. Nichol Smith and E. L. McAdam, Oxford 1941, pp. 30–48.

25. Erasmus Darwin, *The Botanic Garden*, 1789–91, ii, 29.

26. 1850 xiv 296, 281–5.

27. LB II 188–9 (PW II 115).

CHAPTER 9

1x. Lines written on a sheet at the end of Book X of *The Prelude*, probably with reference to Coleridge's 1805 visit to Sicily: see Prel. 609.
2. WL (LY) II 710. Quoted Moorman II 520.
3. From a record by Mrs Davy, 11 July 1844. PrW (Gr) III 441.
4. From a letter to R. P. Graves. PrW (Gr) III 469.
5x. Published separately in 1833 (PW II 288–9) but earlier intended as part of 'Home at Grasmere' (PW V 321). The version here is the MS one.
6. PW II 288 (version published in 1823) and n, 522.
7. 1807 II 90–2; PW II 217–9.
8. PW II 323–30.
9. Cf. my *Coleridge the Visionary*, p. 262.
10. CBL II 218.
11. See my *Coleridge's Poetic Intelligence*, pp. 136–43.
12. E. M. Forster, *A Passage to India*, 1927, ch. xiv, p. 150.
13. Hazlitt, 'My First Acquaintance with Poets': HW XVII 118.
14. Leigh Hunt, *Autobiography* (ed. R. Ingpen), 1903, II, 21 (cited D. Perkins, *Wordsworth and the Poetry of Sincerity*, p. 25).
15. R. P. Graves, 'Recollections of Wordsworth and the Lake Country' (in *Afternoon Lectures on Literature and Art*, Dublin, 1869, p. 288). Cited E. C. Batho, *The Later Wordsworth*, 1933, p. 37.
16. De Quincey, 'Lake Reminiscences from 1807 to 1830', *Tait's Edinburgh Magazine*, 1839, VI, N.S., p. 94 (not in later editions). Cited variatim by Hugh Sykes Davies, 'Wordsworth and the Locke Tradition', *The English Mind* (ed. G. Watson and H. S. Davies), Cambridge 1964, p. 167.
17. See my *Coleridge the Visionary* 1959, pp. 62 and n, 144, 269; and *Coleridge's Poetic Intelligence* 1977, pp, 52, 90, 162, 196,
18. The first was contributed to *The Friend*, 22 February 1810 (Friend (CC) II 334–46), the others added in PrW (Gr) II. All three now appear, fully edited, in PrW II 45–119.
19. John Gough of Kendal. See note, PW V 465.
20. 'Essay, supplementary to the Preface' (1815). PW II 427.
21. See, eg., his *Aids to Reflection*, Spiritual Aphorisms v and x.
22. *Transactions of the Wordsworth Society*, Edinburgh 1882–87, II, 179.
23. Ibid., 182.
24. Ibid., 174; 176. Cf. also John Fox's MS diary, quoting a Waterhead boatman. Moorman II 429n.

List of Abbreviations

BW Blake, *Complete Writings.* Ed. Geoffrey Keynes, 1966 (Oxford Standard Authors edition, reprinted, with a few corrections and additions, from the 1957 Nonesuch Variorum edition).
CBL Coleridge, *Biographia Literaria.* Ed. J. Shawcross, 2 vols., Oxford 1907.
Friend (CC) *The Friend* (ed. Barbara Rooke) *The Collected Works of Samuel Taylor Coleridge,* IV, 2 vols., 1969.
CL *Collected Letters of Samuel Taylor Coleridge.* Ed. E. L. Griggs, 6 vols., Oxford 1956–71.
CN *The Notebooks of Samuel Taylor Coleridge.* Ed. Kathleen Coburn, vol. I—. 1957—
CPW *The Complete Poetical Works of Samuel Taylor Coleridge.* Ed. E. H. Coleridge. 2 vols., Oxford 1912.
Chronology M. L. Reed, *Wordsworth: The Chronology of the Early Years, 1770–1799.* Cambridge, Mass. 1967.
DQW De Quincey, *Works.* 15 vols., Edinburgh 1862–3.
DWJ *Journals of Dorothy Wordsworth* (1798-1803). 2nd ed., ed. Mary Moorman (Oxford Paperbacks), 1971.
DWJ (de Sel.) *Journals of Dorothy Wordsworth.* Ed. E. de Selincourt, 2 vols., 1941.
Exc. *The Excursion,* 1814. (Text from PW, Book V).
HCR *Henry Crabb Robinson on Books and their Writers.* Ed. Edith J. Morley. 3 vols., 1938.
HW *The Complete Works of William Hazlitt.* Ed. P. P. Howe, 21 vols., 1930–4.
LB (1798) Wordsworth (and Coleridge), *Lyrical Ballads, with a few other poems,* 1798.
LB Wordsworth (and Coleridge), *Lyrical Ballads with other poems in two volumes,* 1800.
Moorman Mary Moorman. *William Wordsworth: a Biography,* 2 vols., Oxford, 1965.
Prel. Wordsworth, *The Prelude.* Ed. E. de Selincourt, revised by Helen Darbishire, 2nd ed., Oxford 1959.
PrW *The Prose Works of William Wordsworth.* Ed. W. J. B. Owen and Jane Worthington Smyser, 3 vols., Oxford 1974.
PrW (Gr) *The Prose Works of William Wordsworth.* Ed. A. B. Grosart, 3 vols., 1876.

List of Abbreviations

PW   *The Poetical Works of William Wordsworth.* Ed. E. de Selincourt and Helen Darbishire, 5 vols., Oxford 1940–9.

WL (1787–1805) ⎫ *The Letters of William and Dorothy Wordsworth*
WL (1806–11)   ⎬ 1787–. Ed. E. de Selincourt, revised by C. L. Shaver
               ⎭ and others, Vols. I and II, Oxford 1967–.

WL (LY)   *The Letters of William and Dorothy Wordsworth: The Later Years.* Ed. E. de Selincourt, Oxford 1939.

1799   Wordsworth, *The Prelude, 1798–99.* Ed. Stephen Parrish (The Cornell Wordsworth), Ithaca, N.Y. and Hassocks, Sussex 1977. (See Note on Texts).

1805   Wordsworth, *The Prelude* (Text of 1805). Ed. E. de Selincourt, corrected by Stephen Gill, 2nd ed., 1970.

1807   Wordsworth, *Poems in two volumes,* 1807

1850   Wordsworth, *The Prelude,* text of 1850 (quoted from Prel. above with corrections from J. C. Maxwell's Penguin edition, 1971).

Index

(Page references in italic type indicate central discussions; (sel.) indicates selected references on a pervasive topic.)

227

Poetic identity, 150f, 152
Pope, A., 33
'Power of Music', 195f
'Power of Sound, On the', 196, 208
Prelude, The, 11, 17, 23, 24, 32f,
  38f, 41–3, 46–9, 71, 74f, 79f, 90,
  100, 107, 110f, 119, 123, 132, 133,
  139, 144, 147, 149, 156, 158f,
  164, 167, 173, 180, 183, 186, 190,
  191, 198, 201, 202, 204, 205, 207
Priest of nature, 107, 165, 169
Primal life, 120
Primal sympathy, 116
Primary consciousness, 58, 59f, 70,
  77, 81, 87, 90, 115, 135–7, 161,
  180, 191, 202, 209
Progressivism, 36
Proust, M., 30
Psychology, 87
Psychoscape, 17, 27, 66

Racedown, 23, 48
Rader, M., 10
Rainbow, 116
Rational, rationalism, 26f, 48, 59
Ratzeburg, 79
Rebirth, renewal, 41, 51, 55f, 176.
  See also Self-renewal
'Recluse, The', 183, 195
Religion, 19, 58, 106
Religion of nature, 154f
Renaissance, 15, 31, 35
'Resolution and Independence', 128,
  141–3, 176. *See* Leech-gatherer
Revelation, 71, 206
River imagery, 34, 60, 70, 169, 194,
  214
Robespierre, 46
Robinet, J.-B.-R., 61
Robinson, H. Crabb, 92
Rock imagery, 152, 197
Roland, Mme. J., 34
Romance, 109, 174, 183
Roman Republic, 34
Romanticism, 15, 58
Romantic poets, 184
'Ruined Cottage, The', 18, 62
Rydal Water, 211

Salisbury Plain, 43, 44f, 45, 60
Saturn, 31
Science, 19, 36, 55, 58, 87, 147, 208
Scotland, 117

Sea imagery, 95, 115, 169, 190
Secondary consciousness, 112
Self-renewal, 56, 60, 68, 94f, 96, 136,
  143, 150, 152, 187, 194. *See also*
  Life, Rebirth
Senses, sense experience, 22f, 26, 30,
  40, 56, 77, 83, 92, 116, 201
Severn, 45
Shaftesbury, 3rd Earl of, 172
Shakespeare, W., 11, 38, 75, 110,
  164
'She dwelt among the untrodden
  ways', 80
Shelley, P. B., 37
Simon Lee, 66
Simplon, 131, 157f, 161f, 163, 165,
  185, 202, 204, 207
Skating, 32, 71f, 90, 211
Skiddaw, 173
Snowdon, 186–90, 204
Sonnets, Punishment of Death, 148
Southey, R., 23
Space, 16, 25, 40, 50, 55, 56, 57, 58,
  143, 163, 180, 192, 194
Spinoza, B. de, 54
Spiral imagery, 37, 61
Spirits of nature, 76, 89–91. *See
  also* Genii
Splendour, 22, 185, 192
Spring imagery, 60, 70, 96, 171,
  190
'Star-gazers', 139
Stasis, 129, 150, 152, 192, 206. *See
  also* Fixity
Stelzig, E., 12
'Stepping Westward', 117–19
Sterne, L., 30
Stoics, Stoicism, 35, 116, 214f
Stolen boat, 72–4, 75f, 90, 206
'Strange fits of passion . . .', 80
Stream imagery, 33, 70, 94, 97, 98,
  140, 143, 159, 169, 171, 175, 190,
  191, 193, 214
Sublime, 22, 23, 24, 25, 26f, 33, 49,
  51, 58, 65, 70, 80, 83–5, 105f, 122,
  124, 147, 154, 155, 169, 173, 174,
  175, 181, 183, 192, 208, 209
Suffering, 152
Sun-fountain, 55f, 58, 111f, 138, 173
Supernatural, 58, 64, 79, 93, 118,
  120, 123
Superstition, 92, 132f, 135, 136, 137
Swedenborgianism, 54

Index

Taylor, Henry, 149
Taylor, William, 94
Temple imagery, 34
Temptation, 195
Terror, 49, 74. *See also* Fear
Terror, Reign of, 41, 42, 138
Theology, 112
'There was a boy . . .', 80, 85, 94.
  See also Owls
'Thorn, The', 66, 131–7
'Three Graves, The', 53
Tillich, P., 30
Time, 12, 16, 25, 28, 29–42, 50, 51,
  55, 56, 57, 58, 83, 85f, 98, 109,
  135, 143, 163, 164, 178, 180, 194,
  197, 200
Tintern, 46, 60, 78, 100
'Tintern Abbey', 53, 67, 68, 69, 70,
  75, 84, 96, 111, 166
'To Joanna', 102–7, 125, 126
'To my Sister', 68
Trance, 60, 82f, 84, 105, 142f, 175
Traveller imagery, 184, 189
Tree imagery, 131
Turgot, A. R. J., 36
'Two April Mornings, The', 94

Unconscious, 57
Under-expression, 24
Underflow, 69
Undertone, 21
Unity, 64, 105, 114, 159, 163
Urizen, 24

Vallon, Annette, 43
Vallon, Caroline, 43, 177f
Victorians, 17, 19, 147, 209, 210

Virgil, 96
Vision, visionary experience, 20f,
  24, 32, 45, 51, 52, 60, 83, 84, 85,
  110–19, 135, 138, 143, 146, 159,
  169, 172, 174, 175, 176, 177, 182,
  183, 184f, 187, 195, 202, 204, 205,
  206, 207
Visitations, 77, 91, 117

Waggoner, The, 204
Wandering Jew, 142
'Wanderings of Cain, The', 63
'Was it for this . . .?', 91
Watts, I., 33
'We are Seven', 45, 65, 128
Westmorland, 155, 172
Wheel of Fortune, 35, 36, 38
'White Doe of Rylstone, The', 179
Whitehead, A. N., 19, 20
Wight, Isle of, 43
Wildi, M., 161
Wildness, 101, 102, 107
Wisdom, 75, 78
Wonder, 62, 70, 78, 175, 201
Woolford, J., 12, 88
Words, 193, 196–8. *See also* Naming
Wordsworth, Dorothy, 17, 48, 62,
  70, 71, 72, 100f, 117, 120, 121,
  130, 142, 147, 149, 150f, 153f,
  161, 162, 192, 194, 207
Wordsworth, John, 129, 142, 153f
Wright, D., 142
Wuthering Heights, 27
Wye, Wye Valley, 45, 60, 70, 119

Yeats, W. B., 27, 97, 98, 137, 138